D0343263

YOU DON'T HAVE TO TAKE IT!

YOU DON'T HAVE TO TAKE IT!

A Woman's Guide to Confronting Emotional Abuse at Work

GINNY NICARTHY

NAOMI GOTTLIEB

SANDRA COFFMAN

SEAL PRESS

Cover Design by Kris Morgan
Text Design by Clare Conrad

Library of Congress Cataloging-in-Publication Data

NiCarthy, Ginny
  You don't have to take it! : a woman's guide to confronting emo-
tional abuse at work / Ginny NiCarthy, Naomi Gottlieb, Sandra
Coffman.
      p.   cm.
  Includes bibliographical references and index.
  ISBN 1-878067-35-4
  1. Sexual harrassment of women.   I. Sex role in the work
environment.   I. Gottlieb, Naomi, 1925–   .   II. Coffman,
Sandra.   III. Title.
HD6060.3.N53   1993
331.4'133—dc20   93-12873
                                                                 CIP

Printed in the United States of America
First Printing
10 9 8 7 6 5 4 3 2 1

ACKNOWLEDGMENTS

A number of people read drafts of chapters. We are grateful to Naomi Almeleh, Karen Bosley, Randi Campbell, Marisa Castelano, Ingrid Emerick, Ann Ganley, Alyce Gatlin, Angela Ginorio, Christine Ho, Connie Coffman-Hobson, Kay Frank, Amy Lally, Helen Remick, Cheryl Richey, Linda Roman, Maria P.P. Root, David Summers, Joey Thompson, Maggi Trebble and Kim Yelsa. Their suggestions improved our writing and gave us new ideas. We are grateful to Donna Stringer, Fran Pepitone-Arreola-Rockwell and Tamara Pearl for permission to use the material they gathered for their own study of workplace abuse.

We appreciate the work of Nancy Brandwein, Holly Morris, Jack Slater and Barbara Wilson as they made individual editorial comments on the entire manuscript. Copyeditors Cathy Johnson and Erin Van Bronkhorst improved our writing and we are grateful. Thanks also to Paul McCarthy for keeping us up to date through a steady supply of news clippings about the latest developments concerning work abuse. Anne Nicoll spent many hours with us, shepherding us through the world of computers as we produced multiple manuscript drafts. Carol Brown also provided invaluable after-hours computer assistance.

We also thank especially Faith Conlon, our editor, who patiently worked with us as we reorganized the material several times in the effort to balance the personal and political. We are gratified that she and Barbara Wilson of Seal Press continue to see the importance of books for, about and by women.

Sandra thanks her parents, Jane and Fred Coffman, for their love and their insistence that she always be able to earn her own living; her husband, David, for his love, support and childcare, and her children, Kevin and Sean, for their patience. Sandra hopes they won't grow up to found yet another self-help group: Adult Children of Authors.

Naomi thanks her family and friends for their understanding

as she became completely absorbed in the book, talked excessively about it, and for long periods remained tethered to her computer.

Ginny thanks Ruth Crow for being there always in every sense of the word.

DEDICATION

This book is dedicated to women who experience abuse at their workplaces—in offices, factories, social agencies, restaurants—everywhere that women work, and especially to the women who played a major role in providing material for the book by telling us their stories.

CONTENTS

Introduction   xi

Section I: The Power of Naming Work Abuse

1. What Is Abuse at Work, Anyway?   3
2. Naming Emotional Abuse on the Job   16
3. The Special Case of Sexual Harassment   37

Section II: The Big Picture

4. Are You Privileged, "Other" or Both?   57
5. Myths of the "Working Woman"   81
6. The Double Whammy of Stress and Abuse   95

Section III: Preparing for Action

7. Discover Your Individual Voice   111
8. The Thought Is Mother to the Feeling   132

Section IV: Choosing Your Options

9. Passivity, Aggression or Assertiveness   151
10. Out on a Limb: Risks for You and Your Family   162
11. Going It Alone: Other Individual Choices   177

Section V: Knowing Your Workplace

12. Your Boss and Power   193
13. Shadow Organizations   207

Section VI: Taking Individual Action
to Stop Abuse at Work

14. Target Your Goal   223
15. The Nitty-Gritty of Assertive Confrontation   240
16. Evaluation and Follow-Through   262

Section VII: Action with Others

17. *You Don't Have to Go It Alone*   281
18. *Collective Action*   303
19. *Using the Law and Government Agencies*   320

Section VIII: Conclusion

20. *Where Do We Go From Here?*   341

Notes   357

Index   371

Introduction

The impetus for writing *You Don't Have to Take It!* was our growing conviction that abuse of women occurs not only in homes or on dark streets, but also at *work*. Our political and professional experience persuaded us that many men and women view women's paid work as secondary to their interpersonal relationships. As a result, little attention has been focused on the mistreatment women experience at work. The recent attention to sexual harassment marks a new recognition of the importance of one kind of workplace abuse. In this book, we focus on the many other kinds of emotional mistreatment on the job, so far unrecognized.

Our own workplace experiences have been central to our lives. The three authors' employment has included restaurant and cocktail serving, switchboard operation, office filing, department store clerk, secretary and public assistance aide—virtually the gamut of low paid "women's work," plus short stints of other work such as taxi driving, psychiatric aide and telegram deliverer. In recent years we have been employed as therapists, teachers at a variety of levels, administrators and as a sexual harassment ombudsman. We've been political activists in the women's and other liberation movements. We are all parents and our experiences include single-parenting, traditional marriage and shared domestic duties. We continue to know or remember that domestic work *is* work.

We have seen, politically and personally, the importance of paid employment in women's lives and we feel disheartened by how little attention therapists, teachers and even some feminist theorists pay to the problems women experience on the job. As we discussed our ideas for the book with women friends, colleagues, travellers on planes and commuters on buses (and even a telephone solicitor for cemetery plots!), the almost universal response was, "Let me tell you about what happened to me!" We listened to those stories, interviewed women individually and in small groups, and combed professional and popular literature for more information about abuse of women at work. We found only a few studies of emotional abuse of women on the job.

We conducted a number of "focus group" discussions with small groups of diverse women—women working in the trades, secretaries, managers, child-care workers, nurses, legal assistants, and so on. The women were white and of color, heterosexual, bisexual and lesbian. They were young and old, able-bodied and physically disabled. This same diversity was replicated in the women we interviewed individually. Many of their stories appear in this book.

Some women we interviewed were more than willing to let us use their names, but others preferred us to disguise their identities. In the interest of consistency and caution, we use pseudonyms for all the women we personally contacted. The only actual names used are those that are part of the public record, such as published books or articles, or court proceedings. When we quote stories published by other people we keep the names the authors used, some real and some pseudonyms. We use first names for the women we interviewed and full names for those women whose names are in the public record. Direct quotes are from taped interviews or published reports, or in a few cases, reconstructed from memory.

We have altered facts which would make the women we interviewed identifiable by others. When we changed their jobs or careers, we kept them at the same educational or status level. We did not change anyone's ethnicity, race, class or sexual orientation. When identification of physical disability, race, age or sexual orientation seemed pertinent to the story, we mentioned it, otherwise we didn't. Some of the descriptions are composites of women we've listened to or read about. Each of those composites is designated as such in the Notes section at the back of the book. What remains unchanged are the circumstances of the women's mistreatment at work and specific quotations from their accounts.

When we refer to other writers' works, we place the reference in the Notes section, but we do not interrupt the flow of the text by inserting endnote numbers. Notes can be found by looking for the page and beginning words of the sentence that includes the quote or mention. Lack of an endnote for a personal quotation indicates this was a personal contact by the authors.

We are grateful to the women who contributed their time and often relived feelings of anxiety, rage or grief as they told us of their experiences. Parts of those stories appear in the book. We felt continually frustrated at the necessity to cut the stories to the bones, because each account has important details, complexities and ramifications.

Many of the women's situations combined so many types of abuse, and such complex interactions with so many co-workers and managers that we were forced to omit many parts of their accounts. It is our hope that some women will write longer versions of their experiences, doing justice to their entire situation. Each of the accounts we used, and even those we weren't able to fit in, increased our understanding of the seriousness of abuse at work and helped us interpret what we heard from other women. We regret that we cannot publicly acknowledge each woman by name. The fact that most were not willing to have their names used tells us something about the fear engendered by the abuse— fear that often remains long after women have left their jobs.

The Format of the Book

In Section I of the book, we focus on naming the problem. Chapter 1 gives our rationale for the book. A questionnaire in Chapter 2 provides a framework for naming the particular type of abuse that's nibbling away at—or devouring—your self-confidence and well-being. Chapter 3 identifies sexual harassment as a particular category of emotional abuse on the job.

Chapters 4, 5 and 6 in Section II place workplace abuse of women in a larger framework. Like many other women in similar situations, you may ask yourself, "What is it about me that makes me a target?" Gaining clearer understanding of the social complexities involved can decrease self-blame and can provide fresh energy to challenge abuse. We describe the historical and social changes that have helped and hindered women's economic circumstances, including the stress of women's dual roles as well as the effect of power, privilege and status in the workplace.

Section III lays the groundwork for action. We suggest ways of "getting in training" to stop abuse. You do that by monitoring and changing your thoughts, and separating feelings about past abuse from what is happening at your job now.

In Section IV, we define assertiveness as a basis for our later recommendations to act assertively to confront abuse. To help you consider the possibility of action, the second chapter in this section focuses on risks that affect your family and yourself. Although our bias is toward straightforward assertive action, we then describe other kinds of action that women choose instead of or in addition to assertive responses.

Section V suggests ways to think about yourself in relation to the people you work with. An analysis of the formal and informal systems at your job site can help you to decide what to do about the abusive problems they present.

Section VI provides examples of how to take individual assertive action to confront abuse by a boss or co-workers. It includes suggestions for formulating clear goals and setting the stage by planning and practice. We give examples of assertive speech and action, and discuss how to monitor promises of change.

Section VII discusses joining with others in action. It describes how women in various settings have worked together for change and suggests some principles for small-group organizing. Information is also included about challenging abuse through unions or outside resources such as courts and government agencies.

The final chapter returns to the larger social context. We look at women's changing work experiences, not only in the United States but throughout the world. We focus on the interplays between the personal and the political, the private and public, the local and the global.

The sequence of chapters reflects our conviction that understanding the larger social context and preparing for action give greater assurance that your fight against emotional abuse at work will succeed. But you may wish to read this book in a different order, turning first to the sections on individual or group actions, then working your way back to the social context. Throughout the book we encourage you to consider what action will work best for you.

Our purpose has been to raise public awareness of workplace abuse and to offer alternatives to women confronting such abuse. We hope that others will study the issue in greater depth, increasing our understanding of its scope and complexities.

Ginny NiCarthy
Naomi Gottlieb
Sandra Coffman
Seattle, Washington
April 1993

SECTION I

The Power of
Naming Work Abuse

Chapter 1

What Is Abuse at Work, Anyway?

I had a boss who never stopped pushing. No matter how hard I tried, I always felt as if I was doing something wrong. He said I needed to "learn to piss standing up..."

Debbie Dritz, air conditioner repair apprentice

In one of his chronic outbursts, a restaurant owner tells a waitress: "Move it, you dumb bitch." An hour later he jokes with her in a friendly way.

Co-workers of Jessica, a nurse from India, refer to her as a "heathen." Her supervisor, Babette, forbids her to wear her native sari and puts her immigrant status at risk by failing to complete promised paperwork for her "green card."

California Senator Bill Lockyer, committee chair, interrupts Assemblywoman Diane Watson, speaking to a judiciary committee on the death penalty. He admonishes Watson to stop her "mindless blather," then adds, "I hope I am offensive enough to make you leave."

Male managers at a clothing store focus an audio-video camera on a women employees' lounge, where the women change clothes and discuss personal, private topics.

A customer service representative's boss publicly calls her a "space cadet" and "dingbat" and interferes with her communications with other workers.

An actor's agent says to an African-American actor, "You were obviously the most talented. But you're a nigger black, and Hollywood likes the Vanessa Williams type." The actor notes that "this guy thought he was paying me a compliment."

A university department head assigns a secretary to a new workspace, an unused restroom, where, for seven months, she types while seated on the toilet.

Emotional abuse on the job takes many forms. Sometimes it packs an emotional wallop equivalent to a punch in your solar plexus. Yet it can also blend into work routines with such familiarity that neither you nor the abusive person consciously notices it. Either one of you might excuse even the most outrageous mistreatment: "She's just under a lot of pressure." "He's upset over his divorce." "You know I'm always like this at audit time." "It's the stress of being in recovery." Or an abusive pattern of treatment masquerades as something acceptable, such as "running a tight ship" or perfectionism.

To remove these misleading labels, and to expose abuse for what it is, you have to put a name to it. Then you can decide how to handle the problem. This book enables you to name exactly how you have been mistreated and provides ideas about how to confront abuse. We use the word "confront" to describe the ongoing process of facing the reality of abuse: naming who did exactly what to you, and then consciously deciding what you can do about it. But in the chapters on assertive confrontation we use "confront" in the more narrow sense of speaking out against mistreatment or acting to stop it.

In this book we usually refer to our subject as "emotional abuse at work," "abuse on the job" or one of the specific forms it takes such as harassment, insults or threats. But the problem has many names. You might think of it as harassment, as the boss being "on the warpath again," as "just the normal daily hassle," as mistreatment or as power abuse. Whatever its label, this problem can cause you physical pain and illness, worrisome mood swings or difficulties in relationships and work production. Mistreatment can monopolize your thoughts. Against your will, your mind replays demeaning scenes. You silently repeat clever retorts to the insults at work, promising yourself next time you will state them out loud. But you hesitate, fearing the abusive person's reaction. One woman described her boss as "a spring-loaded gun waiting to go off."

Mistreatment at work can cause you to focus all your attention on the abusive person's moods and idiosyncrasies. You can become so preoccupied with defending yourself that you overlook opportunities to ally with potential supporters. This self-isolation suits a purposely cruel perpetrator just fine. At this point, if you can't yet name the precise action that offends or hurts you, you may feel like you are "going crazy." That reaction occurs so frequently that some people call these tactics "crazy-making." You may invest a great deal of energy doggedly searching for an explanation of why anyone would treat you as less than human. You try to discover just who and what trigger your "crazy" feelings. What is this phenomenon that succeeds in wrecking your peace of mind?

Defining the Problem

Emotional abuse at work is a pattern of intimidation, harassment, emotional manipulation, or excessive or illegitimate control of a worker.

Abuse may include direct, obvious methods of enforcing an employee's isolation from others on the job in order to increase control. Some abusive people invade workers' privacy by asking intrusive questions or making remarks about their appearance or personal relationships. An abusive person may insist on obedience to trivial demands, require impossible levels of performance or require tasks not properly part of the job. He or she may demonstrate power over a worker by humiliating or threatening her in order to induce feelings of inadequacy, shame or guilt. Some bosses and co-workers alternate abusive treatment with arbitrarily timed gifts or privileges which have nothing to do with how well the worker does her job. This pattern often causes a worker to feel grateful to the person who mistreats her, rather than good about herself for working well. Not all perpetrators use all of these methods.

Sexual harassment is another type of emotional abuse.

Though often viewed as a separate form of mistreatment, sexual harassment can include all of the control tactics described above. For example, it can be isolating and threatening as well as humiliating. Some people who sexually harass use their power to gain sexual gratification. Others use sexual harassment to enhance their power. Lewd comments and sexist pictures placed where women employees can't avoid seeing them create a hostile environment. Harassment might consist of repeatedly asking for a date after an employee says no, or regularly paying unwanted attention to a worker's appearance. A worker may be subtly or overtly threatened with reprisals if she refuses the sexual attentions of someone in power.

Sexual harassment has been given more attention during the last fifteen years, and became a major issue after law professor Anita Hill's testimony about Justice Clarence Thomas during the 1991 hearings on his nomination to the Supreme Court. This problem is so pervasive and damaging to women that we devote a chapter to its ramifications. But in the rest of this book we concentrate on other forms of emotional abuse that have rarely been studied.

Methods of emotional abuse don't always fall neatly into distinct categories. Demands for work during lunch and break times may begin a process of isolating the targeted person. A threat may contribute to feelings of isolation, and demonstrations of power often contain veiled or obvious threats. Power abuse can also shock with its immediacy and obvious cruelty. At some worksites it takes the form of "hazing" newcomers, a ritual more accurately labeled "humiliation."

Two male midshipmen handcuffed "midshipman" Gwen Marie Dreyer to a urinal in a U.S. Naval Academy dormitory, while a dozen other male midshipmen stood by snapping photographs, taunting and applauding. Naval academy officials called this treatment "good-natured high jinks." But Dreyer heard via a roommate that "this kind of thing was going to keep happening until we, the female midshipmen, got a sense of humor." Dreyer resigned.

You may want to make it clear to anyone who makes even one abusive statement that it is one too many. An immediate response may save you from additional offensive acts. Nevertheless one mean or thoughtless action does not define a *person* as "an abuser." A normally respectful supervisor or co-worker might "lose it" once or twice over a long period of time, acting in a way that humiliates or intimidates you. That can be hurtful and in some situations it can frighten you enough to cause long-term damage to your work performance. Depending on the circumstances, one act can carry a lot of emotional and financial weight.

We focus our attention on methods of handling the person who *habitually* or *chronically* uses the tactics named above. We define emotional abuse on the job as a *pattern* of large or small acts, a pattern that constitutes an unacceptable degree of control. That doesn't mean it has to happen every day or every week. It might occur just often enough to keep you anxiously wondering when the ax will fall next.

The few studies focused on emotional abuse at work indicate that many women take the risk of speaking out against mistreatment. Yet researchers also tell us that both male and female workers try to bypass offensive, overly controlling people for long periods before confronting them directly.

Because people continue to blame women for their own victimization, women's reluctance to directly confront abusive co-workers or bosses is hardly surprising. Until the 1970s most women were coerced into accepting responsibility for whatever violations they endured. In writing this book we align ourselves with movements working to reverse that perspective. We encourage you to name the problem and to hold accountable the perpetrator, whether a man or a woman. Male workers can also benefit from such encouragement, but in this book we focus on women workers who have been mistreated.

Why a Book About Women at Work?

Why talk only about women, when everyone knows that men—and even children—have been exploited, abused and endangered at work too? Employees of both genders work at the direction of one or more bosses. But within that structure far more women than men work at or near the bottom of employment hierarchies. Their relatively low employment status reflects how little value society places on women in general and their work in particular. Because they are devalued in the marketplace and at home, most women are even more vulnerable to abuse than are most men. Nevertheless we know that male workers, especially men of color and those who are disabled, gay, or considered old, suffer mistreatment at the hands of their bosses.

More men than women are in a position to mistreat women at work, and men's social status supports those who belittle women's contributions to the economy or society. We would like to believe that as women gain power they will change that situation by using their positions responsibly, a tendency some have already demonstrated. But women have mistreated workers, which signals the possibility that, as women gain toeholds in corporate and industrial hierarchies, more abusive bosses may be women. Quite a few of the workers we interviewed told us about mistreatment by women bosses. However, since our material is anecdotal, rather than scientific, we don't know whether the proportion of abusive women bosses described to us equals their proportion in the general workforce.

The stories we relate in the book reflect the roles of women in society and at work. They underline our concern for how women are treated because few of them are in a position to resist abuse without serious financial, career and emotional risk. But the issue that underlies that situation is abuse of power, regardless of who perpetrates it and no matter who is victimized by it. Several aspects of women's lives give us reason to confine our topic to what happens to women who are abused at work, whether by men or other women, whether by bosses or co-workers.

Abuse Stalks Women Everywhere

Humiliation, threats and undervaluing of women at home and in public places affect many women's reactions to abuse at work. Incest, rape and marital battering assail women much more frequently than men, with the result that some survivors become acutely alert to signs of mistreatment in all areas of their lives. They recognize it immediately and take action against the abuse or make a quick exit from the situation.

But many women and girls believe the claims made by those who victimized them: that they deserve disparagement or abuse. They may blame themselves for the treatment they suffer at work, and focus on how to change themselves rather than confronting an abusive boss or co-worker. A researcher of gender-based abuse at work reports women's comments on those connections:

[T]he abuse of power by a respected official felt like incest to a former incest victim. And a former rape victim reported feeling that the only experience emotionally comparable to her victimization by the complaint process was when she had been physically raped.

Sexual harassment, one form of emotional abuse on the job, represents special dangers for women. A government study found that almost three times as many women as men reported being sexually harassed on the job (forty-two vs. fifteen percent). Mary Bularzik, a women's history educator, argues that sexual harassment "is used to control women's access to certain jobs; to limit job success and mobility; and to compensate men for powerlessness in their own lives."

Virtually every woman knows someone who has endured some form of sexual harassment on the job. Recent publicity may have heightened your awareness to the point that you feel like you're threading your way through a mine field every day at work. You may put up your guard against sexual harassment even if you haven't experienced it yourself.

Apprehension about potential sexual harassment can affect your self-confidence when you confront an intimidating or insulting co-worker or boss. Filing a complaint about other forms of emotional abuse sometimes results in attempts at sexual coercion by the very supervisor you ask for help. If you complain to authorities about sexual harassment you may be mocked or humiliated for even bringing it up. This situation presents a Catch-22 for women in particular.

Women Must Work

Not so long ago the belief persisted that men—but not women—*had* to work to support their families, so they were compelled to endure whatever the boss required without complaining. But women also support themselves, and increasingly, several dependents. Low salaries and lack of financial and emotional support from partners make confrontation of abuse a high risk action for many women.

Polly, a licensed practical nurse, found herself in a no-win situation when her son became ill enough to require hospitalization. The doctor said the child might die if Polly couldn't visit him regularly. Her supervisor refused to grant her a leave, and she couldn't afford to resign because she had other children to support. Clearly, Polly's position presented enormous risks if she protested either that decision or the ongoing abuse. Her son survived, but Polly's anxiety took a high toll.

Women's relatively low social and financial status makes them vulnerable to demeaning treatment by people on higher rungs of the status ladder. Because so many women work at low-challenge, low-responsibility jobs, consciously or not, people get the idea that women are less competent than men. Then when insults and contemptuous treatment occur, when the boss looks right through a woman as if she's invisible or isolates her from others, she thinks there must be something wrong with *her*.

Those segregated in jobs still considered largely "women's work" may find it hard to recognize abuse of women on the job. Harassment and humiliations might seem normal, simply because no other group is available for comparison. But even if a woman has a prestigious job, she probably works under one or more male bosses and might be afraid to call attention to herself. She might reasonably fear she will be perceived as a complaining, inadequate *woman*, rather than as an employee with a justified grievance.

A study of emotionally abused nurses found that they often did respond with assertive action. But when they found it had little or no effect, they turned to a secondary tactic of avoiding the abusive person. Most of the abusive people were doctors, with whom the nurses had to work. So the strategy of avoidance created additional problems. Resigning because of verbal abuse played a major role in the turnover rate of nurses, especially nursing directors. Moving from job to job and loss of seniority exacerbates the economic hardship most women already face.

Obstacles to Resisting Abuse

When women resist abuse by supervisors or co-workers, they often encounter more obstacles than men who complain. Abusive people usually recognize who has the power and the tools to resist and who lacks them. They understand that relatively few women have access to influential or powerful people. They take advantage of the fact that many women fear making waves.

Male attitudes toward resisting abuse present a contradictory picture. On the one hand, men tend to take certain risks more readily than most women. They've been trained to accept challenges and handle defeat in ways that help them protect their sense of self-worth. That training has some negative results, but it also conditions men to cope with certain difficult situations. Some men develop tough shells in tune with their ideas about manhood and choose not to complain about abuse, fearing it will earn them the label of "wimp" or "whiner." In the trades and in the armed services, few male apprentices or rookies object to the abuse they call "hazing." Some of them look forward to the time they can inflict similar humiliation on the next group of rookies.

When women brave previously male territories and protest mistreatment, they often encounter even more abuse at every level. Sprinkler fitter Vickie Smith experienced a series of frustrations when she confronted sex discrimination:

> *I took a risk and complained [to the journeyman], but his reaction was very condescending. I went on to the foreman, who reacted by stepping up my cleanup time. At this point I called our apprentice coordinator, who asked if I wanted to be moved to another company or to file a grievance. I didn't really want to do either, so I next approached the superintendent of the company. He ended up writing a bad six-month character report on me over the incident. I also received serious bad vibes from most of the guys on the job.*

In contrast, many men—especially white men—who choose to confront abuse, benefit from built-in support through long-established organizations and "old boy" networks. Labor organizations have typically ignored opportunities to organize in female-dominated jobs and have paid little attention to particular needs of women members.

Studies document that at each step of legal procedures women experience discrimination by all levels of court officers. Women who consider filing grievances rightly fear they will get a less respectful hearing than would a man in a similar situation. Gigi, a tradeswoman, described taking a sexual harassment complaint through the court system as "like an operation. It will hurt, and you get cured much later."

Balancing Family and Work Roles

Even though the movement for women's economic rights is alive and well, the media continues to emphasize women's romantic and sexual relationships. We believe it's time to reverse that trend. Traditionally women were thought to be mainly interested in their personal, family and emotional lives, with work and money taking second or third place at best. But along came the third wave of the women's movement in the 1960s with a different message: it is women's right to work at challenging jobs outside the home and to earn salaries adequate for support of their families.

As a result of movement activities women gradually were admitted to professional schools and a few joined the ranks of workers in skilled trades. Feminists protested and brought court cases to gain economic rights. Activists put a stop to financial discrimination by insurance companies, businesses issuing credit cards and others. 1992 saw the fruits of many years of work in the political arena, as more women than ever before won elections to the U. S. Senate and many other government offices.

The other half of the gender equality issue—that men must share domestic duties, and learn to value *in everyone* the nurturing traits they've assigned exclusively to women—has been less successful. It is still news when a man takes care of a child on a regular basis and an even bigger event when he mends his wife's clothes. Few men have the commitment to leave the fast track and take equal responsibility for domestic duties.

Even as some women's rights continue to expand, a countertrend grows of once more narrowing women's focus to center on family and personal lives. Some feminists as well as anti-feminists claim that women are especially, perhaps even naturally, empathic, emotionally dependent and caring about other people. These messages of women's special virtues, sometimes mixed with the opposing trend that women can "have it all," come across strongly in TV sitcoms, self-help advice, news reports, social science research and tabloid interpretations of those studies.

A look at "self-help" shelves in libraries and book stores show that women are considered to be the ones requiring self-help—especially in the areas of personal relationships and especially with men. Women, supposedly adept at the skills of nurturing and relating to people, still "need" infinite amounts of advice on how to handle them adequately.

It is our belief that women *and men* benefit from improving their abilities to work *and* love in constructive, satisfying ways. But the balance continues to tip in the direction of improving men's ability to gain financial and political power, which they already monopolize, and for women to work on more successful relationships, at which they are already practiced. In *You Don't Have to Take It!* we try to put some balance into the picture.

We present ideas about how to handle work abuse. We suggest ways to weigh the personal risks you take when you act against abuse—and when you decide not to. We hope the stories of women who made risky decisions will help you make the best choice for yourself.

What Can Women Do?

There have always been courageous women and men who refused to submit to power abuse of any kind, even under the most severe deprivation. They take risks and pave a smoother road for the rest of us. A few such women have broken into professions and trades formerly reserved for men. Others, working singly and together, have created public awareness about violence against women and laid the groundwork for stopping it. Women have also worked with men to open a few small cracks in the narrowly based political system. Public protests have persuaded governments to recognize civil rights of people of color, lesbians and gays, of men and women who are old or disabled.

We can learn from the movement against family violence toward women, which has benefited from significant publicity for the past two decades—publicity sparked by women who said "No!" to battering, rape and incest, and who made those crimes political issues. Not many years ago "rape" and "incest" were only whispered words. The phrases "sexual harassment," "sexual exploitation," "sex tourism," "marital rape," "date rape," "battering" and "femicide" did not even exist in the English language. Now—thanks to twenty years of public education and action—these forms of abuse are taken seriously by social institutions and the public.

In contrast, on the rare occasions when emotional abuse at work receives public notice, most media treat it as an individual aberration, rather than identify it as a significant social problem. However, by 1992 a few newspaper stories did at least put a name to it:

> • "Werner Erhard . . . has been accused by former employees . . . of being abusive."
>
> • "The investigation [of a theological school psychologist who sexually abused clients] found a pattern of emotionally abusive and antagonistic behavior by Dr. Finch against faculty, staff, students and clients . . . "

Even these minor references give us hope that abuse at work is beginning to be recognized. There are other signs that the movement to change women's workplace environments has begun. The following are just a few examples:

> • Defying ancient stereotypes and patriarchal cultural obstacles, women activists in an Asian immigrant advocacy group (AIWA) organized Asian-American women and men in the Hotel and Restaurant Employees Union.
>
> • After years of enduring sexual harassment and other forms of emotional abuse, police officer Cheryl Gomez-Preston resigned from the Detroit police department and started an organization to assist other women in stopping sexual harassment.
>
> • Having tolerated twenty years of sexual and other harassment, neurosurgeon Frances Conley resigned her position at Stanford University Hospital. Now rehired, she has agreed to stay on the job, *on condition the harassment stops.*
>
> • Office workers Ellen Cassedy and Karen Nussbaum, along with ten other women, decided against all odds to form the clerical union 9 to 5.

Knowledge of how the cards are stacked against you can deplete your optimism and energy, or you can identify with these women and take the risks necessary to change. Each important advance in women's rights began with the single step of one individual person, when she decided the time was right for her. Many opportunities to take such steps will arise when the time is right for you.

You can: (1) tell a supervisor to stop insulting you, (2) transfer to another department, (3) join with a few co-workers to negotiate for changes, (4) start a union, (5) report abuse to a board of directors, or (6) as a last resort resign from a job. You might begin by labeling the problem as workplace abuse and stating clearly to yourself exactly what another person has done to you. Name the perpetrator. Say it all out loud. Each individual act jump-starts our collective journey of resistance to power abuse.

With this book we begin the process of formally naming the problem of emotional abuse at work. By clearly stating what someone has done to you, you create the foundation for your freedom. The next chapter of the book, "Naming Emotional Abuse on the Job," gets you started doing exactly that.

Chapter 2

Naming Emotional Abuse on the Job

It was so important to be able to know what was going on, to name the abuse. It stopped me from blaming myself so much. And helped me begin to think about what to do next.

Charlotte, city planner

For Charlotte and other women, the first step in focusing on emotional abuse involves naming this problem. Many women find this hard to do, however. Not being able to name the problem kept Shirley, a secretary, confused and immobilized at her job.

Shirley works hard in a medium-sized electronics plant, so she looks forward to her two breaks and lunch hour as times to relax. She uses that important time to phone her two children, run errands or chat with co-workers. She says, "I know I have a right to those breaks so I've explained how crucial they are to me to my boss, Paul, again and again." Even so, Paul regularly demands that she work straight through her break or lunch to meet deadlines he has sprung on her at the last minute. If Shirley objects, Paul raises his voice in anger and threatens, "You can be easily replaced, you know." Yet he's so nice at other times she's afraid she might be judging him too harshly.

She's afraid that Paul may be right that she shouldn't take these problems so seriously. "Maybe I'm making too big deal out of something trivial," she tells herself. "Maybe all the stress of being a single working parent is the real problem." Round and round she goes, feeling trapped.

If, like Shirley, you feel you're treated unfairly by a boss or

16

co-worker, you might not be sure what to call the situation. Since women often assume responsibility for anything that goes awry in personal relationships, we often miss the main part of the problem: that someone else is repeatedly mistreating us.

For many women the first sign of personal liberation takes place in the mind. A woman names a form of oppression to herself. Or she hears it identified by someone else and recognizes its truth. Now she says it out loud, moving from silence into speech and, perhaps, understanding and freedom. This begins the process of naming emotional abuse on the job. Since most supervisors are men, more men can abuse their authority than can women. Furthermore, many men feel threatened when women enter jobs the men assumed to be their territory. Some of these men may retaliate against female "interlopers." In spite of resistance, however, women have begun to rise to supervisory positions and to enter male-dominated professions. Unfortunately, some of these women have become abusive bosses and co-workers. To reflect current changes in management, as well as the frequency of co-worker abuse, we refer to both male and female offenders.

EXERCISE 2A: A Questionnaire To Name Emotional Abuse on the Job

As you read these questions, think of the person you believe abuses you, whether a boss, co-worker or even someone you supervise. Your answers will highlight the presence, or absence, of a pattern of abuse at your job. Check whether these actions apply to you—rarely, sometimes or often. Write in specific examples from your situation in the space provided at the end of each section. The stories following each category include one or more items from the set of questions and illustrate some of the many forms of emotional abuse in the workplace.

ISOLATION

On your job, does this person:

	Rarely	Sometimes	Often
1. Ignore or cancel your requests for meetings or feedback?	___	___	___

	Rarely	Sometimes	Often
2. Stop you from joining or attending meetings of a union or professional organization?	____	____	____
3. Prohibit discussion of salaries or working conditions with other workers?	____	____	____
4. Separate you from co-workers by insisting you work when they are at lunch or on breaks?	____	____	____
5. Cut off support by physically isolating you from co-workers similar to you in important ways (for example, other women or people of your own race)?	____	____	____
6. Isolate you from others who are also angry about the abuse?	____	____	____

7. *Isolate you from co-workers in other ways? Give examples below.*

_____

_____

Rose Melendez worked in the Mission (a Latino neighborhood) as a youth employment counselor when she was recruited to the San Francisco police force by a Latino officer. The police academy instructors let the women trainees know they were neither wanted nor seen as suited to the challenging and dangerous tasks. But the women supported and helped each other survive the seventeen weeks of the police academy.

The worst came next — extreme isolation from the experienced male partners their lives might depend on. Rose recalls that for the first year after her training, none of the men would talk to her.

> *That was the worst. If they had said something negative, I would have dealt with it, but when people just ignore you it's like you're not there. . . . We'd be driving around, midnight till eight in the morning and my partner wouldn't talk to me all night long. Or we'd respond to a call and my partner—it was always a man then—would handle everything and I'd feel like a little shadow asking myself, "Why am I here?"*

THREATS

Does this person:

	Rarely	Sometimes	Often
1. *Repeatedly threaten to fire, demote or transfer you without provocation?*	___	___	___
2. *Threaten to hit or hurt you or your family?*	___	___	___
3. *Hint that she'll reveal something you've confided if you don't do certain things?*	___	___	___
4. *Say he'll deprive you of important responsibilities unless you comply with his demands?*	___	___	___
5. *Threaten to drop tools or use them in ways that put you in danger?*	___	___	___
6. *Imply you'll be sorry if you don't do exactly what she wants, down to the finest detail?*	___	___	___
7. *Tell you about the terrible consequences to him or the organization if you resign?*	___	___	___
8. *Warn you, if you are the first woman on this job, that you may ruin others' chances if you complain?*	___	___	___
9. *Threaten that you'll lose your job unless you do physical work that endangers you or that is impossible for you because of known disabilities?*	___	___	___
10. *Shout, pound the desk, raise a fist, slam doors or talk nonstop to frighten you into submission?*	___	___	___
11. *Imply that you could "never make it on your own" but that if you stick with him, he'll move you up the ladder?*	___	___	___

12. Threaten you in other ways? Give examples below.

    Charlotte moved to a new state to accept a high-ranking position as a planner for city government and was placed on a routine six-month probation period. Initially charmed by her humorous new boss Ken, she grew increasingly dismayed by the frequent temper outbursts he directed at her and others he supervised. As she grew more confident and felt increasingly competent, Ken began assigning her clerical tasks in addition to her professional duties, despite his access to extensive clerical staff. When he was late with a deadline, Ken screamed insults and demands, requiring that Charlotte drop her tasks to do whatever he needed at that second. She tried to discuss the time crunch created by this double duty, but Ken refused. He threatened, "If you want this job, you'll do *exactly* what I tell you to."

    By arriving early and staying late, Charlotte managed to complete a difficult project. Other managers praised the work but Ken took credit, never acknowledging Charlotte's contribution. Ken never indicated that he recognized the high quality of her work, nor did he ever criticize her. So Charlotte was stunned to receive an "unsatisfactory" six-month evaluation. Ken said, "It will be a miracle if you are made permanent," stating that only his good graces could save her job. Another co-worker sought her out and, finding her in tears, confided to Charlotte that Ken always rated new workers as unsatisfactory so that he could keep them off balance and work them even harder.

DEGRADATION AND HUMILIATION

Does this person:

	Rarely	Sometimes	Often
1. Call you names like "stupid," "bitch" or "crazy"?	____	____	____
2. Ignore your ideas and then accept them from a male co-worker or someone else who has more status or power than you?	____	____	____

	Rarely	Sometimes	Often
3. Order you to do things you are ashamed of (for example, lie to inspectors, distort sales claims, make sloppy pipe fittings, neglect patients, withhold information from clients)?	____	____	____
4. Criticize or ridicule you in front of other workers, customers or the public?	____	____	____
5. Tell you no one else would ever hire you?	____	____	____
6. Ridicule your religion, race, age, beliefs, sexual orientation or gender?	____	____	____
7. Ask intrusive personal questions about your family, social life or sex life?	____	____	____
8. Prevent you from having privacy for personal or physical care(for example, restroom use)?	____	____	____
9. Shout or raise her voice to humiliate you publicly?	____	____	____
10. Check and recheck all your work beyond what's necessary for the job, repeatedly questioning petty details or your judgment?	____	____	____
11. Deliberately attempt to embarrass you by repeatedly referring to your race, gender or sexual orientation (for example, referring to you as "a lady," "a dyke" or "too sensitive about racism")?	____	____	____
12. Imply to others that he has an intimate relationship with you?	____	____	____
13. Deliberately give incorrect directions about how to perform a task, then ridicule your failure?	____	____	____

14. Degrade or humiliate you in other ways? Give examples below.

_____

_____

Lydia Vasquez, a single parent who proudly describes herself as a native of Mexico, worked as a machine operator for a truck manufacturer. She had a good working relationship with the swing-shift supervisor but transferred to days when her children returned to school after the summer. The day supervisor, angry that a woman had been assigned to him, constantly made crude sexist and racist remarks. She remembers:

> *That's when I started to learn what discrimination was. One time the supervisor suggested I slip him a five or give him a bottle to get a better job. That disturbed me because I was not used to buying my jobs by bringing gifts or giving money to anybody. . . . Once he said the reason that I was brown was because I drank too much coffee.*

His pal, the lead man, also tormented her. "He always teased me about being short, brown, dumb, and about what an ugly man I made." He told her that Mexicans were "dumb and didn't know what they were doing." Lydia concludes, "Now I understand prejudice. Now I know what racism is."

ENFORCING UNREASONABLE DEMANDS
Does this person:

	Rarely	Sometimes	Often
1. Set unnecessary, arbitrary and impossible deadlines?	____	____	____
2. Assign you all the "dirty," repetitive, dangerous or unchallenging work, or the least rewarding work stations, instead of only your share?	____	____	____
3. Insist you do work that is someone else's responsibility?	____	____	____
4. Assign tasks he knows you haven't learned to do, and refuse to provide instruction?	____	____	____

	Rarely	Sometimes	Often
5. *Routinely insist that work be accomplished in impossible amounts of time?*	____	____	____

6. *Make other unreasonable demands? Give examples below.*

_____

_____

Tina worked as a social worker in a group home for runaway teenage women with a newly appointed director, Marva. When the staff got together to discuss Marva's difficult behavior, Marva learned of their meeting and was enraged. "I was hired to command this agency and that is what I will do," she declared. "If you don't like it you can leave."

Marva then demanded that each staff member account for every minute of her time, including time in the bathroom. Staff meetings involving more than two people were canceled. Tina felt scared and disoriented.

OCCASIONAL INDULGENCES

Does this person:

	Rarely	Sometimes	Often
1. *Offer you special favors (for example, time off, flowers, lunch or high praise) when you're thinking seriously about quitting the job?*	____	____	____
2. *Respond to your intention to resign by making vague promises about how things will change?*	____	____	____
3. *Treat your rights to break times, vacation and so forth as if they were personal favors?*	____	____	____
4. *Keep a formal distance, then suddenly switch to an intimate way of relating?*	____	____	____
5. *Occasionally indulge you in other ways that make you wonder whether the job or the boss is so bad after all?*	____	____	____

6. Offer other occasional and confusing favors or treats? Give examples below.

_____

_____

Muriel, a government accountant, was initially ready to work cooperatively when Bernice was appointed department head, even though she had heard negative rumors about Bernice's management style. Within a short time, Bernice started to harass Muriel. She spent hours each day quizzing Muriel and would humiliate her in front of others. Any attempt at discussion was labeled insubordination and resulted in caustic criticism, often with others present.

In the midst of such harassment, Bernice asked Muriel out to lunch, which made Muriel feel very anxious. Muriel remembers:

> *We had lunch and Bernice was, as I expected, totally charming. I have come to dread these "friendly" encounters most of all: somehow it feels worse to be used and manipulated under the guise of pleasantries.*

Later that same afternoon, Bernice publicly announced plans to greatly reduce Muriel's job responsibilities, without having discussed any of this with her, not even during their "friendly" lunch.

DEMONSTRATING POWER

Does this person:

	Rarely	Sometimes	Often
1. Take credit for your production, work or ideas?	___	___	___
2. Arbitrarily change agreements without consulting or negotiating with you?	___	___	___
3. Demand compliance and loyalty to him when you make complaints about work?	___	___	___
4. Say her recommendation, or lack of it, can make or break you in this company?	___	___	___

	Rarely	Sometimes	Often
5. Require you, more than others, to work in potentially dangerous surroundings without proper protection (for example, around loud noise, chemicals, unsafe equipment or with inadequate lighting or ventilation)?	___	___	___
6. Become irate over issues that others find simply annoying or inconvenient?	___	___	___
7. Insist you get her approval even for small decisions?	___	___	___
8. Keep you late at work, talking about work or unrelated personal subjects?	___	___	___
9. Repeatedly claim he could do your job much better than you can?	___	___	___

10. Demonstrate power over you in other ways? Give examples below.

_____

_____

Rana, an African-American woman, had worked as a middle manager for a large insurance company for almost fourteen years. After a young white man was appointed as her supervisor, he urged her to step down and take a lower position in the firm. When she refused, he gave Rana an unfairly low evaluation, which she answered in writing. He replied, "We're going to get you for this."

During the next year and a half, her boss's power plays and threatening behavior continued. After this, Rana says, "I was so anxious that I hated to even get any message from him, wondering what would come next."

MONOPOLIZING YOUR ATTENTION
Do you:

	Rarely	Sometimes	Often
1. Feel like you're "walking on eggshells" around a supervisor or co-worker?	___	___	___

	Rarely	Sometimes	Often
2. Worry about your supervisor's or co-worker's moods, feel anxious about or afraid of his ever-changing reactions to you or your work?	____	____	____
3. Feel anxious about your faults, even though you didn't feel that way before you took this job?	____	____	____
4. Worry about whether the boss or co-worker will approve of unimportant things, such as the state of your desk?	____	____	____
5. Worry that she will yell at you, or act in an angry, punishing or unexplained critical manner?	____	____	____

6. Are there other ways you give too much attention to the person who mistreats you or to the job itself? Give examples below.

_____

_____

Tina, the social worker at the group home for runaway teen-age women mentioned previously, felt increasingly anxious, always worrying about what Marva, the program director, would do next. She found herself thinking about Marva away from work, and even began having nightmares about her.

Because of her anxiety and lowered concentration, Tina had a hard time finishing her work and would often stay late at the group home. Yet the late hours made her more exhausted and less effective the next day, further lowering her self-esteem. "I was afraid. . . . I couldn't control anything, couldn't predict [Marva's behavior]," she explains.

EXHAUSTION AND LOWERED COMPETENCY
Do you:

	Rarely	Sometimes	Often
1. Work so hard to please that you feel exhausted and find it hard to recover, even on days off?	____	____	____

	Rarely	Sometimes	Often
2. *Often feel sick, especially on work days, even though no signs of physical illness exist?*	_____	_____	_____
3. *Feel less competent to perform job tasks than you used to?*	_____	_____	_____
4. *Drink or smoke more than you would like and more than you did before this job?*	_____	_____	_____
5. *Eat more (or less) than you think is good for you since you took this job?*	_____	_____	_____
6. *Feel so worn out from the job, or distracted by it even on days off, that you don't have time for friends, family, fun or personal projects?*	_____	_____	_____

7. *Are there other ways you feel exhausted or less able to do things that you did before this job? Give examples below.*

_____

_____

Marcia, a highly trained and experienced physician's assistant, works long hours. She frequently takes charts home at night to write notes. This often requires several hours, but seems necessary to please her demanding physician boss. Yet he always demands more. Marcia finds it difficult to identify which of her boss's actions exhaust her. She says, "I usually blame myself instead for not being able to keep up."

She seldom sees women friends any more. All week Marcia suffers from back pain and a nervous stomach. She frequently skips lunch and ends up eating junk food late in the afternoon. She has lost nine pounds, has stopped exercising and feels sad, self-critical and depressed. A complete physical exam shows no physical cause for these symptoms, which lessen slightly on weekends and nearly disappear during her infrequent vacations.

Probably every employee has experienced one or more of the interactions described in the preceding questionnaire at some time in their working life. But a pattern of these inappropriate actions can add up to abuse. We don't mean to suggest that a specific number of items always indicates abuse. Still, the more checks you have under "sometimes" or "often," the more likely you are to be a victim of an abusive pattern of control. Monitoring your physical and emotional health may also provide information about whether or not you are being abused.

How Abuse Affects You

Like Marcia, the physician's assistant, workers often develop physical and emotional problems when they experience abuse on the job. Such symptoms may appear even before a woman can pinpoint what is happening to her internally. For example, you might dread going to work or develop headaches and muscle tenseness shortly after conflicts begin with your boss.

EXERCISE 2B: Possible Signals of Emotional Abuse

Consider whether you've experienced unexplained physical or emotional complaints since you've been on this job. *Check* the items that apply to you.

PHYSICAL EFFECTS

Since you began working on this job or for this supervisor, are you:

_____ 1. *Sleeping too much or too little, or awakening in the middle of the night?*

_____ 2. *Having nightmares about work?*

_____ 3. *Gaining or losing a significant amount of weight unintentionally?*

_____ 4. *Experiencing any of the following symptoms:*
   _____ *Headaches?*   _____ *Allergies?*
   _____ *Stomach or digestive* _____ *Menstrual pain or*
   problems? ("butter-   *Premenstrual Syndrome?*
   flies", diarrhea)   _____ *Hyperventilating or*
   _____ *Back, neck or*   *breathlessness?*
   shoulder pain?   _____ *Hives or a rash?*

_____ 5. *Crying more or unexpectedly?*

_____ 6. *Experiencing higher blood pressure?*

_____ 7. *Developing ulcers?*

_____ 8. *Feeling exhausted and always tired?*

EMOTIONAL EFFECTS

_____ 1. *Have your friendships and/or intimate relationships suffered because of your work or feelings about work?*

_____ 2. *Are you more cynical or needlessly distrustful?*

_____ 3. *Does your self-esteem seem less than in the past? For example, do you feel:*
   _____ *Less worthy of*   _____ *More doubtful about praise or rewards?*   *your own abilities?*
   _____ *More self-critical?*

_____ 4. *Do you often feel trapped, nervous or anxious?*

_____ 5. *Do you feel confused, unable to concentrate on decisions?*

_____ 6. *Are you more depressed, helpless or hopeless?*

_____ 7. *Do you feel angry or more resentful, expressed or not?*

_____ 8. *Do you often feel guilty, often without any particular cause?*

_____ 9. *Are you isolating yourself more from friends and co-workers?*

Understanding Your Responses

Although there's no magic number, a higher number of items or a *pattern* of negative feelings and physical symptoms could be the result of emotional abuse on the job. Of course, they could also be symptoms of other physical problems. Consult a health care provider to help you determine the causes. Be sure you choose a person who understands emotional abuse and stress management issues. Not all health care personnel are experienced in helping workers deal with these issues.

Perhaps you have sensed you would feel trapped if you let yourself look clearly at your situation. Maybe you have been avoiding the very feelings you have right now. Facing the reality of chronic abuse can elicit intense feelings of anger, sadness or even self-blame. You may feel overwhelmed; you're convinced you have to stop being abused, yet you can't see what can be done.

But you *can* do something about your situation. You have just taken the first steps by filling out the questionnaire and exercises and by naming the problem. You can continue to explore the abuse by examining your thoughts.

EXERCISE 2C: Monitoring Your Thoughts

Someone in a position of power may abuse you emotionally by using some of the methods described in the questionnaire on naming abuse. *Check* the following responses which reflect your thoughts:

_____ *1. I am powerless to change this situation.*

_____ *2. I feel worthless.*

_____ *3. I'm different from others and that's why I'm being singled out.*

_____ *4. I'm alone in this situation.*

When you feel apprehensive, powerless, worthless and alone, you've begun to believe what the abusive person has told you. His or her message may have come to you either directly, through words or actions, or indirectly through neglect. You've probably checked a number of items in the categories of "Monopolizing Your Attention" and "Exhaustion and Lowered Competency." You might have gradually changed the way you feel about yourself since you began to work under, or with, the abusive person. But maybe you haven't attributed those changes to the treatment you've received.

"Brainwashing" Can Get Anyone

Each of the headings of the questionnaire, such as "Isolation," "Threats" and "Degradation And Humiliation," identifies a method of controlling others, an abuse of power. If enough of them are used against you, you could become "brainwashed." That is, your thinking could have been changed without your consent, possibly even without your awareness.

Young women, new to the work force, may be at a particular disadvantage because of their work inexperience and desire to get a good recommendation for their next position. Yet, even experienced workers may feel immobilized by abuse on the job.

Kate served as the vice-president of an investment firm for four years. She came into the company as a secretary and very effectively worked her way up the ladder. After ten years of promotions, she became vice-president. For the next four years her boss, the company's president, constantly criticized and insulted her. He would unexpectedly fly into a rage about something she had supposedly done wrong, swearing at her and using obscene language. He undermined her confidence by saying no one could work with her. Kate knew that was not true. Often, after an outburst, he would take Kate out to dinner and apologize. A few days later, the cycle would begin again. Kate recalls her experience:

Why did I put up with it? To begin with, I was astonished, so much so that I was almost mesmerized into inactivity. I suppose I thought it would stop because I couldn't believe it was happening. I really wanted to lose my temper also but was too aware that he had the power and would use it unhesitatingly against me if I did. I also, classically, took responsibility. I kept calm, I worked hard at trying to work with him. Also, because there were no witnesses, I felt helpless. I was trapped— working at too high a level to move to another job easily. Because I had to stay (I was living alone with a big mortgage), I had to keep trying hard with him. Only now do I realize how unhappy I was for four years.

Experienced women employees in high positions, such as Kate, can be as demoralized and uncertain about how to handle the abuse as young women, new to the work force. Experiencing abuse and a tendency to blame oneself can overwhelm many women, whatever their education, experience or job level.

To have been "brainwashed" doesn't mean you've been reduced to some specific psychological or physical condition. It just means someone has subjected you to certain techniques. For example, Kate's boss isolated her, unnecessarily demonstrated his power over her, threatened and humiliated her until she felt completely exhausted and incompetent. Occasionally he would further confuse her with unexpected indulgences.

For a host of reasons, individuals react differently to being mistreated. One person's reactions may not even be the same from one incident to another. Frequently, a woman goes back and forth between these states for some period of time. She first recognizes that she has been hurt or belittled or even over-powered, then denies it in favor of another hypothesis. Then she understands it again. Some strong, independent-minded women suffer self-doubts when emotionally brutalized. Some timid, dependent women experience flashes of insight into their situations.

Because abused workers often describe themselves as feeling crazy, the brainwashing process could also be called "crazy-making." As a result of brainwashing the victim redefines what happens. Thus, women come to believe they are "overly sensitive," "not tough enough" for whatever form of work is in question, or that they "asked for" or "deserved" abuse. The same techniques that for years have kept rape and incest survivors and battered women blaming themselves also serve the needs of abusive people in the workplace.

Do They Do It On Purpose?

A boss or co-worker may or may not consciously use the control methods listed in the questionnaire. Either way, the effect remains the same. But other factors intervene. The techniques are neither perfect nor predictable, and their effects last varying amounts of time. Brainwashing works best in extreme situations. For instance, the more the abusive person succeeds in isolating the victim from people who could provide her with positive feedback about her strengths, the more effective the brainwashing. For this reason, brainwashing succeeds less often on the job than in the home because opportunities for other contacts usually exist at work.

Abuse of power may even be the standard way to treat employees in your organization. This approach may have been taught to the boss as proper procedure for keeping employees in line. Perhaps your manager or co-worker was treated this way by his supervisor, even if it's not standard company procedure.

Regardless of the abusive person's motives, or how they were learned, the effect on you can be powerful. Women who have experienced physical and emotional abuse in personal relationships rate the emotional abuse as worse since it's harder to identify and often results in longer-lasting effects. And at least as important, it can erode your sense of self if you internalize critical messages.

But at some point, after things have gone from bad to worse, something may snap and you realize this self-blame does not tell the whole truth. Naming the problem enables you to understand what is happening. Perhaps you can now hold the perpetrator responsible for his or her actions. You can then decide whether to confront the person, leave the job, or find new ways to handle the abuse.

EXERCISE 2D: Rating Abusive Techniques

To better understand the impact of emotional abuse at your job, we suggest you order the abusive actions from most to least upsetting and debilitating. Seeing what upsets you most (and least) can help you decide what you most want to challenge at this point.

BRAINWASHING TECHNIQUES

- *Isolation*
- *Threats*
- *Degradation and Humiliation*
- *Enforcing Unreasonable Demands*
- *Occasional Indulgences*
- *Demonstrating Power*
- *Monopolizing Your Attention*
- *Induced Exhaustion*
- *Diminished Competency*

Now give instances of the use of the brainwashing techniques that are most upsetting to you. Note their frequency and the effects on you, and whether the mistreatment is increasing in frequency or intensity.

MOST UPSETTING TECHNIQUE

Example: *Enforcing Unreasonable Demands*

Technique	*Frequency*	*Escalating?*
Last minute demands to stay late	*Twice-weekly*	*Yes, daily now*

Your example(s):

Technique	*Frequency*	*Escalating?*

    Now give an example of techniques least upsetting to you.

LEAST UPSETTING TECHNIQUE

Example: *Occasional Indulgences*

Technique	*Frequency*	*Escalating?*
Surprised me with afternoon off	*Once in 6 months*	*No*

Your example(s):

Technique	*Frequency*	*Escalating?*

    Even if you have just one item on this second list, if it occurs more and more frequently, you might want to take action. Working under an extremely critical or overly vigilant boss may leave you feeling crazy or worthless. Facing daily a group of male co-workers who really want you off the job can be overwhelming.

    You gain a sense of your power from deciding what aspects of the abuse most or least upset you. Seeing the frequency of abuse and whether or not it's escalating can help you decide if you want to take action against it now.

Patterns of Abuse and Your Responsibility

    Personal factors may also influence your situation. If this is your first job, you're new at your job or are supervising others for the first time, you might be sensitive to what sounds like unreasonable criticism. Not everything that feels bad is abuse. In fact, you may not be suited to the job you have. If you feel stuck in the job, you may resent any criticism.

Moreover, anger and anxiety about other aspects of your life may distort your view of events at work. A physical or emotional problem can also affect your relationships with co-workers, obscuring the real issues. Considering the following personal issues can help you sort out responsibility.

EXERCISE 2E: Taking Your Self-Inventory

In order to check the likelihood that your actions or attitudes contribute to negative interactions, check the items that apply to you.

_____ 1. *I have experienced similar problems in other jobs.*

_____ 2. *I frequently have difficulties with friends, lovers and family members.*

_____ 3. *I'm often "not speaking to" or feeling victimized by friends or family.*

_____ 4. *Others often find me "touchy" or "paranoid."*

_____ 5. *I think that bad luck always strikes me, and it's never my fault.*

_____ 6. *I carry a grudge against men in general, or women in general, or members of a particular race or religion.*

Consider what your answers might mean about your patterns of relating to others or unnecessarily feeling victimized. The higher the number of positive responses you made to the above exercise, the more likely it is that you contribute something to your work troubles. Perhaps you began, or simply continued, a negative interaction with the boss or a co-worker. Maybe you feel unable to change a pattern of hostile interchanges. An honest appraisal of your part in the interaction represents the beginning of change.

You might have been abused by more than one person or at more than one job. That could make you or your friends think it's your fault. In fact, it may only mean that emotional abuse in the workplace is very prevalent. What do *you* believe these patterns indicate?

No matter how these negative interactions started, if another person continues to mistreat you, you may want to challenge the situation. As you read the chapters on assertive confrontation and legal remedies, remember to include what you know about your own contribution to this negative interaction. You may even decide to acknowledge your own culpability to the abusive person. Faced with your honesty, the other person might be willing to change his or her abusive behavior.

You may want to seek help from friends or professionals to acknowledge your own responsibility and to plan to change your behavior. Only you can determine your priorities in the context of your job situation. But since emotional abuse remains unrecognized, it's particularly important to understand and name what is happening to you when someone emotionally abuses you at work.

Chapter 3

The Special Case of Sexual Harassment

Out there, living and breathing, is a very harmful and dangerous thing that can confront us at any time without warning. We know that it occurs today at an alarming rate. It's not a new thing. It's been happening for years. It happened to your mother and your grandmother.

Anita Hill, law professor

Anita Hill's testimony at the Clarence Thomas Supreme Court confirmation hearings in October 1991 may stand as a national turning point in consciousness of sexual harassment. The image of her televised confrontation with the powerful, privileged white male senators continues to reverberate in the work world and the political lives of women and men. Many women candidates in the 1992 elections attributed their decisions to run both to the inspiration of her actions and to the disrespectful treatment she received in the hearing room as she told of Thomas' harassing behavior years earlier.

Throughout the book we emphasize emotional abuse because that kind of mistreatment has not been widely discussed or named. Although sexual harassment has become more of a public issue recently, it has been "living and breathing" as a serious and special problem for generations. Its particular qualities complicate other abusive situations for women. A construction worker, harassed by her foreman, says:

It began to get weird when he would barely let me out of his sight. At first, he would try to grab at me as long as some of the other guys were around and it would always end in laughter. On one job, he decided

37

that he had to hold on to my belt so I wouldn't fall as I leaned out the window to cut the metal siding away from the trim. Window after window, day after day, he began to put his hand farther and farther down in my underwear. Well, I was scared. Too scared to know what to do. . . . I know I would deal differently with this sort of situation now, but I was only twenty then. Although I felt I could do anything, I couldn't deal with that.

An African-American woman working as a telephone solicitor reports similar harassment by six men at her worksite:

[They] would all come and kind of snuggle up to you in the name of telling you how to use the telephone and things like that. One man stood so close to me that you could feel his penis poking you in the leg. The room was full of people and they just sat there like nothing was going on. . . . [I just felt that] it happened because white men think that black women are whores. . . . Now I feel it's more that I'm a woman, because when I look back on the situation that I was in, you know, it was happening to all the women.

An investigation officer for a human rights commission forfeited a promising career because of the director's sexual harassment. The director had repeatedly made derogatory comments about the man she was dating. On an out-of-town business trip, he pressured her for a date and when she refused, he phoned her hotel room constantly throughout the night. She says: "Right away I started looking for a new job."

These three women were harassed because of unwanted sexual attentions. As a result, the human rights officer quit her job and the construction worker and telephone solicitor endured daily fear and anxiety. The official definition of sexual harassment reflects these women's experiences.

What Is Sexual Harassment?

In 1980, the federal Equal Employment Opportunity Commission issued guidelines defining sexual harassment:

Unwelcome sexual advances, requests for sexual favors, and other verbal or physical conduct of a sexual nature constitute sexual harassment when:

• Submission to such conduct is made either explicitly or implicitly a term or condition of an individual's employment, or when:

• Submission to or rejection of such conduct by an individual is used as the basis for employment decisions affecting such individual, or when:

• Such conduct has the purpose or effect of unreasonably interfering with an individual's work performance or creating an intimidating, hostile, or offensive work environment.

The key words in this definition are:

• Unwelcome
• Sexual nature
• Affecting employment decisions
• A hostile environment.

In 1986 the Supreme Court affirmed that if you are subjected to sexual jokes, sexual propositions, questions about your personal sex life, persistent requests for dates, pawing and obscene gestures, and these are unwelcome to you, your workplace is being poisoned for you. You are therefore, according to the court, a victim of illegal sexual harassment.

Naming Sexual Harassment

Because this book focuses on the abuse of women and what you as a woman can do about it, we describe women as the targets of harassment. Because most sex harassers are men, we refer to sexual harassers as male. An apparently small number of women do sexually harass men, but far fewer men are targets than women.

The following exercise, similar to the ones in Chapter 2, may help you to name the problem of sexual harassment. As with emotional abuse, the person who harasses you may be either a supervisor or a co-worker. Check how often each item in the left column has occurred.

EXERCISE 3A: Identifying Sexual Harassment

On your job, does this person:

	Rarely	Sometimes	Often
1. Tell suggestive stories or sexual, offensive jokes?	____	____	____
2. Stare or leer at you?	____	____	____
3. Make intrusive and sexual remarks (for example, that your clothes or make-up "make you look sexy")?	____	____	____
4. Show you, or leave at your work station, pornographic pictures or stories?	____	____	____
5. Make unwanted attempts to touch or fondle you?	____	____	____
6. Use physical force to touch or fondle you?	____	____	____
7. Try to draw you into a conversation you don't want about personal or sexual matters?	____	____	____
8. Use inappropriate terms of endearment (for example, "honey," "baby doll" or "sweetheart")?	____	____	____
9. Call you offensive names such as "cunt" or "bitch"?	____	____	____
10. Put unwanted items of a sexual nature (such as condoms) in your desk drawer or lunch pail?	____	____	____
11. Request dates, drinks, back rubs, or the like, persisting in these requests even after you've refused them?	____	____	____
12. Specifically proposition you to have sex with him when you've said you do not want this?	____	____	____

13. Suggest you will be rewarded at work
if you accept his sexual advances?   _____   _____   _____

14. Say he will retaliate against you at
work if you refuse his sexual advances?   _____   _____   _____

If someone at your job makes unwanted sexual advances, and if you risk being punished if you reject them, that's sexual harassment. If sexual remarks, pictures, gestures or other actions cause you to feel surrounded by threats and hostility, that's sexual harassment.

How often does this happen to women? Studies vary but nine surveys conducted between 1976 and 1991 found that between thirty percent and ninety percent of working women reported sexual harassment. The women surveyed included federal employees, blue-collar factory workers, workers in the auto industry and social workers, among others. Although younger women are generally exposed to more harassment, age offers no protection. Genvieve, a sixty-six-year-old secretary, objected to her boss's sexual harassment, and then found that his harassment shifted:

He got extremely abusive; there was no aspect of my work he didn't attack. The sexual incidents stopped, except he seemed determined now to prove I was just a stupid steno. I'm absolutely convinced that all the other abuse, the whole vendetta that followed had to do with objecting to those sexual performances in the office. . . . I keep thinking: Is this what I get after forty years?

If you've experienced sexual harassment, it's likely that, like Genvieve, you have faced emotional abuse along with it. You might find it difficult to distinguish between the two or wonder why you need to see the difference. After all, both kinds of abuse represent unfair and inappropriate uses of power.

But distinguishing between the two can help you decide how to respond. Sexual harassment has been declared illegal and you can use the law to stop such harassment. Other kinds of abuse, such as yelling at, demeaning or humiliating you, may be judged illegal, *but only* if they are aimed at you because you are a woman (or disabled, or a person of color, or old).

The sexual nature of sexual harassment carries special and multiple meanings for both men and women in our culture. Although many people privately feel shame or embarrassment about sexual feelings or actions, frank sexuality in public life surrounds us—in advertising, movies, television, music and videos. This outward acceptance of sexuality can become particularly confusing in the workplace, especially in making the distinction between mutually agreeable sexual interactions and sexual harassment. After all, individuals do become sexually attracted to one another, at work as well as other places. Some men charged with harassment may say, "It was a mutual flirtation—just normal office behavior." Playful flirting does occur on the job and many long-term relationships begin at work. How do you tell the difference between mutually agreeable sexual bantering and sexual harassment?

Sexuality in the Workplace

To explore the claim that sexual harassment is just a normal part of the dating game, sociologists studied dating relationships and harassment behavior. They found that harassment is very different from usual man/woman interactions.

First, in dating relationships, a man usually chooses a woman of the same race and near his own age. In contrast, a man who harasses may target a woman on the basis of close proximity or her lack of power. Age or race may not enter into it unless one of those factors adds to the woman's vulnerability. Second, a man who harasses doesn't accept the woman's lack of interest but continues to pressure and pursue. Third, he often has no serious interest in the woman. And finally, a man who harasses often targets several women at the same time. Women's responses differ too. Though initially women may be flattered by sexual advances, most victims of sexual harassment feel anxious, afraid and angered by the attention. None of this resembles ordinary courtship behavior.

Sexuality affects how the game gets played but the real issue is the exercise of power. Catharine MacKinnon, a legal scholar, describes sexual harassment as an "explosive combining of unacceptable sexual behavior and the abuse of power."

Janet, a nineteen-year-old trainee technician in a medical laboratory, found the attention of her supervisor, Hal, anything but natural and comfortable. Hal spent the first several weeks of her training period talking mostly about his personal situation and asking Janet about hers. He assigned her work within his view near his desk, but he never provided the training she expected. Instead, he told her jokes that were humorous at first, but soon became more sexual and offensive to Janet. She tried to work with other supervisors instead of Hal but he prevented this. Once he said to her: "Stand right there so that I can look at your rear end; it's enough to make me fall in love with you." After this, Janet felt very apprehensive when alone with Hal, although her training required his individual attention.

Janet certainly didn't feel free to react to Hal as she would have in a non-work setting. As her account suggests, a woman can't make a real choice to respond to advances when she's worried about keeping her job or concerned about getting needed training.

Many writers and scholars assert that men and women live in different subjective worlds. When it comes to attitudes about sex at work, that appears very true. Men tend to see sexual interactions in the workplace as just a natural part of life. Women feel anxious and intimidated. The differences between men's and women's perceptions form a crucial part of the sexual harassment phenomenon.

Men Wear Different Lenses

Let's look at sexual activity at work first from what we call "a man's point of view." Even though men react in a variety of ways, most learn, as boys and young men, the "appropriate male way" to approach women. A man is raised to initiate sexual interactions, to be the sexual aggressor. Among his teenage friends and later with adult men, he may have won accolades for "scoring" with women or have been ridiculed for "failing." Carol Lindsay, a clerical worker in a small advertising agency, described the response of male co-workers to the boss's harassment of her: "The men in the office all knew what was going on. Their response was to smile and chuckle and to speculate on whether Frank had 'scored' this time around." Men often feel that people exaggerate the issue of sexual harassment. They believe that most incidents reflect just normal sexual attraction.

Some men may even feel pressured toward sexual aggressiveness in their workplace. In male-dominated fields such as the trades and some professions, masculine sexual aggressiveness is expected. If they work in jobs surrounded by many women, they may act sexually aggressive to counter any questioning about their manhood.

A boss may show anger when you, as his secretary, delay his letters or refuse to work overtime again. But his anger smacks of a very different kind of rage when you refuse sex with him or don't respond to his sexual innuendoes. Such refusals can reach the core of how he thinks of himself as a man. You wonder about your reluctance to flatly reject sexual overtures. Even if you haven't verbalized your fears, you may have an intuitive feeling that your "no thanks" will be hard for the boss to take. If you've guessed right, the retaliation could be devastating. Women often try to think of ways to soften their refusal.

If a man is applauded by his male colleagues and friends for his sexual prowess, that applause can be so loud that he cannot hear the woman saying "no." He assumes that he has impressed her and can't understand her unavailability to him. He doesn't see her totally different view of the situation.

Sex-Role "Spillover"

Many men are accustomed to viewing women as wives or lovers or mothers and feel more comfortable interacting with women on that basis. Many women are most comfortable in roles resembling what they do at home and often act at work just like they do in their families. Similarly, men often don't differentiate roles at work from those at home. This has been called "sex-role spillover." A female flight attendant says:

> *"I like to think of the cabin [of the plane] as the living room of my own home. When someone drops in [at home] you may not know them, but you get something for them. You put that on a grand scale—thirty-six passengers per flight attendant—but* it's the same feeling.

Women's and men's behavior on the job also mirrors the home situation when it comes to power. Many couples may not acknowledge that one of them has more power than the other. If you asked the average man if he uses power over his wife, he would be astounded if not insulted. Yet many men still exercise the power to make major decisions about their families' lives. Few question these power relationships at home.

Furthermore, if a man is insensitive to his wife's needs and feelings (a frequent complaint by women about their husbands) then he may not consider the feelings of the women targets of his power plays at work. It doesn't require a big step for a man to ignore the power issue on the job as well as at home, and to consider a female co-worker a convenient outlet for sexual interaction.

The Lenses of Women

Some women like flirting at work, bantering with "the boys." The atmosphere where you work may have a playful sexiness—an atmosphere you enjoy. At first, you might be flattered by sexual attention from a boss or co-worker. If you admire him or are impressed by his high status, his attention may seem immensely flattering. But when the pressure continues even after you reject the advances, you may become fearful and anxious. A graduate student says:

> *I would say half the women I know are like me, ideal victims of sexual harassment. . . . We've been told all our lives that male attention is flattering. Nobody ever talked about how humiliating and coercive it can be at times.*

Like some women, however, you may decide two can play this game and you may consciously use sex as a strategy to get ahead. You may have found that sexual attractiveness has previously gotten you what you wanted: a marriage, relationships with men outside of work or better working conditions. You may know that in the real world the "casting couch" is not just a figure of speech. Even though these "rules" are not written down anywhere, many women understand and follow them. It takes courage to resist. A filmmaker recalls her responses to a director who suggested a weekend together to "talk about the film":

> *[To his invitation], I said, I don't know. I don't know. But inside my head was 'I want that job'. . . . I really was considering it. I didn't want to sleep with him, but he was holding it over my head and I was*

*willing right then to sleep with him in order to get the job. I finally
came to my senses. He called me back and I said, 'No, I just can't do
it.' Of course that was the end of the job.*

Like many women, you may have learned to accept men's
unwelcome sexual overtures in order to avoid hurting their feelings or triggering their anger. At work, you may follow that pattern and allow a man to control the interactions between you.
You feel reluctant to challenge a man because of his power position but his behavior still makes you uneasy. You may see a
whole range of sexualized actions as hostile rather than exciting,
actions that spoil your work environment.

Even if you made it clear that you didn't want the sexual attention, you may blame yourself and feel ashamed and embarrassed after a harassment incident. You may tell yourself that if
you had acted differently, the behavior wouldn't have continued.
The myth that women should control men's sexual behavior dies
hard. You may believe that somehow you have the sole responsibility for what happened. You think to yourself: Maybe I flirted
without realizing it, maybe I dressed provocatively, maybe I
laughed too hard at a sexy joke. Although you feel you should
have managed the sexual behavior differently, you also have the
gnawing feeling that you really have little control over the man's
behavior. Even quite self-confident women experience a sense of
powerlessness when harassed. Women say that, whether the harassment was severe or not, their feelings of self-worth decreased
significantly as a result of being harassed.

The tendency to blame yourself, or other women, can vary
with the situation. If a woman has been seriously harassed, she
may feel less responsible for the incident. And once women endure sexual harassment themselves, they are less likely to blame
women in similar circumstances. If a woman blames herself, she
is likely to protect the perpetrator. Women have said they didn't
want to embarrass the men publicly or to get them into trouble.

Because of this sense of responsibility, a harassed woman
may not tell anyone about the incident. She may not even mention the harassment to her husband or boyfriend—all too often
with good reason. Men often blame the woman for the harassment, believing that she somehow encouraged it. Friends and co-

workers may also believe myths about women's responsibility for men's sexual behavior and they may not be particularly sympathetic. Even when a woman tells someone, she will often leave out the sordid details. Anita Hill's delay in recounting the lurid specifics of the encounters attributed to Clarence Thomas until she was called to testify at his confirmation hearings jibes with the accounts of many women victims who do not reveal the truth until many years later.

Lesbians may have different encounters with sexual harassment. A closeted lesbian is usually assumed to be single, heterosexual, and therefore fair game. Closeted lesbians experience more incidents of harassment than do lesbians who are open about their sexual identity. A lesbian may fear that she risks her job or her standing at work if she discloses the real reason why she does not desire sexual interactions with this man—or men in general.

Regardless of sexual orientation, many women try to ignore unwanted sexual overtures or remarks at work, hoping they will stop. One study found that seventy-five percent of women victims did just that. But if the woman decides not to tell anyone about the incident, tension, fear and anger build up internally. Job performance suffers, and time and energy go into warding off future trouble without creating a stir.

When women simply ignore men's overtures, men may interpret this, however wrongly, as indirect encouragement and actually increase the harassment. On the other hand, confronting the perpetrator about his unwanted behavior may also increase the harassment. As we discuss in other chapters, you need to understand your own work circumstances so you can predict whether your challenges to harassment will go well or not. Understanding your workplace will help you predict whether your challenges will be effective. With knowledge of the alternatives for action as well, you can choose a strategy with a good chance of success.

When the Job is Sexualized

Sexual harassment can happen anywhere, at any kind of job. But many jobs actually encourage sexualized behavior. Some jobs demand that you at least pretend to like the sexualized environment. Standardized sexual attractiveness may be a job requirement for those who serve the public, for example, receptionists or flight attendants. A flight attendant makes airline passengers feel comfortable, so she may believe it inappropriate to protest sexy jokes or banter. This reinforces the notion that women in these jobs may invite sexual advances.

• A waitress's tips may depend on accepting customers' sexual banter and physical touching. And a cocktail waitress is often required to wear a sexy costume. That garb, along with excessive drinking by patrons, puts her at risk for receiving sexual overtures. But her job security and income depend on not making waves. A cocktail waitress talked about how she "must manage to turn [the abusive customer] off gently without insulting him, without appearing insulted. Indeed [you] must appear charmed by it, find a way to say no which also flatters him."

• The recording industry markets sex and has been widely criticized for degrading women in videos and on album covers. In some recording studios, sexual jokes are rampant. A secretary in a major recording company charged that her boss masturbated at her desk and physically blocked her exit. One male executive commented, "We're an industry that hasn't grown up, that's made up of a bunch of guys going through puberty at forty."

• Some television beer commercials portray scantily clad and voluptuous women as an added attraction to men as they hunt, fish and drink beer. At a beer company, a machinist complained that her male co-workers placed pornographic pictures on her tool box and on her mirror. She charged that a direct connection existed between the sexual exploitation of women in the company's ads and management's insensitivity to sexual harassment.

• A former head of production for a major Hollywood studio says:

Sex is in the air. We create the myths here—romance, passion, glamour—with which America is obsessed. Because it can be hard to separate real life from myth-making, you see a lot of sexually oriented behavior.

• A stripper has to fight against the widespread assumption that her work invites and justifies sexual harassment. One stripper concludes:

The real problem is the way society views stripping. They see strippers as hunks of meat, the dregs of humanity, without feelings or dignity. The general view is that we are nymphomaniacs ready to go to bed with anyone. It's simply not true. . . . As far as I'm concerned, all women are exploited. Prostitution and stripping aren't the causes of sexism. They are the result.

Co-workers and Customers

The power of the man who harasses you may not flow from his formal position. In fact, in many work situations, co-workers rather than those with formal authority harass women.

Sometimes, co-workers gain power when people in charge don't stop the abuse or indirectly condone it. During the first week of Gigi Martino's work as a merchant sailor, a seaman propositioned her. Upset, she consulted with the chief engineer: "He consoled me by saying that if he were a female on a ship and didn't get propositioned, then he'd start worrying."

When Cheryl Gomez-Preston, a woman of African-American and Puerto Rican descent, became a Detroit police officer, her co-workers sent her written racial slurs and threats, such as "Die, bitch," "Nigger bitch" and "Go back to Africa." When she appealed to the commanding officer, an African-American man, he casually explained that "this was the mentality of the white boys over there." Then he suggested that she have sex with him if she wanted him to help.

Clients and customers also engage in sexual harassment. When they threaten to retaliate for the refusal of sexual advances, the consequences can be severe: they can withdraw their business or cancel contracts with your company. Workplace sexual harassment can occur in any kind of business relationship where one person controls the benefits for, and reprisals against, another person.

Why Women Don't Complain

Even if you've experienced serious harassment, you probably didn't make a complaint; most women don't. Many times women don't even identify the behavior as harassment. Even when they define it as harassment, women often tell no one.

Some women do confront the harasser individually and many of them find that effective. Of 20,000 federal employees surveyed in 1987, forty-four percent of the women who reported sexual harassment said they had tried to stop the harassment on their own. Sixty-one percent of those women said objecting "made things better." Yet, only fifteen percent of the harassed women reported this to any one in authority. Less than five percent made a formal complaint.

Why don't more women make formal complaints? The reasons are many and compelling. This exercise helps you explore the reasons for not confronting sexual harassment.

EXERCISE 3B: Reasons Not to File a Complaint Against Sexual Harassment

Check those that apply to your situation.

_____ 1. *I can't take the risk. I need the job and am frightened about possible retaliation by the boss or co-workers.*

_____ 2. *I'm not sure what steps to take to complain, and I'm pessimistic about the outcome.*

_____ 3. *A previous complaint I made got me nowhere, so I'm not about to try that again.*

_____ 4. *I've been told all my life not to argue or to fight, so I avoid conflict whenever possible.*

_____ 5. *My friends, co-workers and even my family will assume that I'm somehow responsible. They'll say I shouldn't get into these situations.*

_____ 6. *I feel I need to protect the man involved since the assault on his ego would be too much for him to bear.*

_____ 7. *I can't depend on my union to support me. The men in charge would probably not understand.*

_____ 8. *I'm afraid that I'll be dismissed as a "spurned woman," as was Anita Hill.*

_____ 9. *I assume that the people hearing the complaint will take the side of the person I'm accusing.*

_____ 10. *I'm afraid they will call me a troublemaker and say I am bringing a trivial charge or just being malicious. I may be given poor work evaluations.*

Each fear in this long list comes from the unhappy experiences of other women. Go over the answers you checked and ask yourself:

What's the evidence this will happen?
If so, what are the most likely consequences?

Even if only a few of these fears ring true for you, your reluctance to start a complaint process is understandable. In fact, even if you start a complaint process, you may experience what has been called "filer's remorse"—second thoughts about making the harassment public. You may just want to forget about the whole experience after the harassment has ended. Maybe "forgetting" is one way you've dealt with the pain of past abuse.

But not speaking up prolongs the existing Catch-22 situation. You and other women don't say anything, so the company head doesn't know about the incidents. When you do decide to tell him, he denies the existence of any problems because no one has ever come forward. You predict he'll deny it, so you don't challenge the abuse. And the cycle continues.

People in the sexual harassment field say that very few women bring false charges. The fallout from complaining often seems too big a price to pay. Officials who deal with sexual harassment charges often find that there's no disagreement about the actual facts. The person charged will acknowledge that his behavior or his language was exactly what the victim reported. Investigators of sexual harassment at a major university reported that the two parties agreed about the specific behavior in ninety percent of the cases. The difference: He believed his behavior was flattering to the woman, whereas she felt intimidated and frightened by it.

If you've thought about making an official report, you know that this often results in a "he said, she said" kind of situation. Many times, sexual harassment occurs out of the sight or hearing of others—in private offices, in a restaurant, or perhaps in a car on the way home from work. Without witnesses, it's one person's word against the other. However, the courts now take the harassed woman's perceptions more seriously. The Supreme Court has ruled that victims' statements can determine whether sexual harassment has created a hostile working environment.

One Result: She Quits—He Stays On

When women experience sexual harassment, quitting their jobs frequently seems the only realistic way out. Elaine, a Native American nurse, had just taken a job at a health clinic and was having her first conversation with the director. While telling her that he valued the views of women on his staff about women's issues, he stared constantly at her breasts. She says, "The whole idea of his talking about the importance of women's issues and then looking at my body all the time was just too much." He did this several more times and she became apprehensive when she had to be alone with him to discuss work issues. She liked her work and believed she was making a contribution to the Native American community, but she soon left the job, primarily because of the director's behavior. Ironically, in many such situations the perpetrator stays and the woman leaves.

Depending on her job and personal circumstances, resigning affects each woman differently. The server in a fast food store or the line worker in a factory may have little trouble finding another job. But if a downturn has affected the economy, quitting could pose an enormous problem. A waitress remarks: "It reaches a point where it's too much of a hassle and you quit and take something else. But when you have children and no support payments, you can't keep quitting."

Studies show that about seventy percent of women experiencing sexual harassment leave their jobs. They either quit or are fired in retaliation for refusing sexual advances. We also know that on average, sixty percent of working women report being sexually harassed. So if *sixty percent* of women are sexually harassed and *seventy percent* of those women must leave their jobs, we have a problem of considerable consequence to millions of women. In fact Sally Kaplan, a social researcher, cautions that if something isn't done about sexual harassment to prevent many women from leaving their jobs, the United States won't be competitive in the new international markets. Through years of affirmative action policies and through individual persistence, women have gained a toehold in many occupations. That progress can be seriously endangered if many sexually harassed women leave their jobs. Also, when women want to complain about harassment, they may find that long-term employees will be taken more seriously. Going from job to job doesn't give you that permanence. So quitting puts a damper on both the progress and the possibility of effective complaints.

Some Reasons For Optimism

Maintaining a long view over time gives us some optimism. Men have enjoyed centuries of freedom to harass women sexually. Coined only in 1976, the term "sexual harassment" now defines a social issue, not just a personal problem. Legal changes signify considerable progress in recent years. Courts define sexual harassment as illegal sex discrimination. The courts also give considerable credit to the woman victim's perceptions. Employers now are held responsible if sexual harassment occurs in their workplaces. Women have won large monetary settlements because of the effects of harassment and can now sue for compensatory damages when harassment occurs.

Women's organizations have been in the forefront of the fight against sexual harassment. The women's movement and the significant influx of women into all areas of the work force have brought positive changes for women workers. Many women now in prominent positions in government and industry have been fighting for the end of all kinds of sex discrimination, including sexual harassment.

After Anita Hill's grilling by the Senate Judiciary Committee, a question was heard again and again: Would any woman come forward now? Some women may feel intimidated by Anita Hill's experience, but the anger of others will energize them to action. Following the Clarence Thomas confirmation hearings, human rights commissions reported being inundated with calls. Letters deluged newspaper editors, and businesses and other organizations were under increasing pressure to stop sexual harassment. More and more women have brought legal suits. Organizations as diverse as city councils, transit systems and the military instituted very tough rules about dismissing harasssers and providing training for employees. Four admirals and the Secretary of the Navy lost their jobs in 1992 on charges that they mismanaged the inquiry into blatant sexual harassment know as the "Tailhook" scandal.

On this basis, we can feel some optimism about future attention to sexual harassment and the other kinds of emotional abuse which constitute the focus of this book. Our society has come part of the way toward establishing a safe environment for working women. Those cartoons showing the boss chasing the secretary around the desk have largely disappeared. Instead we have recent accounts of men, such as the one quoted in *The New York Times*, who now make serious attempts to change their traditional sex-laden work behavior.

> *A word like "Hon" becomes a friendly nickname. But that can be offensive, and I stopped using it a couple of weeks ago. I'm not sure I'd like to be called that at the workplace either.*

Barney Rosenzweig, TV producer of "Cagney and Lacey" and "The Trials of Rose O'Neill," says: "Like most men I tend to forget that what we regard as kidding around, being cute, can be very off-putting for women."

As you consider action against sexual harassment or other kinds of abuse, you may also want to think about how your individual situation is influenced by political and social factors. Placing your circumstances in that broader context is the purpose of the next several chapters.

SECTION II

The Big Picture

Chapter 4

Are You Privileged, "Other" or Both?

*Speaking Korean in an Anglocentric, monolingual culture made me
"other." I wanted to be like the other children in my class. I had learned in
this country that to be different—from the standard of whiteness and maleness—to be other, meant to be inferior and bad. Everything about me was
bad.*

Hyo-Jung Kim

Abuse at work doesn't occur in a vacuum. Power and privilege
and the confusion about each of them sometimes contribute to
maintaining abuse. Identifying your privilege and power, or
your status as "Other," can affect your fear of abuse and your
ability to decide on the next steps.

Who Are The Privileged?

A qualified man reaps the benefit of his privilege when management encourages him to compete for an important position,
while overlooking an equally proficient woman. An interviewer
dismisses a sixty-year-old as a competitor for a sales job, but
hires a young person. Conference coordinators choose white
male scientists to participate on committees and panels of experts, ignoring equally accomplished women. A woman of color
may be considered for even fewer of those opportunities. What *is*
this thing called privilege?

Privilege *is a benefit or advantage enjoyed by a particular person or
elite group of people. Privilege usually grants protection against some
problems and inconveniences, and exemption from certain obligations.*

The privileged *are those who have special benefits, advantages, exemptions or protection usually as a result of their social status (class, sexual orientation, gender, age, race).*

Many people associate privilege with power, but the two concepts differ. The ability to distinguish between those who have power and those who have privilege can help you see clearly how each relates to abuse. How you respond to control and humiliation may depend on your understanding of another person's status and privilege, relative to yours. For instance, you might acquiesce, either gracefully or resentfully, to demands of a privileged man, even if he's not in a position of power over you. You might respond to his upper class accent or his status as a male or an older person *as if* he actually has the power to control you. Or maybe he *believes* his privilege gives him authority over you, and you follow his orders because you don't want him to feel embarrassed by your refusal to recognize his authority. If you convince yourself that you must do what this prestigious man stipulates, you give your power away. You attribute power to him, but it may be your attitude toward his privilege that causes the major problem.

Like lots of other people, you might prefer to avoid thinking about these issues. Maybe you fear that acknowledging your privilege or someone else's will bring out your feelings of envy, guilt, powerlessness or unwelcome responsibility. But trying to escape full awareness of your emotional reactions to privilege makes it harder to confront abuse in the way you choose. Amelia, a licensed practical nurse, said about an abusive supervisor who was African-American, "The racial differences caused me to wonder, 'Is this part of my racism or our cultural differences?' It was useful to do that, but when I talked to other workers about him, I realized it wasn't just me." Clarifying the possible relationship between her white privilege and the supervisor's male privilege helped Amelia make a decision. She decided to resign but when she left she reported her complaints to her supervisor's boss.

When You're The One With Privilege

You may, at a tender age, have identified the privileged people in your neighborhood, even if that word was never used to describe them. Maybe their high social status was signaled by a slight shift in tone of voice when they were mentioned. You got the message to keep a respectful distance. When you needed to speak to them, you did it ever so politely. Think about who those people were. The mayor? A doctor? White people? Did they live in certain neighborhoods, belong to the country club, attend private schools?

Which people might you, even now, feel a little anxious about approaching socially or for a business transaction? Focus for a moment on reactions of uneasiness or self-consciousness you would experience in the homes or offices of certain people. If one of those people invited you to a party, would you worry about saying the "wrong thing"? Using the wrong fork? Some symbols of high social status take obvious forms. The privileged live in cloistered neighborhoods or attend events considered socially newsworthy by the local paper. But some of those who evoke your nervous reactions may not enjoy wealth nor appear exceptional to everyone. They may have just succeeded in climbing one rung higher than you on the status ladder.

If you are one of the people who benefits from privileged status, you tend to see someone like yourself mirrored back when you look at television news, advertisements featuring successful people, or arts and entertainment features. Those people may appear more glamorous, better dressed, a little older or younger than the advertising models, but if you squint your eyes you see someone more or less like you. A quick perusal of newspapers shows similar portraits of people considered politically or financially important. Most of them are male and most of them are white. Since these are traits that can't be controlled, the significant questions about privilege are "How does the person use it?" and "How does it affect you?"

The Shield of Privilege

Privilege works as a kind of shield. To the extent you have it, it protects you from some strains and hardships. It paves the way for opportunities. If your status is high you probably know other people who have similar privilege. They might offer you opportunities to make money or interview for a better job. It seems natural for a friend to introduce you to someone who can help you. You consider the favor so ordinary that you don't even identify it as privilege. That personal introduction may give you a boost of confidence, which enables you to present yourself in the best light. You make a better impression, and that enables you to get the job or make the sale. You ignore the fact that privilege doesn't shield other people from having to present themselves as strangers when asking for something.

When you look for a job or advancement, you'll be lucky if you're interviewed by another privileged woman. She sees someone like herself. She's likely to hire or promote a person she feels comfortable with, and because she sees you as a familiar type, she tends to feel at ease with you. So the advantage of the initial introduction may lead to higher status and even more privilege.

Imagine the job market as a marathon foot race. A male runner would be given the privilege of a thirty-minute advantage. So as a woman entering this race, you'd be half an hour behind the lead man. But when you took off at the starting gun, you might not notice the others placed behind you, scheduled to start even later. You might have been granted a half-hour head start over some of them on the basis of your privilege as a white person. Or you might have started earlier than others, because you were presumed to be heterosexual or able-bodied.

In the "rat race" of the work world, a white male benefits from automatic advantages similar to those we noted in the hypothetical foot race. Depending upon your class or race, you might have taken the position right behind that white man. You might enjoy your place on the privileged receiving end when the time came for assignments, promotions or raises. Other more subtle experiences, such as living in the "right" neighborhood, going to the "right" schools or knowing the "right" people could give you the inside track. If someone asked you how you got a head start, you might not know what they were talking about. "Just lucky, I guess," you might say. "Well, I guess I'm just faster than most people." You probably wouldn't want to know that special privilege determined when or where you started the race, because getting special treatment seems unfair.

Quite a few people in the United States have increased their privilege by earning more money than their parents and moving into a higher class. Some women advance their status simply by marrying wealthy men. So money often brings privilege in its wake and lots of money brings lots of privilege. In addition, privilege permits you to enter fields offering economic promise. Economic comfort interacts with other privileges to form a cycle of advantages.

Who Are The Others?

But you may be one of the people who rarely, if ever, enjoys privilege. You may feel intimidated by people at work because you are aware of your relatively low status. You see yourself as one of the women who don't count much. One of the *Others*. You may recognize the injustice of other people's judgments on the basis of traits you can't control. Still, you hesitate to object to unfair treatment, and against your will, you feel grateful to have any job at all. Or maybe you don't buy any of that, but you realize people of privilege look down on you. That makes you sad, but you tell yourself, "It's just life." Or it makes you mad, and you continually fight the urge to snap at anyone who treats you with less than full respect. Perhaps because you don't want to acknowledge such a painful situation you act as if all people have equal opportunity to create whatever social reality they want. You refuse to admit the existence of Others and disassociate yourself from them.

> The Others *are people often judged to be less important than the privileged.* Others *tend to be invisible in popular media or portrayed only in a narrow range of roles—those roles considered insignificant in power circles. They are rarely hired for jobs of high authority or adequate pay and often excluded from scientific studies.*

You might often feel like one of those Others, or perhaps you look upon certain people as Other. You might experience either one or the other vantage point, as your circumstances change. When you were growing up, your parents may have instructed you to avoid certain people considered "trash," "different," "not nice" or just plain "low class." Think about the people whose well-being you now assume you needn't bother about, the ones less successful than you, who wear "tacky" clothes, don't "speak correctly," who are "different" or "stick with their own kind." They may live in dangerous neighborhoods. You think they speak too loudly or stand too close to you in conversation. You view them as unattractive. Perhaps you learned as a child to avoid such people. They are the Others, in comparison to you. Their race, ethnicity, class or religion probably differ from yours.

If your status is Other, you look in the television glass and see, not a mirror, but people from a different world. If you're over fifty, you may feel "out of it." All the consumers of products on television seem to be young, blonde and as thin as low-cal crackers. These able-bodied people holding athletic poses suffer from nothing more devastating than the common cold or body odor. There is no obviously disabled person showing off her freshly shampooed hair. The models' skin color, hair texture, noses, cheekbones and eyelids are nearly uniform. Most of the models are trying to captivate or please young white people of the opposite gender. When models of color appear in advertising, they often look a great deal like their white counterparts.

EXERCISE 4A: What's *Your* Status?

What is your quick answer to this question: Are you mostly privileged or Other?

Privileged _____ Other _____

Some people are unwilling or unable to choose just one of the two categories. Maybe you identify yourself as somewhat privileged, but also realize some aspects of your status are considered "Other." Whether you chose one of the categories or both, try to determine the reasons for your choice.

This exercise can help you clarify your Privileged/Other status. It might be your first step to understanding your status relative to your boss or co-workers. Look at the categories below, and check the ones that describe you.

PRIVILEGED/OTHER CHECKLIST

PRIVILEGED	**OTHER**
_____ *White*	_____ *Person of Color*
_____ *Man*	_____ *Woman*
_____ *Heterosexual*	_____ *Lesbian/Gay/Bisexual*

PRIVILEGED	OTHER
_____ *Native-Born*	_____ *Immigrant*
_____ *Healthy*	_____ *Chronically Ill*
_____ *Slim*	_____ *Fat*
_____ *Young Adult/Midlife Adult*	_____ *Adolescent/Old*
_____ *Able-Bodied*	_____ *Disabled*
_____ *Christian*	_____ *Jewish/Other*
_____ *Middle- or Upper-Class Parents*	_____ *Working-Class Parents*
_____ *Mentally Healthy*	_____ *Mentally Ill*
_____ *Intelligent*	_____ *Not Intelligent*
_____ *Conventionally Attractive*	_____ *Not Conventionally Attractive*
_____ *Employed*	_____ *Unemployed*
_____ *Wealthy/Financially Comfortable*	_____ *Poor*
_____ *"Standard" English-Speaking*	_____ *Regional or Foreign Accent*
_____ *Formally Educated*	_____ *Not Formally Educated*
_____ *Manager/Professional*	_____ *Worker/Non-Professional*
_____ *Property Owner*	_____ *Renter*

Count your check marks on each side of the checklist. Do they indicate mostly privileged status, or Other? Does your answer match the one you gave to the question about your status before you completed the checklist? If not, take time now to explore the reasons for the difference.

Uncovering Hidden Status

Some women who have completed the Privileged/Other exercise found their responses to individual items obvious—yet they were shocked at the total picture. Some of the women knew full well the individual ways in which society considered them Other; they also recognized some of their privileges. Yet, until

they looked closely at each side of the checklist, they didn't realize how heavily their traits of privilege outweighed the Other
categories.

"I just can't believe I have all these privileges," Carolyn said
after completing the above exercise. "Sure, I know I'm a successful lawyer, but I still think of myself as one-down because
I'm a woman and I grew up next to a migrant camp." She shook
her head in dismay seeing how many traits she checked on the
Privileged side of the chart. She hadn't thought about her status
as white, young, heterosexual, able-bodied, Christian, intelli-
gent, employed and educated. When several colleagues confirmed that they saw her as an upper-class person, Carolyn faced
a completely new idea of who she was.

People who seem anxious or hostile in your presence may
cause you bewilderment until you discover their assumptions
about your status. Debra Matsumoto, a publishing company
employee, learned valuable lessons about how another employee
viewed her.

> *I eventually began to see that Jill [a co-worker] was envious of me as a*
> *person and that I threatened her self-esteem simply by being who and*
> *what I was. I learned from others that she thought of me as a privileged*
> *person and was jealous because my life, in comparison to hers, had been*
> *much easier. I have never thought myself intimidating, and it was a*
> *new experience for me to be viewed as a threat as well as a member of*
> *the elite.*
>
> *I thought of how I had felt trying to compete with my privileged*
> *friends . . . and remembered my own hostility. . . . I learned to empathize*
> *with some of Jill's feelings and discovered that we were actually a lot*
> *alike.*

In contrast to Carolyn and Debra, some people surprise
themselves by the number of Other traits they check. You might
be a person of color, disabled or in some other way considered
Other, but at some point you may have decided not to acknowledge those characteristics. Maybe that way of adapting has
served you well for a long time, but in doing the exercise, you
discover you've checked *several* Other traits as descriptive of your
status. Your socially determined place on the Privileged/Other
Checklist might help explain why you sometimes feel "one-

down." You might puzzle over why you feel intimidated or shy around certain people. You've tried to ignore or deny your status, but now looking at the list, the reality of your Other status stares you in the face. You may not want to admit that people look down on you for characteristics you can't control. Or that you look up to them. Maybe you're reluctant to admit that you look down on yourself, as Other. At some periods in life, denial of class or other biases helps you endure what must be endured. At other times your efforts to bury part of your reality make things worse. Abuse often triggers old hurts, and sometimes old ways of adapting as well. But those techniques that helped you endure in the past may be inappropriate in dealing with an abusive co-worker now. Once you uncover what you've hidden from yourself, you can use the information about both the old hurts and your ways of dealing with them to make effective plans to face abuse.

Perhaps you decided not to do the Privileged/Other exercise at all or to postpone it until later. Maybe, like Carolyn and Debra, you prefer to think that people judge each other on their merits, not because of accidents of birth. But an honest look at status in your workplace might explain some of your discomfort or conflict, including how you react to mistreatment by a boss or co-worker. Sensitivity about your status or that of your boss could lead to misjudging his intentions. It might even cause you to make a mistake about whether you have been abused. If, like Carolyn, your status has changed without your realizing it, you might imagine a boss sees you as Other because that is how you continue to see yourself. Your economic status, like that of many women, may change throughout life as a result of career changes, marriage or divorce, which affect how others view you.

Status Shifts

None of the items on our Privileged/Other Checklist absolutely defines any individual's status. In some situations the categories of "privileged" and "Other" could even reverse places. For instance, we place young and midlife adults on the Privileged side of the checklist, because most business and professional managers devalue both older employees and teens. Yet in a particular job, such as personal or investment counseling, your maturity, associated with knowledge or experience, might give you an edge. Many traditional cultures respect the wisdom of elders. In an organization specializing in work with Others, your own status as Other could be an advantage.

Although some employers would see deafness as an advantage in an agency serving deaf people, Zoe, a social worker at just such an agency, found otherwise. Her boss, Terry, a hearing person, abused Zoe and the other deaf staff, which surprised Zoe, since Terry had made it clear when she hired Zoe that Zoe's deafness would be a benefit to the agency. Two other surprises: Terry never held against Zoe the fact that she was openly lesbian, but *did* discriminate against her as a female. Terry claimed that because Zoe was a woman she should use her interpersonal skills more effectively than an inept male colleague. She also expected Zoe to take over part of the man's job at no extra pay, and demanded less of the man because he "had a family to support."

You may encounter a similar mix of common biases and surprising individual attitudes that run counter to majority biases about privileged and Other status. Our Privilege/Other Checklist suggests only the most commonly held ideas about social privilege and Other status, which also change from time to time and in different situations.

If you enjoy the esteem of colleagues for your privileged status in one situation and then don't find it in another, you might resent the loss in the second situation. Say you are a thirty-year-old Wellesley graduate with a background of awards for professional achievements. You have become used to treatment as an accomplished person. When your new sixty-year-old boss says, "Take care of that today," you react as if you've been attacked. Because the boss gives you orders instead of looking up to you, you feel as if you have been abused. You are angry even though the boss has issued a legitimate order, and has not spoken to you abusively.

On the other hand, you might have been enjoying the privileges of relative youth without realizing it. Suppose you reach fifty or sixty, having achieved impressive career goals. But gradually you notice that certain younger colleagues treat you and your ideas as irrelevant. You feel abused. If you work in a youth-oriented business such as entertainment, advertising or computers, you may have legitimate cause for concern. Maybe you have lost your previous status. But loss of privilege is not the same as being abused.

Know the Person Who Abuses You

Just as you may deny your own status, you could either exaggerate or underestimate the importance of a controlling person's privilege. Think carefully about his or her status in relation to your own. Status is relative, so you can't see the whole picture without acknowledging the status of everyone in it.

EXERCISE 4B: What's the Abusive Person's Status?

Mark the Checklist for categories that describe the person who has abused you. Base your responses on information rather than assumptions. If there's more than one abusive person, make extra columns for each.

PRIVILEGED/OTHER CHECKLIST

PRIVILEGED	OTHER
_____ *White*	_____ *Person of Color*
_____ *Man*	_____ *Woman*
_____ *Heterosexual*	_____ *Lesbian/Gay/Bisexual*
_____ *Native-Born*	_____ *Immigrant*
_____ *Healthy*	_____ *Chronically Ill*
_____ *Slim*	_____ *Fat*
_____ *Young Adult/Midlife Adult*	_____ *Adolescent/Old*
_____ *Able-Bodied*	_____ *Disabled*
_____ *Christian*	_____ *Jewish/Other*
_____ *Middle- or Upper-Class Parents*	_____ *Working-Class Parents*
_____ *Mentally Healthy*	_____ *Mentally Ill*

PRIVILEGED	OTHER
_____ *Intelligent*	_____ *Not Intelligent*
_____ *Conventionally Attractive*	_____ *Not Conventionally Attractive*
_____ *Employed*	_____ *Unemployed*
_____ *Wealthy/Financially Comfortable*	_____ *Poor*
_____ *"Standard" English-Speaking*	_____ *Regional or Foreign Accent*
_____ *Formally Educated*	_____ *Not Formally Educated*
_____ *Manager/Professional*	_____ *Worker/Non-Professional*
_____ *Property Owner*	_____ *Renter*

Write the answers to these questions:

1. *On which side of the checklist did you mark the most traits?*

> Privileged side _____   Other side _____

2. *How many kinds of privilege characterize the abusive person?* _____

3. *How many traits considered Other does she or he have?* _____

4. *Do you or the people who mistreat you have more privilege?* _____

5. *Which of you has more Other attributes?* _____

6. *What, if any, surprises did you find in the number of privileged or Other categories you checked for your boss or co-workers?*

_____

_____

7. *Did any surprises result from assumptions you made earlier, rather than real information about the abusive person? What assumptions?*

_____

_____

8. *Why do you think you made those assumptions or guesses?*

_____

9. What thoughts or feelings do you have about the abusive person being more or less privileged or Other than you previously thought?

If in the past you've attributed more privilege to an abusive person than now seems accurate, that might explain why you feel more fear of him or her than has seemed reasonable. If, on the other hand, you see that someone who has mistreated you has even greater privilege than you estimated, that could give you a clue to the origins of his hostility. You might have assumed the hostility stemmed from something you had done. Now you might consider whether the person's attitude results from a negative view of a certain group and his assumption that your identity as part of that group is who you *are*. That is, his privilege has narrowed his view, so he can only focus on his belief that you are inferior to him. Instead of seeing you as a competent secretary, lawyer or teacher he's aware only of his fear or anger at you, a person of color. Or she recognizes you only as relatively old and disabled—conditions intolerable to her—not as the creative designer or reliable computer programmer you are.

In some situations, you might try speaking openly about differences and cultural biases that stand between you and a more privileged person. In other circumstances the atmosphere may be so threatening or the privileged person so negative about new ideas that you decide not to risk it. But the second choice doesn't mean you have to accept abuse. Perhaps you can persuade higher authorities to enforce guidelines that mandate respectful, fair treatment. Many biased workers have been forced to learn to treat others justly, even though they maintain their prejudicial attitudes.

EXERCISE 4C: Does Privilege Trigger Adrenalin?

Review the traits listed on the Privileged/Other Checklist again. *Consider* these questions and write the answers:

1. Does thinking about some of these traits you checked arouse more anger, hurt or fear than others? If so, which ones?

_____

_____

2. Why are your feelings so strong about that trait?

_____

_____

3. Do your co-workers see this characteristic as important?

_____

_____

4. What early experiences impressed you with the importance of the characteristic you feel strongly about?

_____

_____

5. What, if any, relationship do you notice between your strong feelings about certain traits and whether they can be changed (such as age, education, financial comfort)?

_____

_____

Some people who have completed this exercise and some community organizers believe those targeted for harsh discriminatory treatment have either the most visible or the most unchangeable Other traits, such as race and gender. Those people maintain that invisible Other traits such as religious affiliation or sexual orientation are not quite so hard to endure because they aren't apparent to other people. They also believe discrimination on the basis of traits that change, like age or education, is more tolerable than discrimination based on traits that remain for life. Other people are just as adamant that "there is no hierarchy of oppression." That is, one type of institutionalized discrimination cannot be judged as worse than another. They say oppression and abuse are equally deplorable, regardless of what triggers the mistreatment.

Your individual job may determine which form of privilege or Other status affects your position the most. It's possible that all your co-workers view one of your traits that differs from theirs as overwhelmingly significant. Depending on the job and culture, you may be seen only as a person of color, as "just a woman" or "the disabled person." If you accept being defined in that way and go along with the belief that one trait outweighs all others in importance, you can lose track of the complexities of your overall status. Such a narrow perception may also profoundly affect your attitudes toward the possibility of change in your workplace.

How you react to privileged and Other status reflects a partly subjective, and partly objective, reality. A man's personal opinion of your social value compared to his may affect how he treats you and how you feel about it. But it's just as important that social institutions like business, education, medicine and law treat you differently according to your status. No one can entirely escape the impact of institutional treatment according to gender, color, age and so on. Even though some people can rise above biases, barricades to success at work confront many people both on and off the job. Women who sue employers experience court procedures as a painful revisiting of abuse. African-Americans and Latinos suffer discrimination in getting loans and insurance and in disproportionate jailing. Business managers frequently manipulate old people into retirement before they're ready. Lesbians and gay men suffer violence and housing discrimination. Disabled people and those who are fat may not even be considered for many jobs. Even though individuals usually don't know the statistics on such treatment, nearly everyone recognizes some aspects of social status. That awareness affects our expectations of the privileged and the Others. Even so, privileged social status does not equal power, which takes more direct and inescapable forms.

Power or Privilege: Which Causes the Problem?

People with a strong feeling of being Other sometimes give in to demands of the privileged even when it isn't necessary. Their ideas about being Other bring on feelings of helplessness followed by the assumption that nothing they do will stop abuse by a privileged person. To avoid giving up your ability to control at least some of your work environment, keep in mind the differences between power and privilege.

> Power *is the ability to change the way another person acts, feels or thinks.*

Danger Ahead: Power

Our definition of power has its limitations. Many kinds of power exist: sexual power, the power of persuasion, economic power, among others. But we're concerned here with power *over* other people, not power *to* control one's own life. In many work situations women find themselves confronted with the power of men, simply because men hold more jobs that permit or require the giving of orders. When supervisors, whether men or women, can fire or demote you if you don't do as they say, that's power. Although even this power is limited and in the process of being socially redefined by laws regarding discrimination and union rights, in general it is considered a legitimate power of an employer or boss. When co-workers intimidate you with words backed by a show of muscle, that's power. When they purposely drop a wrench an inch from your head, that's power—illegitimate power.

These people definitely have the ability to change you in some way. You move out of the way; you give them what they want; you decide not to complain. Or you resign from the job. If you stand up to the abuse by taking legal or other action, you take protective measures first. You still have choices, though they may be limited. Power can be defined and its effects described with considerable accuracy. The consequences of power often loom larger than those of privilege.

Ruth's boss peppers her with orders, which are "almost tyrannizing," she says, "as if I were a servant, not a colleague and a capable colleague at that." Ruth takes pride in her position as the first woman city desk editor on a metropolitan newspaper in her area. But her boss, who has the power to fire her at will, chronically subjects her to public humiliation by intruding into her staff meetings, criticizing her judgment and ridiculing her.

Understanding the power he holds to make or break her position, Ruth plays her cards carefully, rarely confronting him directly, determined above all to protect her job. Her success has taken an emotional toll.

Like Ruth, you might have a completely reasonable fear of confronting an abusive boss. But even though he or she can decide to fire you, it's possible you can circumvent that control. For example, you can change the balance of power by organizing people whose collective strength may be greater than that of one person or even an institution. You might borrow or reflect someone else's prestige. This can be done through the advocacy of a mentor or intervention of a formal organization such as a union. Such responses to other people's *power over* you offer examples of using your *power to* increase control over your own life.

Confusion Ahead: Privilege

Privilege often presents a more subtle problem. Yet some aspects of it were not too subtle for the U.S. government to address. The 1964 Civil Rights Act addressed the unfairness of privilege. It prohibited discrimination against people of color and women; later it was amended to include old and disabled people. The act implicitly recognizes, and tries to compensate for, the unearned privilege of whites, the relatively young, able-bodied people and males. The regulations against unfair exercises of privilege have seldom been adequately enforced, however, and many workers believe privilege is even more difficult to recognize and confront than power.

Ruth's struggle to rise in the ranks of previously male newspaper management has toughened her. Yet facing the male privilege of other managers continues to require courage. She's had to deal with insults by her male colleagues differently from the way she handles those that come from her boss. Her fear of the colleagues as privileged, influential *men* initially inhibited her ability to set limits on their demeaning treatment.

One of the managers follows Ruth around the newsroom with a thick notepad to keep track of her mistakes. But she counters anxiety about his "tailgating" by reminding herself, "This kind of thing will occur throughout my life. I can't stop that sort of stuff that goes on in millions of workplaces, and all

across the continent. If I let it affect me, I cannot do my job."
She has learned to recognize the limits of privilege by itself and
she now uses her own power to stop abuse of herself and her
staff.

Dynamite Ahead: Power Plus Privilege

Privilege, though sometimes limited, may give birth to
power and control. A complex chain of connections binds the
concepts of privilege, power, illegitimate control and abuse.

Privilege ◆ *Legitimate Control (Power)* ◆ *Illegitimate Control* ◆ *Abuse*

Although people who exercise legitimate control or power
over Others may be Other themselves in some respects such as
women or people of color, they usually enjoy some important
kinds of privilege such as class status, education, light skin, etc.
Their privilege may have positioned them to be noticed when a
managerial job became available. The power that accompanies
permission to "manage" employees gives them a certain amount
of control over workers' output. They exercise the legitimate
right to tell employees what tasks to do and how and when to do
them. They do not have the right to mock, humiliate or insist on
work beyond that contracted for. But some managers overstep
the boundaries of their legitimate power. They try to control personal aspects of employees' lives or to coerce them by intimidation or humiliation. That's illegitimate control. When it occurs
as a pattern it constitutes abuse on the job.

You may encounter the power of a boss or a group of male
co-workers who abuse their power by insulting or sexually harassing you. Their actions might include expressions of sexism,
racism or other prejudices that are so automatic that they don't
realize how hurtful their comments are. But their actions might
also constitute a purposeful campaign to drive you out of the job.
The privilege that accompanies their race, class or gender—or all
three—may reinforce their illegitimate power.

When Privilege Opens the Door to Power

Like Ruth, you may worry about what male co-workers can
do *to* you. Or you might think about what they can do *for* you if
you're willing to toe the line. But their ability to harm you is usu-

ally limited unless you give them some of your power. As men they have privilege but if they can't hire or fire you and can't control your work flow or paycheck, they probably don't have legitimate power.

One exception to this generalization emerges if the higher status of a majority of your co-workers gives them access to power. Because of their status and greater numbers, they can turn their privilege into power. Women in the trades and in some high-level professions frequently encounter this situation. People of color are still formally excluded from centers of power such as private clubs, although movements to prohibit such racial and sexual exclusion have reduced some inequities that result from this illegitimate use of power. In the trades, some men use the illegitimate power of physical threats and manipulation of dangerous machinery to intimidate women workers.

Your responses to the Privileged/Other Checklist can help you evaluate the role played by privilege in your feelings of intimidation. Possibly your fear that privilege can be turned to power reflects the situation exactly. Might some co-workers' privilege translate into power because those workers can hurt your reputation or damage your career? Do they wield enough influence with the boss to have you fired? Or does the major problem lie in your interpretation of the risks in your position? If you answered no to all but the last of those questions, maybe the many levels of co-workers' privilege combined with your Other status obscure their lack of actual power.

You might discover by checking the Privileged/Other Checklist that you too are privileged and have no reason to be intimidated by other workers' high status. That might leave you more room to focus on the power that could be used against you.

Never Underestimate Your Own Power

Mary Ellen, a hairdressing instructor, knew her boss had absolute power to fire her, so she backed away from telling him to stop yelling insults in the midst of her teaching. In his late forties, he owned the business and had plenty of money. By contrast Mary Ellen was in her mid-twenties, poor and a lesbian. She felt the power and the privileged status of her boss as stacked heavily against her, and saw herself as powerless. Yet, when the boss publicly humiliated her once more than she could tolerate, Mary Ellen shouted at him, "I will not put up with such treatment any more!" Then she walked out. Mary Ellen's aggressive response and decisive exit surprised her almost as much as her boss. It reflected her gradual realization that she would give up her job if necessary to get out from under her boss's abuse. At that point neither his power nor his privilege as an older heterosexual businessman could affect her. To her surprise the boss followed her out of the building, saying, "Look, I blew it. I'm sorry. I really want you back and I won't shout at you again. You can't walk out and leave me with all these students. Please!" Mary Ellen's skills as a cosmetician and teacher gave her power she hadn't recognized. It had not occurred to her that the boss needed her as much as she thought she needed the job. Your particular place on the power and the privilege continuum, as well as your economic situation and career plans, will affect the risks you decide to take.

You might also recognize that, like Mary Ellen, your ability to perform gives you power you hadn't recognized. Or an individual quality might shift the balance of power that social status seems to dictate. Jessica, a nurse, said of her abusive supervisor, "She had status power, but she realized early on that I had strong personal power. Her only area of power was castigating me for the number of visits I made (to patients in their homes). My final response was 'This is a control issue, not a real issue.' "

A woman of color abused by a powerful boss whose white privilege provides him an additional shield may be wise to keep up her guard against racism, whether expressed directly or not. Abusive people may use any tactic at hand. On the other hand, in such a situation, unfounded assumptions may be made about the other person's racism. Acute awareness of hundreds of years of oppression can translate into paralyzing fear or rage. This particular boss may be an equal opportunity abuser who directs his temper at anyone in his path. If a woman assumes that supervisor or co-worker is reacting in a racist way, she may be thrown off the best course for handling the situation. For instance, she may overlook possible alliances with white workers, who are also abused by that person.

The power and privilege situation with abusive co-workers

can be complex. You may be a lesbian, an immigrant, disabled or significantly younger than an abusive co-worker, or in some other way assigned low social status. You may be treated as Other because co-workers know this is your first job or your first one at a professional level. If an abusive co-worker has privilege similar to that of the boss, she could use her status to turn the boss against you. If you complain to the boss, her privilege might gain her more credibility. The combination of her privilege, her friendship with the boss and his power could be dangerous for you. But this scenario is only one among many possibilities.

Privileged Status Plus "Otherness"

Once you've become aware that your fellow workers' privilege stems from race or gender status, for example, don't stop there. You might incorrectly decide "he's privileged and I'm Other." But the Privileged/Other Checklist allows us to appreciate how many types of privilege affect our lives, and to realize that most people have a mix of privileged and Other status. White women can be so absorbed in trying to wrest a bit of power from men that they ignore their privilege as whites. A poor woman of color can become so aware of being at least "three-down" on the social status ladder that she ignores how hazardous life can be for a white woman who is also old, disabled, an immigrant or chronically ill.

Maybe you don't like to admit to relatively high status compared to your co-workers or boss or to acknowledge that those differences are significant. By hiding certain aspects of your status from yourself you might unknowingly trade on your social privilege, even if you don't intend to. Your boss from the same status level may, for instance, listen to you more than to your co-workers because she perceives you as being like her. Maybe your sexual orientation or ages are similar or you attended the same private school. You may try to ignore those connections, but your co-workers probably will not. They may resent them. Declining to consider the significance of such connections might easily cause you to misjudge the entire situation. Once you recognize that your class or color gives you influence with powerful people, you can decide how to use those privileges, and for whose benefit.

Recheck Assumptions

Take another look at the list of privileged and Other traits you checked for the person who abuses you. How do you know that person is of a certain class, age or ethnicity? You might, for example, assume your boss's upper-class background makes it impossible for him to understand anything about your experience growing up poor. Your assumptions might add to your anger about his abuse.

Anger doesn't necessarily represent a problem, unless it stems partly from false information. Then it can lead to unwarranted trouble. Your guess about the boss's upper-class family could be dead wrong. Or you may have hit the mark, but he suffers from an invisible disability that causes him pain and fear about his ability to function well. Or maybe he's Jewish and feels outnumbered by what he perceives as a sea of "WASPs" (white, Anglo-Saxon Protestants), of whom you are one. The goal here is not to excuse his abuse because of his problems. You need an accurate perspective on how much power he exercises and how much privilege he has.

Check out your hunches or assumptions. You could discover a co-worker is not much more privileged than you, or that she has several privileges, yet also many disadvantages. If you occasionally have lunch or coffee together, try a question about where the person grew up or went to school. If you proceed cautiously, she may eventually reveal enough to be useful.

Seeking information about another person's status can be risky. To learn more about the other person, you may have to tell more about yourself, which might make you vulnerable to further mistreatment. In some cases, though, the revelations can help the abusive person see you as an individual, not just as part of a category. It's no fun exchanging personal information with abusive people. But once in a while, taking the risk of short-term anxiety brings long-term rewards.

Alana, an African-American community college teacher, understood that she and her abusive Latino boss operated from different cultural bases. She wanted the boss to accept her view that their conflicts did not illustrate a simple matter of right (his opinion) and wrong (hers). She hoped he would see that their male/female, Latino/black cultural experiences resulted in different perceptions of how the job should be done, and that their ideas could be discussed with that awareness. Although she was not unduly optimistic about succeeding, Alana determined to stretch herself and take a risk. Her boss refused to discuss the subject, but making the effort proved helpful. Alana knew she had done her best to analyze the situation, and became even more clear about who was responsible for the problem. Her experience of meeting the boss more than halfway boosted her confidence when his abuse escalated later and she became embroiled in a major altercation with him.

Risk Creative Alliances

You may develop connections with co-workers who have more (or less) privilege than you by noticing personal similarities not listed on our Privileged/Other Checklist. You might decide you have a good reason not to protest abuse—in order to gain long-term rewards, for instance. You could then try a long-term tactic of gradually eroding the abusive person's hostility toward you by broadening the way he or she sees you. You might find ways to bridge obvious differences. Maybe you both love baseball, feel frustrated by the transit system or like to gobble up science-fiction stories by the dozens. This tactic requires treading an emotional high wire, since the other person may misinterpret your action as acceptance of the abuse. You may need to object to specific abusive behavior at the same time you respond positively to other aspects of the abusive person. You'll need to set clear limits and stick to them. It may be worth the effort if you get the person to see that you're not just a "dummy," a "broad" or a "dyke." Relating to you as a more complete person makes it hard for the person to abuse you.

It is never easy to determine whether the discomfort of reaching out to an abusive person might be worth potential long-term gain. Anything you learn about the person might help you decide to try for a positive connection or to move in the direction of a new job or more radical action. If you decide to make a formal complaint to stop abuse, your demonstrated efforts to go more than halfway could strengthen your case.

Accurately identifying the power and privilege of particular people will enable you to evaluate how the continuing shifts in women's and men's economic roles affect your struggle against emotional abuse at work. Keeping track of individual and societal changes can help clarify your options, even as the picture grows more complicated.

Chapter 5

Myths of the "Working Woman"

As women we're trained to always doubt our feelings. In order to humiliate, you have to have a person there who can be humiliated and I think women are more easily humiliated. To some extent the men here do this to everyone. But women are more targets than others.

Ruth, newspaper editor

During the 1970s and the 1980s many women had "click" experiences. Their personal circumstances, they discovered, were tied to society's pervasive attitudes about women—the personal was political. Many women stopped wholesale self-blaming and—click—spotted the connection between individual change and social change. That same process may occur as workplace abuse is recognized.

Taking individual action against abuse may improve your work situation. Yet, ultimately, similar problems are likely to arise throughout your working life and those of your co-workers until women—and men—join together to make systemic changes. We're all in the midst of major social turmoil about women's roles. Naming the problem of workplace abuse is part of this important change. Abuse is a *social* problem, not just an individual aberration. Abuse is ultimately tied to the way society's institutions view and treat women.

In this chapter, we challenge myths about women's work roles. We show how society shapes everyone and how people continually affect each other, by supporting, contradicting or enacting traditional and contemporary roles. The individual personal view remains important. But the political and social realities also have important ramifications for how abuse is viewed in the workplace—and for what can be done about it.

We answer each myth with facts and questions that reflect current upheavals. For example, many women continue to receive traditional messages about what work they should choose and about expected behaviors at home and at work. But we know that many other women now get very different messages. Social scientists disagree about women's "essential nature" on the one hand and the impact of society's strictures on the other. During the seventies and eighties, many of us in the women's movement thought we had found easy answers to women's problems. We were right about some solutions. Others haven't been seriously tested, and still others present increasingly complex dilemmas.

MYTH: *After several decades of the women's movement, most women can now have whatever jobs they want.*

CHALLENGE: Women's progress in the workplace from the 1970s to the 1990s has been significant but limited. As important as these advances have been, they still affect only a small percentage of women in the paid work force. They primarily benefit professional, middle- and upper-class women. Some women have broken through gender barriers to such high-paying or high-ranking jobs as police chiefs, fire-fighting battalion heads, neurosurgeons, company executives and government leaders. As a result of class-action discrimination lawsuits, the doors have opened wider for women in a range of jobs. More women today work as stockbrokers, plumbers, electricians, lawyers and ministers.

But millions of women still perform low-paid jobs and work at occupations in which women are the majority. Women comprise:

- Ninety-nine percent of all secretaries.
- Ninety-seven percent of all child-care workers.
- Ninety-six percent of all licensed practical nurses.
- Ninety-four percent of all registered nurses.
- Sixty-eight percent of all sales and retail service workers.
- Sixty-eight percent of all social workers.

This narrow range of choices means that many women will not find a good fit between their abilities—current and potential—and the jobs open to them. With limited choices, many women work at jobs that don't use all or many of their capabilities. As a result, millions of women are "underemployed." Many women would prefer to do different kinds of work while others would certainly prefer jobs that pay more money. Most women are still confined to low-status jobs where the abuse of power—including emotional abuse—adversely affects them.

MYTH: *If the "social revolution" of the last thirty years didn't change these work roles, nothing ever will.*

CHALLENGE: A look at history shows the possibility of change. When large corporations developed in the last century, men did the office work. They had respect, received good salaries and expected to move up to be managers. Corporations then hired more and more women for office jobs, primarily because those in charge considered women more adept than men at operating the new typewriters. Those same jobs then paid less, with no expectation that women would move up the management ladder.

The telecommunications industry has a similar history. Originally, men served as telephone operators. Then one company decided that men were sometimes "noisy, boisterous and rude." Women would act more politely. And women agreed to work for two-thirds of men's pay. Before long the operator positions became "female" jobs, just like office work. So work arrangements can and have changed, even though some of the results haven't panned out well for women.

Change can also benefit women. During World War II, with millions of men serving in the military, government and industry actively recruited women for manufacturing and construction work to support the war effort. Numerous advertisements showed women doing riveting on battleships and a wide range of dirty, physically demanding industrial jobs. Because of the national emergency, "appropriate" work for women quickly became redefined. Half a million women worked at non-traditional jobs during those war years. And many of the wartime workplaces provided on-site child care.

Even though the World War II experience lasted just a few years, it demonstrates that significant social change in the workplace is possible. Americans are so accustomed to women receiving less pay than men that it may be hard to imagine a different scenario. Yet in a number of industrialized countries, greater wage equity exists than in the United States. For example, in Italy and Denmark, women earn eighty-six percent of what men earn. In the United States, women still earn only seventy-two percent of what men earn. However, young women are gaining ground. Women between the ages of twenty-four and thirty-five now earn eighty cents for every dollar earned by men of the same age. Economists noted in 1992 that a new generation of working women have secured better jobs with higher salaries by working more continuously and obtaining more education than in previous generations.

Legislation can make a dramatic difference. In 1972, Title IX of the Education Act passed by Congress made it illegal to discriminate in educational programs on the basis of sex. In 1971, just before that law was passed, women constituted *nine* percent of medical students; in 1989, that proportion increased to *thirty-three* percent. In law schools, the proportion of women rose from *seven* percent to *forty* percent and in dentistry, from *one* percent to *twenty-six* percent. Women with talent for these professions had always existed. Their proportion in these fields has changed because politicians and lawmakers—both women and men—succeeded in banning discrimination in professional school admissions.

It seems clear, from American history and the experiences of other countries, that national policy can transform the work circumstances of American women.

MYTH: *Although some women perform non-traditional, "men's" work, most women are naturally suited to the helping "feminine" work role.*

CHALLENGE: Women don't develop a "feminine nature" by chance. Most girls and boys receive the message that different behavior and attitudes are expected of them according to their gender. Walk by any preschool or elementary school play yard and you'll notice boys playing aggressive games with other boys.

Girls in those playgrounds congregate with each other and play quieter games.

We find now that these patterns can vary. At times, children's behavior seems to depend on the gender of their playmates. Some boys act less aggressively if they play with a group of girls; some girls are more assertive if they mingle with boys.

From the start, most parents handle their newborn boy and girl babies differently. From the minute a newborn baby girl gets wrapped in a pink blanket and her brother in a blue one, the two children receive different treatment. Adults use different tones in cooing over the two cribs. The differences continue as the father mock wrestles with his baby boy and plays more gently with his "fragile" daughter. Mothers handle and talk to their girl infants more often than their sons. Social scientists say these patterns lead to more independent, rough behavior in boys and more dependent, empathic behavior in girls. As a result, most boys tend be more aggressive than girls. Girls become generally more verbal than boys.

Toys—trucks or dolls—clearly represent the different expectations parents have for their sons and daughters. Some new toys exaggerate these expectations. Mattel has developed a toy car for boys that thoroughly mutilates dummies in a crash. For girls, Mattel has made a doll which can be strapped to the girl's midsection to create the illusion of pregnancy.

Social scientists continue to argue about how much of children's and adults' behavior comes from natural development and how much from training and encouragement. In any event, society reinforces differences which develop between the usual behavior of boys and that 'of girls. By the time people reach adulthood, the fact of gender controls much of their behavior, on and off the job. That behavior depends on continual messages about what's appropriate. But scientists also discover much overlap in the behavior of men and women. Even when there is a tendency for boys to develop one trait more than girls, a considerable proportion of boys and girls may not fit what is considered typical.

Race and ethnicity add another dimension to this picture. For example, many observers have noted that gender roles are more fluid in African-American families. There, many husbands and wives share in decision-making and household responsibilities. Many African-American mothers present a non-traditional model for their daughters. If you are an African-American woman who grew up in this kind of household, you probably received a clear message about the independence and competency of women.

Sociologist Norma Williams' study of Mexican-American families in Texas shows that roles are becoming more flexible in some Latino groups as well. She states:

> *Husbands continue to wield greater power than their wives. [But] working class women... are breaking from the traditional culture wherein a woman's identity stemmed from being solely a wife and a mother. Women in the professional class take their newfound sense of personal and social identity for granted.*

MYTH: *Sex stereotyping has largely disappeared in today's schools.*

CHALLENGE: Traditional images and expectations have changed in some school systems, often because of protests and hard work by women in those communities. Publishers have revised textbooks to show girls and boys doing equally valued tasks and sharing in all aspects of living. If you have a daughter in grade school, check to see if she is still using unchanged elementary school books. If so, she sees that text and pictures depict boys and men doing many different kinds of work, much of it requiring an adventurous and daring spirit. The girls and women in those traditional books spur them on and take care of them when they return from their adventures. With such models, many girls continue to absorb the lesson that their destiny means caregiving on life's sidelines.

Despite some progress in reading materials and other non-sexist practices, gender bias in schools continues to affect the educational experience of girls. Studies disclose that African-American girls, even those with high potential, are the least reinforced and encouraged by their classroom teachers. Schools also emphasize traditional sex-role stereotypes among Latina girls. In 1991 and 1992, two educational reports confirmed that bias against girls still prevails—in classroom interactions, in textbooks, in encouragement toward achievement, in incidents of sexual harassment. Susan Chira, a *New York Times* reporter, cites the 1992 study:

> *Teachers pay less attention to girls than boys. Some tests remain biased against girls, hurting their chances of scholarships and getting into college. School textbooks still ignore or stereotype women.*

By the end of high school, the girls in these studies have lower self-esteem than boys and lower expectations for their own achievements, especially in math and science.

While you were in school you probably observed that, for the most part, women were the teachers, while the school principal was a man. This situation has shifted somewhat, as women move into administrative roles and some men teach in the lower grades. Yet for the most part, such models still reinforce other messages about the place of women and men in the world of work. And the "place" for many women turns out to be lower-paid, nurturing jobs—in less powerful positions, more susceptible to abuse.

If you are over thirty years old, you were probably discouraged in high school from taking shop classes. Because of current efforts to make schooling "gender-fair," more girls now have shop classes available to them. However, peer pressure may continue to encourage traditional sex-stereotyped choices. Many young women are still not encouraged to explore lucrative positions as are young men. For example, they may be subtly discouraged from advanced science courses. Even now, women of all backgrounds and races are counseled away from preparation for high-paying work in scientific fields or the trades.

A woman may decide she wants to work as an electrician or a pipefitter, or repairing appliances, all jobs paying more than usual "women's" jobs. But then she often discovers she didn't receive the necessary technical background in high school. Without math and science in high school or without help to overcome "math anxiety," high school graduates find they do not meet the requirements for admission to three-quarters of the departments at many of the larger universities. Many Native American, African-American or Latina girls may not even be counseled to train to be a clerical worker, whereas white girls are generally given that option.

MYTH: *The nurturing role that most women assume is not only natural to them but serves them well.*

CHALLENGE: Caring for and about other people should have high priority for everyone. But the situation gets sticky when girls and boys come to believe that nurturing others constitutes the main task of girls and women, even at the expense of taking care of themselves.

Different cultural groups can give women different messages about roles. Even though Asian families typically adopt traditional sex roles for women and men, they also emphasize educational and occupational achievement for their daughters. Paul Brandon, an education researcher, followed a group of Asian-American and white students after high school and found that Asian women completed college at almost twice the rate of the white women—thirty-three percent for the Asian women as contrasted with eighteen percent for the white women. As one example among Native Americans, Navajo children don't expect that there will be that much difference between men's and women's behavior. The Navajos have a long-standing tradition of flexibility in male-female work roles.

Beliefs about their future work and family lives have shifted for many young women. In her study of young women from the ages of twelve to twenty-five, Ruth Sidel, a sociologist, identified the "New American Dreamers." Optimistic about their futures, these young women expect to combine careers and family roles easily. They place great emphasis on material well-being, but exude confidence that their careers will bring material success and that they can go it alone if necessary. Sidel found an "incredible mixture of the old and the new." One eighteen-year-old African-American woman says:

> *I want to be a model. . . . I want to have a big, BIG house and a BIG family—three girls and two boys. . . . [My husband] will be a lawyer. He'll be responsible, hard-working, and sensitive to my feelings. And he'll take the little boys out to play football and I'll have the girls inside cooking. That will be a dream come true.*

Other young women (Sidel called them "Neo-traditionalists") also expect to have careers but place family life first. Their ideas of mothering seem to reflect family ideals of the 1950s. Significantly, another group of young women from poor families, often women of color, had no clear hopes for the future.

As the world of young women shifts, some expectations remain constant. Most mothers continue to encourage their daughters to show sensitivity and empathy to others. You may remember your mother urging you: "Now be nice. How would you feel if you were Mary?" So a girl learns that she must care about other people's feelings above all. An adult woman speaks of her teenage years:

> *Underneath I wanted to be a great person. I had a lot of talent in various directions . . . but then this passive, outside part of me took over. . . . I tried and tried all the time to understand everybody, so I lost myself. I got a sense of self from doing for others. I didn't know who I was. I was just an understanding person.*

If these traits become entrenched habits, the young woman remains at a disadvantage in the workplace, especially if she encounters mistreatment there. She turns the other cheek before even examining the effect of the abuse or what she might do about it.

Power plays an important part in workplace abuse but power also influences women's personal traits as well. Carol Tavris, a social psychologist, maintains that empathy and understanding is "not a *female* skill; it is a *self-protective* skill," since people in powerless positions need to be alert to the needs of people who can control their lives. Much of women's stereotypical behavior may result from the different types of work that women and men do and their different levels of power. Sara Snodgrass, a psychologist, suggests that "women's intuition" should properly be called "subordinate's intuition."

MYTH: *Women don't want the "dirty and heavy" work that many men do. That work does pay more but it deserves higher pay because of the demands.*

CHALLENGE: Most people believe that a garage mechanic, or steel worker or plumber should be paid well because he has to deal with oil or grime and must lift heavy objects. They think the jobs women usually do just don't compare with the unpleasantness or exertion of men's work. But think about a nurse or nurse's aide who must clean up urine, feces, blood or vomit, and lift heavy bodies all day. The difference between the mechanic's job and the nurse's comes not from the dirtiness or the energy used. The difference? Society considers one "women's work" and values it less than "men's work."

A truck driver or a plumber earns far more than a daycare worker or an aide in a nursing home. Handling machines commands a higher price than caring for the young and the old. And the truck driver or plumber may resent women entering his field. The woman who wants a non-traditional job with better pay may find the doors closed to her. And the woman who succeeds in opening the door may find her male co-workers emotionally abusive because they resent her presence.

MYTH: *Women make their own individual choices about the work they will do.*

CHALLENGE: When you were a child, what paid work did you expect to do as an adult? Your ideas may have reflected the traditional women's jobs in the work force. So perhaps you thought you would work as a nurse or secretary or teacher. And you would marry, have children and be supported by your husband. Or you might have received the very different message that you could choose any work you wanted. More and more women, socialized to wider possibilities, have made inroads into a variety of workplaces.

Whatever the expectations, most women continue to work in a small number of jobs where women are the majority. This doesn't sound like free choice by each individual woman. Instead it points to serious restrictions placed on women by society and by workplace practices. Even when today's young women are told that they can work at a myriad of jobs, they still face the reality of limited workplace options. A business administration college graduate reports in 1991 on a job interview: "I interviewed for an agent position at an insurance company. They looked over my application and offered me a position as secretary."

Economists argue about what aspect of the structure of work

leads to this outcome, but the outcome remains the same. In fact, the future could reinforce current patterns. The increase predicted in the work force will occur mainly in the poorly paid service sector, where most women work.

Some women experience special circumstances in the work force. If you are a lesbian and came out early, you probably knew you had to support yourself, even if you hoped to live with a partner. But you were still limited by a smaller number of occupations available to women and still earned less than men. If you came out as a lesbian later in life, you probably received and believed the traditional messages as you grew up. In any case, homophobia—fear and hatred of gays and lesbians—may constrain you at whatever work you do.

Disabled women face additional restrictions. If you are disabled, you may have experienced problems being accepted in the work force. You may have been taught to show gratitude for whatever job was offered. And if your job required special training and work preparation, you may still have felt on trial even with that training. If you appeared discontented or angry, you might have received the label: "not work-ready." Challenging women's traditional roles or abuse may pose hazards to your job security.

Depending on the class position of your family—working class or middle class—you may have developed different ideas about future work. You may have thought of your future work the way a working-class woman interviewed by Lillian Rubin, a family counselor and social researcher, described it: "I never had any goals to be anything, except I always figured I'd get married and have kids and that would be enough for anybody."

As a woman of color, you may have developed other ideas about work and family expectations, running counter to those held by white women. For example, African-American women have a longer history of being in the paid work force than white women. But that longer history, greatly affected by racism, hasn't necessarily resulted in greater choice of jobs or higher pay. Over the years, more women of color than white women have had to combine work and family. They often have not had the choice of staying home to care for their children. One African-American woman said:

I'd never known a woman who stayed home with children. . . . I did not know any housewives. That form of life was kind of alien. I did not even know that was possible. When I found out that people actually only stayed home and did nothing but raise children and clean house, I thought that was fascinating. . . . I always assumed I'd work and have children.

The idea that women have "free choice" of what work they will do is overshadowed by messages they receive about appropriate work for women, and by restrictions in the work force.

Socialization is Complicated

Women's expectations about certain work and family roles derive partly from images presented in the media. But all of us participate in socializing each other and reinforcing stereotypes. A woman may teach her daughter to behave in ways she deplores, because she fears the daughter won't attract a husband if she doesn't learn submissiveness. A beautician, asked if her husband ever helps around the house, replies:

No, and I wouldn't want him to. I'd rather do my own cooking and housekeeping. I don't believe in women's lib. And I don't believe in all that crap—making a husband do half the work.

When asked why she wouldn't expect this since both she and her husband work at outside jobs, the beautician explains angrily:

Because I was raised that way! My mother taught me it was the responsibility of the woman to clean the house and cook and clean the clothes and everything.

You can purposefully reflect on what other people model for you. You can become conscious of the behavior you model for others. Then it may be possible to see what impact these socialized roles have on your work situation, particularly as you think about challenging abuse. You can decide whether you want to continue playing out those roles and what risks you face if you decide not to. You can also become more aware of what part of your workplace role comes from the larger picture of bias and barriers to women's advancement.

Maybe you don't fit traditional roles. As you grew up, you may have received messages different from those of the girls and women around you. You might have developed a different attitude from your friends about the kind of work you expected to do. You also may also have known men who don't fit the traditional mold at all, men who support you in the nontraditional work you chose. And you may have been appropriately assertive with men who criticized your choices.

But even women like yourself find their strength limited. Strong women (and strong men) sometimes weaken in their resolve after a period of harassment, humiliation or intimidation. Seeing yourself in the perspective of all women's lives should help you to achieve a useful mix of faith in yourself and understanding of socially imposed difficulties.

The Zig-Zag Course of Change

Progress is mixed. Consider the following contradictory signals:

• A 1990 *Time* magazine poll noted that many women reach adulthood with the clear conviction that they will have both paid jobs in the work force and a family life. Still, fifty-one percent of the women polled valued having a long and happy marriage and raising well-adjusted children ahead of career success. This ordering of priorities is not necessarily a bad thing. But until most men share family responsibilities equally with women, women will continue to take a back seat in commerce. In 1992, Carolyn Cowan, a research psychologist, found that even when couples planned to provide care equally for a coming child, "men did less child care and women did more than either had predicted during the pregnancy."

• In 1991, a national poll found that girls have lower esteem and lower career expectations than boys. "Boys dream big dreams and hold onto them," the pollsters reported. "Girls start out with dreams, but they give them up sooner and tailor their ideas to what they can become much more narrowly than boys." The poll also revealed that girls argue with teachers less than boys do even when the girls know they're right.

• In 1991, ABC-TV decided to discontinue the cartoon show *New Kids on the Block* because of its popularity with "the wrong kids." Only girls watched the show and "you have to have boys watching a show if it is to succeed," according to the network. ABC-TV also decided not to have any female lead characters in a Saturday morning show. Why? "It is well known that boys will watch a male lead and not a female lead, but girls are willing to watch a male lead."

• In 1992, three economists reviewed the evidence of women's work force experience in the 1970s and 1980s and asserted that much progress has occurred. Examples: Women hold forty percent of entry-level and middle-management jobs, double their share in 1972. (Time will tell if these women can increase the proportion of women—now only three percent—who serve as top corporate managers). Half of accountants are women, as are one-sixth of doctors. More and more women now plan a lifetime of work.

• The number of women elected to government positions has increased dramatically in the past twenty years. After the November 1992 elections, there were six women senators, forty-seven representatives, three governors, eleven lieutenant governors, nine attorneys general, sixteen state treasurers and many more women in state legislatures. President Clinton appointed six women to Cabinet and sub-cabinet posts in his new administration.

Change for women appears to be taking a zig-zag course, with progress in some areas and stagnation in others. As you watch the fluctuations, it's useful to gain a heightened awareness of assigned roles. The way women are socialized intertwines with the economic system, still trapping many women in jobs with little power and income. This makes women vulnerable to abuse and hesitant to challenge it.

Restricted roles are not the only society-wide problem for women at work. We turn now to another aspect—the strain many women feel because they have two jobs: one at home and one in the work force.

Chapter 6

The Double Whammy of Stress and Abuse

Who is the worker? The worker is a person with children and child-care responsibilities or aging, needy parents; a person with a part-time, flex-time or full-time work schedule and a life outside the workplace; a person with a wide range of skills and experience who may change occupations as well as jobs. The worker is a person whose career is interrupted by the demands of family life.

Wendy Kaminer, lawyer and journalist

Most women know the strain of having two jobs—the one they're paid for and the one at home. That strain can sometimes make it difficult for women to challenge abuse at work.

You might postpone taking action against an abusive boss because you can't find the time and energy even to consider the alternatives. You need to plan your approach and to assess the risks. But high stress and straight thinking often don't go together. As a working woman, you somehow can't call on the energy and concentration needed to think through a plan of action and make a decision.

Like most women, you may think the stress you experience is strictly a personal problem. But many women tell us that once they realized their situation was related largely to their role as women and that the problem was not "just me," they felt both relief and a surge of energy to address abuse.

Multiple demands on working women do have positive aspects. Some studies show that women who have several roles—mother, wife, working woman, community volunteer—experience less depression, have higher self-esteem and greater life satisfaction. Coping with many demands can give you a sense of competency. Moving from one role to another can give you energy. As Faye Crosby, a social psychologist, asserts in her book, *Juggling,*"Women feel enriched as well as stressed by juggling occupational and domestic responsibilities." Lisa Silberstein, a social researcher, also found that some women "are vitalized by . . . swimming upstream and succeeding at it."

But the impact of the overload shifts as the situation changes. When your children fall ill, when your job does not go well, when your adolescent gets into trouble, then struggling with all the demands exhausts rather than exhilarates you. Family members and the larger society can't be counted on to give practical help when working women have too much to do. Husbands and children often don't pitch in at home. We have not yet legitimized programs such as child care and family leave to relieve burdens for working women. When you are stretched to the breaking point, challenging abuse on the job just doesn't seem feasible.

Working conditions can add to the overload. Many people believe that the high-stress profile is a problem peculiar to high-powered executives, but recent research uncovered some surprising findings. Think for a moment about your work:

> • Do you have many demands made on you on the job?
>
> • Do you think you are capable of doing much more than the job requires?
>
> • Do you have little control over the decisions made about your work?

If you answered yes to these questions, these factors—many demands, little opportunity to work at your full capacity and little control over your job—probably cause you as much or more stress than executives experience. Applying the criteria above, think of the strains in these jobs: nurses' aide, word processor in a large office, fast-food dispenser, or receptionist in a hospital. Women in supervisory positions know that many demands also come down on them as well. But the *combination* of higher demands *and* less decision-making power adds up to great stress.

Juggling Work and Family

More women work outside the home than ever before. In 1960, twenty percent of women with children under six worked outside the home. By 1991, that figure had soared to fifty-eight percent. Some families make adjustments to this change. Public opinion polls show that young adults expect to share in home tasks when they become parents. Also, many couples in their twenties and thirties now participate more equitably in home responsibilities.

Magazines and Sunday newspaper supplements show husbands who share household and child-care responsibilities with their wives. A *New York Times* story in 1991 pictures Gordon Rothman, a CBS producer, at home on parental leave, caring for his infant son. But in that same newspaper account, Fran Rodgers, the president of Work/Family Direction is quoted as saying:

> *The few fathers who take a couple of months off from work tend to end up on covers of magazines. So it looks like a trend but it isn't. There is no company where very many men are taking months off.*

For most working women, the home remains primarily their responsibility. Women who are full-time homemakers do eighty-three percent of household tasks. Yet, women who work outside the home still do seventy percent of those tasks. Until more families catch up with the changing work scene, most working women will have considerable home responsibilities. They straddle two worlds, with pressures from each. Linda, a beautician, reports:

> *My work, it's hard because of the job but also because of having to get my husband and my daughter up and out. I get up at 6:15, and then I get my husband off to work—I make his breakfast and fix his lunch . . . Usually about eight, I wake my daughter and give her a bath and feed her and help her get dressed . . . and then I'll straighten the house a little and then . . . we'll walk up the street to the babysitter . . . and then I'll walk the ten blocks to the shop. By the time I get there I feel like going back to bed.*

Ann, a highly paid vice-president of a large firm, finds herself on the verge of quitting her job because of concern for her daughter:

Right now, my twelve-month-old daughter is very clingy as a result of an ear infection. . . . If I don't hold her, she screams. I'm supposed to go on a business trip tomorrow, and I have a strong urge to say, "I'm not going," . . . but I can't tell my boss my child is sick. The worst thing I could possibly do is to acknowledge that my children have an impact on my life. Isn't it ironic? I'm on the verge of quitting the company but I can't even tell my boss I don't want to go on this trip because my child's sick.

Some groups have a rich network of extended family members to support the single mother. But without that support, stress multiplies for many single mothers because they have to manage all of the demands without another adult to help. Since twenty-nine percent of all American families are headed by one parent—the vast majority by women—millions of women go it alone and you may be one of them. If, as a single mother, you endure emotional abuse on the job, the lack of another adult at home for a sounding board can add to the strain and make challenging the abuse doubly hard.

Beyond the Immediate Family

Other kinds of family obligations can also create pressures on working women: Lillian, a fifty-eight-year-old widow, works as a salesperson in the women's clothing section of a large department store. She constantly worries about her thirty-three-year-old daughter, Colleen, whose husband had been physically abusive to her during most of their marriage. After Colleen finally left him, he went to court and obtained physical custody of their three children. Lillian used all her savings to pay for Colleen's legal fees during the four-year custody battle. She regrets she couldn't do more. She says: "I should have taken time from work to accompany Colleen to a crucial court hearing. I was afraid to ask for time off." Even at work, the thought of her grandchildren never leaves her mind. All of this affects her job performance, and she's worried about being able to keep her job.

Melanie, the business manager of a carpet store, is an only

child. All the care and worry about her elderly parents, both ill and frail, fall on her. She arrives at their home at seven each morning, gives them their medications, and prepares breakfast and lunch. Returning later in the day, she makes their supper. She regularly takes her parents to their doctors, using vacation time to do so. Even so, the owner of the carpet store becomes testy when she misses work too often. She hasn't even had time to keep up with friends who might provide her with needed moral and emotional support.

Melanie's care of her parents mirrors the situation of many women. Media reports focus attention on old people in nursing homes, giving the impression that most elderly and infirm people are in such institutions. In fact, only five percent of elders who need care are in nursing homes at any one time. The rest— ninety-five percent—are at home cared for mainly by women relatives. Melanie is one of those women.

Other situations increase the strains between work and home. You may have a chronically ill or disabled partner who requires considerable care. If you've never married, your siblings may assume you are "free" to care for your mother. As a divorced woman, you may retain emotional ties and a strong sense of responsibility for your ailing former mother-in-law.

The work arrangements of some professional women may give them some leeway in handling these pressures. But many more are afraid of appearing "not serious" about their careers or suitable only for reduced responsibilities if they take time for family. If you are the first woman of color or the first out-of-the-closet lesbian to be hired by your company, you may perceive the risk as even greater.

Managing Two Worlds

If your situation resembles the plight of any of the women just described, you know what it feels like to be caught between work and home. When you feel burdened by these pressures, you might have trouble separating normal irritants of the work world from serious emotional abuse. You might chalk up the real abuse you experience to "women's lot" and their unalterable burdens.

You also may know the tension of keeping your two worlds

separate. During your hours at work, you must concentrate on your job. You must try to ignore your concern that your son has behavior problems at school or that your mother, who has had a stroke, becomes more frail every day. Moreover, at home your family wants you to leave work worries at the office. You are expected to do all the home tasks and to help the children with their homework with energy and high emotional involvement. You may have learned very well that home does not provide respite for women, as it usually does for men.

So when women go out of the home to work, they lose whatever leisure time they've had. Sometimes women say they just need more time to do everything, when what they really need is less work. Nina, a company executive, put it this way:

I say to him, "Do you want to bathe the kids tonight or do you want to clean up the kitchen?" That's the way I usually put it to him, because if I don't, he'll go watch TV or read the paper. Usually he does the kitchen but he doesn't want to do the bathing, so I end up bathing and reading to the kids.

Ann, the vice-president mentioned earlier, describes her nightly schedule and its effect on her relationship with her husband.

I come home at six-thirty, take care of the kids, cook dinner, go to bed, get woken by the baby. I get totally exhausted. I can't stand it anymore. Then I dump on him for not keeping up his fifty percent of the bargain and causing me to feel so harassed all the time.

When Arlie Hochschild, a sociologist, studied fifty two-job couples from 1980 to 1988, she found that in eighty percent of those homes, the men did not share in housework and child care. Wives say that the men consider housework to be the "woman's job," leaving wives to have to ask for help. A husband in another study remarks:

Men aren't supposed to do things like that—caring for home and children, but it's what women are supposed to be doing. It's natural for them, so they don't mind it.

Marilyn French, a feminist author, may have had this husband in mind when she commented that: "It never seems to occur to men that taking care of themselves and raising their children should be everyone's work, not solely women's."

You may have chosen a job for its location convenient to home, in order to decrease work or home strains. But by doing so, you may lose out on advancement possibilities and better pay in another job some distance away. You may have arranged your work to fit your children's schedules. Edna, a waitress, adjusted her work schedule to accommodate the needs and ages of her children, something almost no other job would have permitted her. In her children's younger years, she worked the dinner shift, while her husband took care of them at home. When they started school, she worked breakfast and then lunch, arriving home just before they did. Louise Howe, an analyst of workplace issues who interviewed Edna and many other waitresses, writes: "What was typical was how their family responsibilities...had shaped their work patterns and schedules." Many chose waitressing because of family demands on their time, even though sexism and racism in the restaurant business usually prevent women from advancing into higher-paying jobs.

Ironically, when women develop considerable skills in handling many tasks at once, even those abilities go undervalued. Because they juggle many demands and move from situation to situation, women often get criticized for being "scattered," rather than praised for handling so much. Men, on the other hand, receive compliments for their ability to focus single-mindedly on one task. Gwen, a corporate administrator, sums it up:

> *Women have a whole myriad of priorities they have to deal with, whereas men are only trying, often, to manage one, so they can be very focused on that. We are able to do ten things at once and do most of those things well. Because of the corporate structure, which is primarily male, they look at that and call it scatterbrained.*

What Can Employers Do?

Ignoring the fact that most women work because they have to, many employers still act as if women have a choice about working. Like most women, you probably work because you must. Many married women—in both low- and middle-income families—need to supplement their husbands' salaries. Single women must support themselves. Many women with children have total financial responsibility for their families. Others earn money to create a buffer zone of independence between themselves and controlling partners. But we can't measure the imperative to work solely in financial terms. Women also work to maintain their self-respect, to use all their talents, to contribute to society or because work itself gives them pleasure. Work is rarely a trivial matter for women, any more than it is for men.

Many businesses offer part-time work, which might seem a useful choice for women. But many women need full-time pay, and part-time work rarely provides important health and other benefits. So the message gets across that part-time workers don't count. Your employer may think that if you don't count, it doesn't matter whether you face abuse. You may feel that when you experience mistreatment as a part-time worker, you have no right to object.

Even professionals who can afford to work part-time face difficult dilemmas. Nina, the company executive mentioned previously, works part-time in order to spend more time with her young daughter. Nina's boss says her unwillingness to return soon to full-time work makes her vulnerable to dismissal. He claims she isn't committed to the job. She sees it differently and instead says, "I am committed to the company—on a part-time basis."

Changes in the Wind

While most employers assume that all workers can meet demands of both work and home without flexible hours or work conditions, some businesses now pay attention to women's dual roles. An executive of a major corporation tells a newspaper reporter:

> *It used to be that what happened to your employees when they went home at the end of the day was their business, but today, that worker's sick child is your business, because if she's worrying about her child, and calling in sick when she isn't, and probably feeling resentful because she had to lie, she isn't going to be productive.*

In 1986, more than 2,000 employers sponsored services related in some way to child care. This represented a jump from 415 in 1982. Services ranged from informational seminars about finding care all the way to child care facilities at the worksite. Such a substantial increase over four years bodes well for the future.

Sometimes it looks as if the nation moves forward and backward at the same time. Bills that would help women handle work and home responsibilities have been introduced for years in Congress. Even introducing such proposals represents an advance. For the first time since World War II, when women were needed in the work force, government has begun to recognize working women's family needs. After several vetos of similar bills by President Bush, The Family and Medical Leave Act, which provides workers some respite from work in order to care for young children or sick or elderly relatives, was finally passed by Congress and signed by President Clinton in February 1993.

Flex-time—allowing workers discretion in arrival and departure times—was a radical notion just a few decades ago. It first appeared in the United States in 1972. But by 1985, thirteen percent of all women employees worked on a flex-time schedule. Some businesses in the United States have begun to offer benefit packages that acknowledge home-care responsibilities, using the benefits as a recruiting device to attract higher-level personnel. Until recently, corporate employees who refused a transfer to another city because of family considerations risked being considered unambitious. In 1990, a corporate vice-president asserted that "turning down transfers is such a common occurrence that it is unlikely to have a significant impact on a person's career." Progress may be uneven but the trend toward recognition of the family needs of working people continues on an upward swing.

Daycare and National Policy

If you've searched for daycare for your children, you know that quality, reasonably priced daycare facilities are not readily available for all families who require them. From your experience, you may not be surprised to read the following report of child care availability.

Ten million children under the age of six have two working parents or a single parent who supports the family. . . . And yet, in 1986, there were only 40,000 day-care centers and 105,000 licensed day-care homes watching over 2.1 million chidren.

Low-cost, high-quality daycare may seem like a dream. And you may assume you have no right to expect governmental solutions to your personal problems. But some countries, such as Sweden and Italy, assign high priority to the welfare of children and their parents. Many industrialized countries, some with far less wealth than the United States, provide a wide array of programs and policies that help parents deal with the conflicts between family and work. Consider this description of daycare in Sweden:

Child care in public day-centers is of very high quality. The centers are generally open ten to twelve hours a day five days a week. Costs are paid by the federal government (fifty percent), municipal government (forty percent), and parental fees (ten percent). Fees are charged on an income-related basis: e.g., a parent earning $500 a month or less may leave a child nine hours a day five days a week for as little as $16.00 a month . . . . This fee includes three hot meals a day plus snacks.

Sweden is only one of many countries helping to reduce women's dual role stress. In 1971, Italy passed the Law on the Rights of Working Mothers, providing legal protection for working women beginning at the time of childbirth and when young children become ill. Under this law, a woman cannot be fired during pregnancy or during the first year of her child's life. Maternity leave extends to five months and provides eighty percent of the woman's wages. Mothers receive two years' of credit toward a variety of seniority rights each time they give birth. By contrast, the United States has not established any similar programs to help working women. Also, in contrast to most other industrialized countries, this nation does not provide a cash subsidy for raising children.

Continued public action is needed to increase understanding that work in the home concerns everyone and that the care of children should involve all citizens. Someday this nation may join the seventy-five other countries that guarantee parental leave for infant care. But meanwhile, your difficulty in juggling work and home does not signify some deficiency on your part. You experience those pressures partly because national policy doesn't yet support working women.

Stereotypes Complicate Your Struggle

Handling many responsibilities is not the only way that women's roles lead to stress. We mentioned "sex-role spillover" in the chapter on sexual harassment. This means that men and women act in stereotypical ways in the workplace as they do elsewhere. The "spillover" can complicate women's work performance and make it difficult to confront abuse. Men at work may view you in a personal way, not simply as a co-worker. They bring their outside-of-work attitudes about women into the workplace.

Ann Hopkins, an independent woman of strong character, served as an accounting firm manager at Price Waterhouse. She was denied partnership even after she received the highest possible evaluations of her technical skills and her ability to attract new business to the firm. Of eighty-eight nominees for partnership, "she had generated the most business and billed the most client hours." But one partner suggested she "take a course at charm school." Another counseled her to "walk more femininely, talk more femininely, dress more femininely, wear make-up, have her hair styled, and wear jewelry." Hopkins sued the firm for sex discrimination. On May 14, 1990, a federal court ordered Price Waterhouse to award her a partnership.

Maybe you work with men who have mixed expectations of you. They want you to be flirtatious, or to take care of them as their mothers did, each by turn. Women firefighters report that male colleagues treat them in a variety of ways but rarely simply as co-workers. One woman firefighter reports:

> *The men have to know, do they relate to you as mother? Aunt? Girlfriend? Sister? . . . They have a hard time fitting you into a category. . . . We want them to see us as co-workers/sisters. . . . That's the role we choose.*

How women react to men at work also has complicated results. Many women feel they need to please others and to do what's expected. They go along with the flirting or teasing when men act inappropriately personal. Women may choose this as the best way to get along. Also, verbal sexual games can be fun; they can make work enjoyable and relieve monotony. Some personal interactions at the office will continue to lead to happy, healthy intimate relationships.

But when work relationships are personalized, differences in power can come into play. For men in power positions, sexual games represent low-risk activities, but for women they can become potentially unnerving, especially if abuse occurs. Your sexually tinged behavior might lessen the possibility that men will see you as a competent work colleague. To bring a successful complaint, you need to shift from a traditional woman's role to one where you present yourself in a straightforward and serious manner as an employee.

Women also bring other well-ingrained personal attitudes to the job. Because we frequently worry about the emotional well-being of our families, partners and children, we often do similar worrying at work. We may act as if we have full responsibility for the emotional climate at work, and assume the role of keeper of the emotional peace. A woman working as a landscape architect reported:

> *One of the bosses was having emotional problems and taking it out on all the other employees. The other two bosses were totally unaware. I brought it to their attention and said, "We've got to find some way to deal with this."*

Sometimes, this caring tendency at work traps a woman into taking care of the co-worker or boss who abuses her, often at her own expense.

A real estate agent whose boss yelled at her and humiliated her in front of others decided that his personal problems caused him to act this way. She says:

> *After I tried humoring him for a while, I realized that the problem was his marriage. So I sat down and talked with him about it.*

Identifying more clearly the roles you play will reduce tension and enable you to take action against abuse. The stress of two jobs, "spillover" and role tensions are all factors in your decision. For the remainder of the book, we assume that you intend to confront abuse at work in some way. You may not know exactly what you want to do, so we offer a series of alternatives.

SECTION III

Preparing for Action

Chapter 7

Discover Your Individual Voice

I wasn't a quitter. I was a cop, and cops don't whine and cry. Cops don't quit.

Cheryl Gomez-Preston, police officer

Only when you hear your *self* clearly can you assess your situation at work accurately and decide whether you want to confront an abusive boss or co-worker, wait it out or something in between. Your ideas about status, privilege and "appropriate" roles come to you filtered through social institutions, family members and friends. Such messages create a kind of mental static and interfere with your ability to hear your own voice when it cautiously whispers that someone at work mistreats you. Or when it timidly suggests you speak out against abuse. The "jamming" of true messages by uninvited voices poses a problem common to many people. In this chapter we suggest ways you can cut through the jamming.

Your Silenced Voice

People considered different or Other—such as women, people of color, lesbians and gay men—sometimes feel as if they're interlopers in a dominant culture. Surrounded by the din of the majority, their own voices take a secondary role, becoming almost mute. You may feel an uneasy split in striving to accommodate alien values while maintaining a clear sense of your own personal universe. As a woman living in a male-dominated economic world, you may experience what activist-historian W.E.B.

Du Bois called "twoness . . . this sense of always looking at one's self through the eyes of others, of measuring one's soul by the tape of a world that looks on in amused contempt and pity."

Du Bois spoke as an African-American living in a white world. But some of those tapes that "measure one's soul" prescribe roles for women and men, the old and the young, people of certain social classes, as well as ethnic groups. They tell us how to behave in large and small ways. They apply to women in trades or professions where people with power tolerate or encourage abuse of women workers. You may have heard from colleagues, a supervisor or professor, for example, that a loud voice, foreign accent, breezy manner, plain (or too attractive) appearance give the "wrong impression for a woman in this profession." If a colleague mistreats you at work, you think of all the things you might have done wrong, and decide it must be your fault because you "don't look right" or "don't sound right."

If you step out of the identity assigned to those of your social status, others may judge you as even worse than simply flawed or "bad." You are "deviant," "weird," a "freak," or not really a woman, Christian, American, Asian or whatever. Perhaps you are told, "Women can't handle high stress." "Asian women aren't aggressive enough for sales work." "A good Christian woman wouldn't be working with an otherwise all male team." So if you do handle a stressful job, you *are* aggressive or you *like* working with men, then you can't claim to be a "real woman," a "real Asian woman," or a "good Christian woman."

People either inside or outside your culture may assign your role. Your relatives may admonish you, "Indians of this tribe do not call attention to themselves." As an assertive Native-American woman of that group, you don't really belong—according to this definition—to your tribal community. You may have learned that in your culture, "You never tell an older person what she should do." That might mean you have no right to complain about an older co-worker's abuse. If you deviate from the prescribed description, you automatically fall outside the group identity. U.S. Ambassador Julia Chang Bloch explains the double pressure on her: "I know every time I'm given a job, it's not just Julia Chang Bloch. It is a woman, and an Asian, also being tested."

Static Dominates The Mind

You open up room for other people's biases to fill your mind whenever you silence your own opinions and impressions of reality. Your mind is never blank, but other people's words can speak so loudly they drown out your own thoughts. Assumptions about your place as Other in the world may have taken up residence in your mind so early in life and with such power they seem to equal The Truth. They require no evidence to support them.

Some messages reflect family expectations, including assigned family roles. The more insidious assumptions go beyond stating what you should and should not do: they *define* your identity for you. "Betty the bungler. She messes up everything she handles." "Marilyn is so timid, she wouldn't contradict the cat!" Though some family members intend their definitions to be complimentary, even positive messages can lead to trouble if they're someone else's idea of who you are. "Liz can take anything and never bend or break." If you are Liz, you may hear a lot of mental static about how "you can really take it." You may even tolerate abuse, believing a strong person doesn't complain. Perhaps no one ever told you that flexible "bending" can indicate greater strength than stubborn endurance. On the other hand, resistance to negative family messages can compel you to prove the family wrong at any cost. Detroit police officer Cheryl Gomez-Preston absorbed the message that "cops don't quit." She says the negative attitudes of her family inspired her:

> *I used to constantly hear that I was going to be like my biological father, who was Puerto Rican. I now call myself Gomez-Preston to honor that heritage, but at the time I was ashamed. They used to tell me that I would wind up being nothing. I was told I was the worst of two ethnic groups, Black and Puerto Rican.*
>
> *I couldn't let them be right. . . . The police department became a way for me to prove myself. . . . When you come on the force, you have no rights, and you have to take your licks, keep on, pick yourself up and dust yourself off when you fall.*

Gomez-Preston's determination to "keep on" nearly cost her her life.

[T]he threats started coming. I started receiving written racial epithets. . . . [T]he hostility got worse. . . . [Faced with an armed robber] I looked over my shoulder for my backup, but there was no one there. . . . My husband couldn't comprehend what was happening to me. He kept telling me to quit, but it wasn't as easy as that . . . I was a cop, and cops don't whine and cry.

An urge to commit suicide put Gomez-Preston in the hospital for six weeks and finally she agreed to resign her position. Only then could she turn her life around dramatically. She no longer had to show her family that she wasn't a "quitter."

Perhaps early in life you chose silence as the least dangerous reaction to emotional, sexual or physical abuse. When faced with abuse as an adult you may call upon that familiar method of self-protection. In an effort to ward off threats or lacerating criticism, you might strive to read the mind of an abusive person and to predict moods, demands or capricious decisions. You put your *self* on hold until your work day ends, attempting to be invisible as well as inaudible. Any time the threatening person nears your work area, you set all senses at red alert. If you regularly tune out your own impressions and tune in to his or hers, you can feed the abusive person's desire to monopolize your attention, a brainwashing technique.

To discover what you really believe, you might have to stifle temporarily the uninvited messages from society and your family, including the parental judgments that intrude even when your parents are no longer living.

Your Mind, the Saboteur

Perhaps you anticipate with pleasure certain activities, yet you regularly procrastinate getting them started. "*This* time I'm going to speak up for myself for sure. . . . Well, wait a minute. I'd better talk it over with Don first, anyway this job has to be finished now, so I'll think about it later." The next time the idea enters your mind, you decide it's too petty to bring up so long after the fact. How did it slip out of your mind? Did some soft-spoken message cause you to forget the issue until it seemed to late too act on it?

You may almost feel that an alien self propels you in a direction opposite to your desires, sabotaging your intentions. Remember the movie, *The Invasion of the Body Snatchers*? The film you've been starring in could be titled, *The Invasion of the Mind Snatchers*. Perhaps the alien voice insisted, "You're not important enough to contradict authorities. You always did have pretentious ideas, as if you were better than the rest." But you can write a new scenario by exploring who snatched part of your mind, and how you can get it back. Let's say you persist in repeating negative self-judgments and gloomy predictions about your prospects at work. Feelings of anger, depression, resentment, guilt, helplessness—or all of the above—will almost certainly follow. Such is the power of negative thinking.

Besides coping with insults or intimidation from co-workers or your boss, you increase your problems by repeating insults you heard as a child. Voices in your head imply you deserve abuse and nothing you could do would stop it. You begin to expect mistreatment. Every error, accident or misfortune gets chalked up as evidence to support your negative thoughts. You think maybe your family said it right, when they claimed that you "ask for trouble." Maybe you should have stayed "in your place" as they defined it. Your pessimistic family has snatched your mind out of your control. At their most extreme, alien thoughts result in your unintentional cooperation with abuse. You sabotage yourself.

Suppose your day begins with your boss shouting, "You don't even belong in this business!" You tell yourself, "She's right. I never should have tried to do this job." You feel ashamed. You open up your psychological kit bag and tuck in the boss's statement along with negative judgments of your character and the feelings those judgments generate. You carry them with you all day. They act like a magnet, collecting opportunities to repeat the emotional reaction. A co-worker arrives late and doesn't smile or say "Good morning." "See?" you say to yourself, "She thinks I'm not worth talking to." Developing a defensive strategy, you stop greeting her, and for good measure, others too. Pretty soon other co-workers stop saying hello. You interpret that as more evidence for your developing case that people mistreat you. The magnet works efficiently. With a kind of perverse satisfaction, it attracts any sign of hostility or rejection in the atmosphere. Anything hinting of hope or good cheer bounces away with the strength of a negative force. As you gather "evidence" that no one values you, you begin expecting the worst of everyone, including yourself.

Is This "Asking For" Abuse?

The short answer to that question is no. To make mistakes or to put yourself at risk unintentionally does not imply you "asked for" abuse. *Yet to some extent* you can contribute to predictions coming true. If you picture yourself performing poorly, those visions can act like a rehearsal. Like most people with a habit of thinking negatively, you probably harbor a faulty definition of "failure." Anything you do less than perfectly labels you unworthy. Now, you're the director of a movie in which each error becomes a frame labeled "failure." In imagination, day after day, you experience the actions, words and scenes of the script you wrote and produced. You've rehearsed your role and learned your lines well. Eventually, the lesson you have studied most conscientiously is called "how not to succeed."

Daily practice of this role can hype you into a state of anxiety. At a crucial moment, your fear that you can't perform well enough interferes with a confident presentation of your ideas. Later, instead of evaluating yourself accurately, you verbally flog yourself. "I knew I'd ruin that opportunity. I should have let Fred do it. I'm not qualified for this job." By expecting to botch the job, you actually contribute to presenting yourself in a poor light. Then you compound your problems by declaring yourself "no good" or "stupid." The spiral of negative thinking spins downward.

But just because you talked yourself into putting your worst foot forward does *not* mean you "ask for trouble" or that you don't want success. That's much too simple. In the first place, you may not have failed at all. Maybe you didn't perform as well as you hoped to, as impressively as the boss thought you should, as Mary or Fred might have. Executing a task imperfectly differs significantly from failing. And even botching a particular job does not equal failure as a worker or a person. The way you carry out your work doesn't define who you are.

True, your unintentional self-sabotage may have created additional problems to resolve. But many factors affect how well you perform at work. A real world exists out there. Although some individuals show concern about your welfare, others care only about their own power or prestige. The power of your mind may be limited by (1) events you can't control and (2) by the power of other people's thoughts and actions focused on accomplishing what *they* want. Several abusive co-workers or a threatening boss can interfere with your best efforts to perform a task well. But they can't stop you from treating yourself respectfully, unless you let them. You can choose to make the effects of abuse worse than they already are by accusing yourself of "asking for it," or you can decide to take control by replacing negative thoughts with factual statements.

Can You Really Control Your Mind?

The answer to this question is complicated, but our short answer is yes. And, also, no.

A currently popular idea suggests that everyone can rise above her environment by deciding to change and regularly making uplifting, forward-looking statements or "affirmations," such as: "Visualize success and success will be yours." "You can take charge of your life." Some people benefit from this practice. Reciting the words increases confidence and generates hope. Those attitudes, in turn, enhance the person's ability to speak up for what she wants; other people then take her ideas more seriously. "Positive thinkers" tend, as a result, to achieve more of their goals than those who expect the worst. Then success reinforces the affirmations and inspires still more optimism. Ruth reacted with strong feelings to her newspaper boss's attempts to shame her.

> *No matter how strong I am, I still wonder some days what I'm doing in this job. "I must be here by accident. I'm not capable of doing the job." These thoughts used to plague me thirty days a month.*

But Ruth learned to use self-affirmations for quick recoveries:

Now I remind myself, "I'm doing a good job. My imagination, my energy, my risk-taking ability, my 'people' skills are great compared to the men I work with."

You can control more aspects of your life—including your thoughts and feelings—than you may believe possible. You needn't even learn to "think positively." You can make significant life changes simply by thinking *accurately*, by putting an end to negative exaggerations and devastating self-criticisms. When you speak truthfully to yourself, you minimize the impact of other people's vilification. When you remove your load of self-criticism, you expand your available energy. Increased vitality opens you to new opportunities, which, combined with rational self-evaluations, set the stage to challenge abuse. This potential chain of thoughts, feelings and events comprises the "yes" part of our answer to the question about controlling your mind.

Is It Really That Simple?

For some women, changing an established pattern of thought requires courage. When you modify long-standing ideas about the world, you risk delving into the unknown. Anxiety about giving up the comfort of familiar habits can stall well-laid plans for improving your life. Change also requires self-discipline. Each person maintains a threshold of fear and obstinate attachments to the pain and stress that feels familiar. People vary in their abilities to follow through on action plans. Some can envision more easily than others the satisfactions possible from new ways of coping. In addition, each person differs in her degree of energy and perseverance in learning new skills.

Those idiosyncratic traits all affect our yes and no responses. Yes, you can control your mind, if you're willing to work on it consistently. But, no, our exercises won't help if your attachment to negative thoughts makes you too reluctant to give them up. No, you won't modify your feelings if the process takes more work or time than you choose to invest or if you recite affirmations without believing them. Since many people find it hard to believe positive, optimistic statements about themselves, our exercises encourage you to substitute neutral, factual statements for habitual self-destructive comments.

You may think your hesitancy to give up negative self-evaluations indicates a serious character flaw. But ambivalence about making changes plagues many people. If you've believed for quite a few years that you're a person who "can't," who "isn't good at," defining your limits may provide security. You needn't even recognize certain possibilities. You may fear that if you stop your global self-criticisms, you'll lose motivation to improve. But probably the opposite will occur. As a result of substituting self-respectful treatment, you'll move in a direction that brings you satisfaction.

Tune in to Your Messages

Pay close attention to your words when you talk to yourself, especially when you feel either "down" or angry. You might discover you have insulted yourself without even noticing. "You fool! You really messed up that whole project. You're never going to get anywhere." If your boss or co-worker had demeaned you that way, you would have reacted with resentment, hurt or fear. You might not mind much being told you neglected to deal with a problem soon enough, underestimated the price of an order, used the wrong tool or said something undiplomatic to a client. But "messed up the whole project"? You did nothing right at all? Who wouldn't feel angry or despairing if they believed such a criticism? Yet you don't protest your own disrespectful words. Calling yourself a "fool" or other names that imply you're totally beyond hope of improvement exemplifies abusive language. Such name-calling can do even more damage when it comes from within you than when someone else hurls an insult at you. You may chronically abuse yourself in such a soft tone that you don't quite hear the message. Your barely audible words make an especially powerful impact.

Other people's insults are loud and clear, so you can talk back. But since you don't hear your own voice distinctly, you can't even contradict it. Your own messages can come through nearly twenty-four hours a day, whereas at least the abusive boss, your mother or your husband has to leave you alone once in a while. Negative comments can convey devastating self-criticism, hopelessness and helplessness. You might have already become a one-woman verbal demolition expert, blowing up any hopes of improving your life or feeling good about yourself the moment they appear.

To find out whether you've been verbally abusing yourself, listen for any judgments you make about what you do or fail to do. "You can't do anything right." "You never were any good at sports." Pay special attention to name-calling, such as "stupid," "fat slob," "lazy." Watch for comments that make very general statements about your character or performance, as well as negative predictions about the future. "You sure did a lousy job of that." "You'll never make it at this job." "You shouldn't have tried to compete, you're out of your league. Stick with the losers."

EXERCISE 7A: Record Your Negative Thoughts

List the negative comments you've recently made about yourself:

Example:

I'm a fool.	*You messed up the whole project.*	*It's hopeless.*
_____	_____	_____
_____	_____	_____
_____	_____	_____
_____	_____	_____

When asked to do this exercise some women instantly pour a torrent of self-abuse onto the page. Others have trouble hearing their muted voices. At first they rely on sentence fragments or brief flashes of visual images for clues to destructive messages. If you can't grasp much at the beginning of this process, listen for sighs or muttered swear words. They often indicate the presence of negative statements. Try to recall what went through your mind just before you uttered a gasp or some other sound indicating disgust or frustration. If you recapture even part of a silent self-critical or hopeless message, write it in a special notebook.

Gradually you'll become more alert to your nearly silent messages, as well as the more obvious ones. Your list will grow longer. *Keep a daily record* of how you speak to yourself. Then *read it aloud.* Listening to your negative talk may be hard to take at first. As you become aware of your harsh criticisms, you might feel embarrassed at how you've treated the most important person in your life—you. At their worst, your self-accusations resemble the insults of the person who abuses you. Disgust can make you want to abandon the exercise. But allowing abuse of yourself to slip underground again will further damage your self-confidence and plans to change. *Keep writing your thoughts.* Remind yourself that hearing and recording them are the first steps toward excising them.

Trace Negative Thoughts

Suppose you aren't even thinking about your job or competency or self-worth. You're strolling down the street, gazing absently into store windows when an unwelcome notion intrudes on your peaceful mood: "There's no way out. No one will ever treat me any better than this." Although the "invasions" of such destructive messages seem mysterious at first, with practice you can trace them to triggering events. Scoldings or negative predictions might take the form of pictures in your mind rather than words. They can whiz by so fast you don't even notice them until you've practiced alerting yourself.

Suppose you're watching television, and a deep sigh escapes you. Instead of ignoring it in favor of watching the movie, you take a few minutes to consider what generated that sigh. You remember saying to yourself—in the middle of a frothy TV romance—"I'll never get a decent job." That tells you why you sighed, but where did that statement come from? What did you think about a moment earlier? Write or record on a cassette whatever you can remember about what passed through your mind. Then do the same with the idea, picture or fragment before that, and the one before that, tracing the train of associations back as far as possible. It's essential to get the record down immediately, because these conversations with yourself can be as elusive as dream fragments. Nearly silent thoughts can contribute to depression or anxiety, compounding your externally imposed problems. In this instance you might remember thinking, "I'll be lucky to even have a job tomorrow." Retracing your thoughts before that, you realize you muttered, "Mr. Harrington was furious today. He'll never give me a good recommendation." You hoped you had put that part of the day's work out of your mind. Then you recall that a moment earlier you admired an outfit worn by the movie's major character. You said to yourself, "I'll never be able to afford anything like that," followed by, "I have to get a better job, but I'll never get a decent job." The rest of the negative predictions quickly followed. A message of hopelessness such as "I'll never get a decent job" saps energy and sabotages action as much as does self-criticism.

If you had simply dismissed your dispirited mood during the movie, you might have tricked yourself into believing you felt secure about your job. But anxiety about the impending doom would have surfaced eventually in some form, and to explain it away you might have told yourself, "I guess I'm just anxious (or depressed) again." Possibly, in an effort to adapt to an unsatisfactory job, you have insisted that you don't need or want more money. But coveting the clothes you saw on television indicates you do want to be paid a good wage. Tracing feelings to their source at your job enables you to name the problem and consider what changes it calls for. This process provides hope—in contrast to suffering depression or anxiety presumed to have no cause and therefore no cure.

Automatic Thoughts Get You Off Track

Those negative and self-critical responses you write in your notebook constitute *automatic thoughts.* They spring instantly to mind, without examination. Since you've been thinking many of them all your life, you don't ask whether they make sense. They often flourish when you face a crisis or a wrenching decision, including how to cope with abuse at work. They take various forms.

Global Thinking: These are generalized ideas made without qualifications. Global thinking allows for no shades of gray: "all," "never," "completely impossible." Few such generalizations can be supported by evidence. These mental bumper stickers work well for rousing the troops, in this case the ego demolition crew. But their statements about people's lives and successes rarely stand up under questioning. What people? What women? Whose life? Whose success? Under what circumstances? When you catch yourself making such statements (aloud or silently) challenge yourself with those questions.

Automatic Negative Predictions: This error involves predicting dire consequences without sufficient evidence. "They won't hire a woman/ Latina/ lesbian/ deaf person." "I know it won't do any good to complain." You might be right, but you need to check for evidence before assuming you know what will happen. Some companies that wouldn't hire Others in the past have changed their policies. Even if an employer refused to hear complaints in the past, times may have changed enough to make a difference.

Here is an example of correcting an automatic thought:

AUTOMATIC THOUGHT	ERRORS	RATIONAL (QUALIFIED) THOUGHT
I'll never find a job where I'm not abused.	*global word (never) negative prediction*	*Now that I'm learning to recognize abuse sooner, it's possible I'll find a job where it doesn't happen.*

Unqualified "Shoulds": The word "should" can introduce a helpful guideline when accompanied by another word such as "if." "I should hurry if I don't want to be late." When "should" stands unqualified, it insists you do something without stating either a goal or reason. "I should feel grateful to have a job at all." If your boss mistreats you, why should you express gratitude for the job? Does your statement mean you should count your blessings? Why? Because you feel better when you do? Because you've decided you can't stop the abuse right now? Those qualifications *might* provide a reasonable case for not complaining. You could then revise the statement: "If I want to feel good, I should look at the positive aspects of my job." Now you have a built-in check on the statement's usefulness. If you don't feel good, either you can't adhere to the guideline or it doesn't balance the negative impact of abuse. Either situation indicates a need for further analysis.

"Women new to these jobs shouldn't make waves." But why shouldn't women make waves? Maybe that statement really means, "If you don't want to be noticed as the only woman, then you shouldn't make waves." Your particular "shoulds" and "should nots" may have guided you to morally acceptable actions for a long time. But sound moral judgments sometimes get mixed up with social restrictions. The statement about not making waves may disguise an outmoded idea about "ladylike behavior," such as: "Nice girls/good women shouldn't call attention to themselves."

If you have a persuasive moral reason for acting a certain way, stating it will help you evaluate it. "I should never take a day off from work" doesn't have the same power as "I shouldn't take time from work unless I'm sick, because it isn't fair to collect wages I haven't earned."

AUTOMATIC THOUGHT	ERROR	RATIONAL (QUALIFIED) THOUGHT
I should be able to take this treatment.	*unqualified "should"*	*If I want to stay in this "man's job," I might have to learn to take this treatment until I establish my qualifications.*

Other forms of automatic thoughts can influence your emotions and decisions:

All-or-Nothing Automatic Thoughts: This type of faulty thinking assumes no middle ground. If one thing happens, the consequence will be massive or global. "If I don't get the promotion I'll have to resign." All-or-nothing statements often threaten impending catastrophes. "If I can't even do this job, I'll never be promoted." "If I don't get an excellent evaluation, I won't get anywhere in this business." Global words, such as "always" and "never" often make their way into all-or-nothing thoughts.

Personalizing Automatic Thoughts: In this error, you assume that whatever someone says must mean you. A co-worker who has abused you says, "Women aren't serious about careers. If they were they'd be putting in the extra hours." You immediately think he means you. Maybe he does, or maybe not. Check the evidence.

EXERCISE 7B: Substitute Rational Thoughts

Write your automatic faulty thoughts and correct them with precise, appropriate qualifications.

AUTOMATIC THOUGHT	ERROR	RATIONAL (QUALIFIED) THOUGHT
Example:		
There's no escape from abuse.	*Negative prediction*	*Some people do. I might.*
_____	_____	_____
_____	_____	_____
_____	_____	_____
_____	_____	_____

Perspective and Proportion

Abusive people—perhaps including you when you mistreat yourself—tend to treat all errors or vexations as equally important. Even minor mishaps carry the emotional impact of disasters. This loss of perspective robs you of the ability to solve problems. So keep an inner dialogue going, continually modifying how you speak to yourself. After a while you'll find you've formed the habit of respecting your own thoughts and feelings. When you've trained yourself to hear your own voice loudly and clearly, you can then weigh others' opinions against yours to see which make the most sense. Achieving a balance between "alien" voices and your own enables you to arrive at objective facts and a plan to handle abuse.

Underlying Ideas

Notice patterns in automatic self-criticisms and other negative messages. You might hear yourself regularly make the same two or three comments or variations on the same basic theme, such as: "I'm stupid." "I'm incompetent." "I should never have tried to do this job." The pattern can point you toward an underlying idea about what you expect from life, what you think you deserve or how you expect other people to treat you. These three examples, for example, may point to an underlying idea that, "I'm too inadequate to do anything well enough to succeed." You may have rehearsed those statements for so many years they seem second nature. If pushed to explain your opinions you might say, "That's just the way it *is*," or "That's just who I am." Achieving distance from these assumptions helps you evaluate their truth and usefulness.

Martha, an ecologist, gave herself the repetitive message, "I can't write." She assumed it stated a simple truth. After struggling for years with feeling inferior to colleagues, she finally uncovered the underlying idea, "Working-class people can't write," which supported it. Although her statements contained no global words, the underlying idea contains an implication that all working-class people can't write. She substituted a far more complex, rational guideline: "Some working-class people learn a language style unacceptable to many publishers. If they want to publish in professional journals, they may have to learn a different, more academic way of writing." Notice all the qualifications. Martha reminded herself many times of the truth of her revised statement. Finally she was able to say with conviction, "I come from a working-class background *and* I'm an educated person. I write as well as my middle-class colleagues."

Negative Patterns in Underlying Ideas

If negative messages persist, even after a serious effort to modify them, look for the underlying ideas. You may have to take several steps to uncover the long-standing ideas that slant your basic view of the world. Deeply held beliefs provide a platform for automatic thoughts such as, "I can't speak up against abuse" or "I'm responsible for how other people treat me." Here are some examples of fundamental assumptions that might guide you through life: "Whiners never get anywhere." "Don't play victim." "Smile and the world smiles with you." "You get what you ask for." These underlying ideas, which can be called a "philosophy of life," may take the form of spoken reminders. But sometimes their power lies in their silence. How can you argue with them, if you can't hear them?

EXERCISE 7C: Explore Your Underlying Ideas

1. *Record* the automatic thoughts and self-criticisms that most resist change, even after you've worked at revising them for several weeks.

\
\

\

\

---

2. *Underline* the words or phrases that share common themes. For example, "scared of my shadow," "gutless" and "wimp" have more or less the same meaning.

3. *Put a check mark* in front of those that indicate faulty automatic thoughts, and add initials for the type of thought—e.g. "N.P." for negative predictions, "G.T." for global thoughts.

4. *Write* one statement that summarizes the automatic thoughts you grouped together as similar. For the examples in number 2 above you might say, "I lack courage," "I'm often afraid" or "I haven't learned to stand up for myself."

\

\

---

5. *Answer* the following questions about your summary statement from 4:

   A. If it suggests a guideline for people in general or those of some particular group (Others, privileged, Americans, etc.), what would that guideline, or maxim be? For instance, the statements in number 4 above might be translated to, "The squeaky wheel gets the oil" or "The Lord helps those who help themselves."

\

B. When did you first adopt that idea? (Take the time to remember whether you believed it at an early age.)

_____

_____

C. Who told you that, or who made it seem clear by actions?

_____

_____

D. What happened that caused you to believe it?

_____

_____

If you still have trouble identifying the underlying idea, try exaggerating one of your most common automatic criticisms or statements of hopelessness. Make the statement thoroughly irrational by adding as many global generalizations as possible. For the thought "I'm stupid," you might substitute, "I am the most stupid person I know about everything, and I always was and always will be." "You got what you deserved" might become "Everybody gets what they deserve every time they do anything." You might have assumed a trait said to be typical of your family. "All the McGregors are cowards." Keep playing with irrational statements until you find one that sounds like an underlying idea that would explain the automatic thoughts it supports. *Write* it here:

_____

_____

_____

Crystal's Story

In Crystal's family the desires of her five brothers came first, as their mother or one of the three girls in the family tried to fulfill them. In this poor, rural, African-American family Crystal's mother worked hard both in and outside the home and expected little help or cooperation from her boys. They remained "boys" to her long after they grew up, and they knew they could always find a handout at her doorstep. Four of them grew up to sell drugs. When deals fell through and their mother had little to offer beyond room and board they turned to Crystal for "loans." She borrowed from the bank and went short to bail them out of trouble or to indulge their extravagances. Often that meant that Crystal gave up her serious study of piano for a few weeks or months because she couldn't pay for lessons. To support herself and her music study she eked out a living caring for children in a private home.

The couple Crystal worked for, the Addisons, expected long, arbitrarily set hours, and treated her as if she had no other life beyond her job. Mr. Addison undermined her in the presence of the children, contradicting her discipline and calling her names. At first Crystal couldn't explain to herself why she continued to work for people who didn't value her. But a therapist helped her make the connection between her inability to say no to her brothers and her unwillingness to confront the boss.

Mr. Addison frequently insisted she work late to help out with a dinner party, and Crystal told herself, "If I don't stay, it will be a disaster." (All-or-nothing thinking and negative prediction.) This request sometimes meant serving meals, a task not included in the original work agreement and for which she did not receive extra pay. She worked as late as the Addisons desired, and a pattern began of their expecting overtime at their whim. Occasionally Crystal felt a hint of anger emerging, but then admonished herself, "Mr. Addison doesn't know better."

In therapy, Crystal realized she had inherited powerful early messages. "Those boys just can't help being the way they are." "Women have to take care of things and pick up the pieces." "Women are strong; women have to be able to take it." Although her mother hadn't verbalized most of those messages, she had acted them out. Crystal began to understand how underlying messages steered her toward postponing her own ambitions to meet the immediate demands of others. Searching for evidence that the underlying ideas were true, she could not turn up persuasive arguments.

Eventually Crystal realized that women, including herself,

can *choose* the times when they will care for others. But breaking her habit of automatically saying yes to men remained a challenge. She had to ask herself regularly if she really wanted to take care of someone else at her own expense. She forced herself not to succumb to other people's requests for help unless she could prove to herself it was really her choice. That was especially hard when the men in her life "explained" that one loan or one night of overtime at work constituted a special emergency situation. Her next step was to recognize that men *can* take responsibility for the way they act, just as women can. When Crystal modified long established underlying ideas, shifts in her automatic thoughts were achieved more easily. Then her feelings changed from helplessness to optimism. She resigned her job in favor of one that paid better and offered more respect.

EXERCISE 7D: Check the Truth of an Underlying Idea

To discover whether your underlying idea is reasonable, *answer* these questions:

1. What is my underlying thought?

_____

_____

2. What is the source of that belief? (Who said so?)

_____

_____

3. How reliable is the source?

_____

_____

4. Do some people disagree with these opinions or experiences? What are their reasons?

_____

_____

5. How reliable is the original source compared to people I know now who disagree? For instance, which of the people know me better, which know the world or my situation better? Who cares more about my welfare?

You might find there's a small grain of truth in an underlying idea. Suppose you tell yourself, "You'll never make it in the advertising business." You know the statement is too general to defend rationally. You understand that it exemplifies an unsupported negative prediction, but you can't get it out of your mind. You ask yourself who gave you that message and what evidence supported it. A recurrent thought from the first job you took emerges: "You don't have what it takes to withstand stress." Then you consider the evidence for that. The advertising business often presents a kind of three-ring circus of crisis management. You realize you've felt anxious and stressed about three-quarters of the time you worked at the last two agencies. That covers eight years of work, usually accomplished well in spite of unwelcome tension. The truth stares you in the face: You *don't like* pressure or tight deadlines. You can handle the stress if you want to, but you may not choose to stay in this career much longer. This series of statements enables you to move on to a decision about your career without a negative evaluation of your character.

Completing the exercises above can remind you that changes in your life come about when these goals guide your actions: (1) to treat yourself with respect; (2) to give yourself messages that are rational and true; (3) to talk to yourself in ways that get you moving. If noises from the past interfere with following those guidelines, you may discover that childhood feelings are jamming reception. That discovery leads you to your next two challenges: How to stop the jamming and prepare for action.

Chapter 8

The Thought Is Mother
to the Feeling

The reality was, when one of my instructors got dogmatic, like my dad, that person got the anger that was intended for my dad. . . . If I asked you to go out on the street and ask a three-year-old how she wanted to manage her life, you'd think I'd lost my mind. Yet we let the three-year-old we used to be run our lives.

Nan, mental health specialist

The connection between thoughts and emotions has powerful ramifications. Taking a close look at that link gives you an opportunity to discover why you react strongly to insults, even when you don't respect the person dishing them out—even when he or she has little power or privilege. Once you have identified the source of the feelings, you can change how you react to insults and actions that now intimidate you. Getting in training to confront abuse sometimes requires uncovering early memories that influence current thoughts, feelings and decisions.

Feelings Follow Thoughts

It often makes a lot of sense to dismiss a bad mood or periodic slump as unimportant so you can "get on with it." But if you make a habit of denying strong feelings, you might be in for some problems down the road. Paying close attention to your emotional reactions might help you stop abuse or even prevent physical ailments that result from suppressed feelings. Feelings often appear to stem directly from events, but an important step intervenes between action and feeling, one you can easily overlook. That step is the *meaning you give* to something that happened. To become more aware of how you interpret an event, work your way backward from the feeling. Rather than tell yourself you're "upset" or "confused," search for a more precise word to describe the experience. Obviously, "upset" indicates you don't feel good, but it doesn't provide you with enough information to be useful. So ask yourself if you're even a little bit angry, hurt, ashamed, afraid, sad or helpless.

Once you notice and name an emotion that makes you uncomfortable, try to recall what you thought just before you experienced that feeling. The sequence might look something like the following interpretation of Bill's comments to Irene:

EVENT triggers ⬧ **AUTOMATIC THOUGHT** triggers ⬧ **FEELING**

Bill said I'm incompetent	*I'll be fired.*	⬧ *Fear*
and shouldn't have this job	*I'm a failure.*	⬧ *Shame, humiliation*
at all.	*I'll always fail.*	⬧ *Hopelessness*

It isn't difficult to understand how fear, shame, humiliation and hopelessness follow from Irene's *automatic thoughts*. But they don't flow from her co-worker Bill's comment, which constitutes the *event*. Her feelings rest on faulty interpretations of the meaning of his statement. Many people would make quite different interpetrations, some of which might focus on whether Bill is competent to judge Irene's work.

If Irene—or you—can create negative interpretations of events, those interpretations can also be modified. Since negative thoughts tend to bring on unwelcome feelings, your modifications can change your emotions to be more in line with what you want. *You can't control how another person treats you, but you can control your thoughts and consequently, your feelings.* If you were Irene you might reinterpret this situation in more logical terms. See how the feelings would then shift:

SITUATION	**NEW THOUGHT**	**FEELINGS**
Bill said I'm incompetent and I shouldn't have this job at all.	*Bill might influence the boss. I'd better be careful and watch what Bills says and does.*	*worry alertness caution*

The new feelings won't provide you with comfort. But so long as worry leads to being alert and careful, the possibility exists of responding constructively to Bill's insults.

EXERCISE 8A: Feelings ◗ Follow Thoughts ◗ Follow Events

Record a disturbing feeling you recently experienced. Then jot down the thought it stemmed from. Next, determine what event triggered the thought.

FEELING triggered by ◗ **THOUGHT** triggered by ◗ **EVENT**

_____	_____	_____
_____	_____	_____
_____	_____	_____

EXERCISE 8B: Interpretations Change Feelings

Write down an event and the thought that followed it. Use the principles from Chapter 7 for changing automatic thoughts to rational ones as a guide, and rewrite your thought. Then notice how you feel. *Record* your changed feelings.

EVENT	MODIFIED THOUGHT	CHANGED FEELINGS
_____	_____	_____
_____	_____	_____
_____	_____	_____

"I'm just a whiner, a loser," Patty said to herself over and over. Three of her bosses had habitually insulted and belittled her during her several years of tending bar in a casino. In the same period two lovers controlled more of her personal life than she liked to think about. Labeling herself a "hopeless target" and too "messed up" ever to change, Patty developed a habit of muttering to herself, "No one will ever give me a decent job. It's hopeless." She alternated negative predictions and self-abuse with angry statements blaming bar managers, especially, for act-ing like "drunks and selfish pigs." When the most important aspects of her life—work and relationships—spun out of control Patty felt like going to bed and hiding under the covers. It was either that or try something completely new to improve her situ-ation. She decided to change her automatic thoughts.

PATTY'S ORIGINAL STATEMENTS	FEELINGS
1. Everybody has always abused me; it will never end.	*Hopelessness*
2. These bar managers are drunks and selfish pigs.	*Anger*
3. I just don't see that I'll ever learn any kind of useful skill.	*Despair*

PATTY'S MODIFIED STATEMENTS	FEELINGS
1. My mother and Frank and Ben each called me names, said I couldn't do anything right. But Henry, Joan and Marta talked to me with respect.	*Sadness*
	Relief
2. Bart is not an alcoholic. The dealers are the heavy drinkers and about half might be alcoholics.	*Surprise*
3. Except for Bart, the managers seem more interested in their careers than in being fair. I wish I had a career.	*Envy*
4. I'm skilled as a bartender. But it's time to learn another skill that pays better and increases my self-respect.	*Resolved*
	Energized

Although some people can change their internal monologues after just a few weeks of practice in modifying interpretations, Patty found it a tough job. But she stuck with the task. After sev-eral months she succeeded, and discovered that her revised thoughts improved her confidence enough to test a new type of job. When that didn't work out, she took another, which didn't satisfy her either.

Then Patty revived a childhood dream of working as a nurse, which made her realize she wanted to go to college. She was stunned at the amount of money required, but wasted no time lashing out at herself for being poor or for being a "loser," as she would have earlier. She trained herself not to say she'd "never be able to afford college" and that, at thirty-five, she was "too old." Instead, she practiced making factual, neutral statements: "The first year of school will cost X number of dollars." "If I want to go to school I'll either have to work double shifts to save enough for my first year or get a loan and scholarships. Or else I'll have to find a part-time job while I'm in school that will pay enough to live on and pay for tuition and books."

Those thoughts led Patty to plan, rather than founder in self-criticism and hopelessness. For the first time in many years she felt energetic and hopeful. She accurately described the challenges ahead as neither "a piece of cake" nor "an impossible dream." Most importantly, she no longer accepted the proposition that she was destined for abuse by employers, lovers—or herself.

Patty gradually developed an independent voice and optimistic outlook. Careful planning enabled her to enter college at the age of thirty-seven. Each summer she worked double bartending shifts, heartened by the knowledge the job would not be permanent. She saved nearly half her wages, and moved beyond the ideas that had kept her from pursuing a career. After five years of struggling on a demanding budget she began work as a hospital nurse. By that time her improved self-confidence and practiced skills enabled her to solve problems as they came up rather than assuming she would be victimized by them.

Feelings From the Past (Mis)guide the Present

Even though you are not responsible for abuse by another person, the more you understand the origins of your emotional reactions to it, the better you'll be able to handle it. When you're insulted or bullied you may experience anxiety, anger, shame or humiliation. Loss of confidence and lowered self-esteem may follow and decrease your ability to handle the problem effectively. When a reaction to abuse is emotionally overwhelming, it may point to a childhood experience that resulted in a similar feeling.

As we saw in Chapters 4 and 7, when Ruth was shamed by

male editors at her newspaper, she reverted to childhood emotional reactions. She realized she would have to work at silencing her mother's voice, a voice that had in fact become her own. She had never thoroughly explored the impact of her mother's emotional abuse, so, she says, "At forty-two I decided it was time to look at all that."

In therapy Ruth found visualization and meditation useful. She emotionally revisited some of her painful childhood experiences. She realized how they directly affected the reactions she brought to her boss's verbal abuse, the feeling of being "walked all over with army boots." She learned to separate the past from the present, and says she gradually reduced the devastating impact of her boss's treatment:

> *Therapy gives me a better sense of worth and the understanding that it's not my fault if an error has occured. I don't so much blame myself. I'm much better at speaking up in a one-to-one situation. I still have trouble speaking up in a group, but I feel much more secure about my ability to do the job. A year ago I was running around trying to please everyone all the time. Now I'm much stronger about cutting down on the number of inane demands and orders. I just say, "I didn't get to it today, Len."*

By exploring emotional relationships between past and present you can defuse your emotional responses to disturbing events. "Defusing" doesn't mean eliminating reactions, but rather gaining control over them, so they won't harm you. Ruth doesn't always tell her boss what she thinks of his behavior, and sometimes she decides a confrontation would be counterproductive. But more and more, she speaks up to her male colleagues, refusing to be intimidated by their "egos the size of barns."

EXERCISE 8C: Focus On Your Feelings

Find a place to be alone and quiet for an hour and a half. Allow time after this exercise to reflect on the experience. Read the Relaxation Message and Guided Fantasy into a tape recorder or ask a friend to read them to you as you relax. If you already have a favorite relaxation routine, use it instead. Then go directly to the guided fantasy. If you're not accustomed to relaxing, you may want to practice a few times before you continue with the rest of the exercise. Whether you use a tape or your friend reads the instructions for you, allow plenty of time. Be sure that the reader speaks in a very slow, calm voice.

Count slowly and silently to three each time you see three dots in the script. Count to five when there are five dots. You and your friend might reverse roles on alternate days. Choose a partner for this exercise whom you can trust completely, because if unexpected feelings emerge, you may feel vulnerable.

Settle down in a comfortable chair, but not one so cozy you'll fall asleep. Bring to mind a situation in which you felt abused at work. Then put it aside to return to later in this exercise.

The Relaxation Message

Settle comfortably into your chair or sofa. Uncross your legs and let your arms lie flat. Take a deep breath and hold it to a count of five . . . . . 1 . . . . . 2 . . . . . 3 . . . . . 4 . . . . . 5 . . . . . Let your breath go out slowly . . . . . Imagine yourself in a place that is peaceful and warm, where there is nothing to do and you have complete trust in the environment . . . . . It may be a place you have been or it may be one you have visited only in your imagination . . . . . It is a place where there is plenty of time to relax . . . . .

Frown tightly and close your eyes tightly . . . hold it for a moment or two . . . breathe in, count to three: . . . 1 . . . 2 . . . 3 . . . and say to yourself, "Relax now . . . . . ," as you relax your forehead and your eyes . . . Tighten the muscles of your jaw . . . Breathe in, count to three: . . . 1 . . . 2 . . . 3 . . . and say to yourself, "Relax now . . . . . ," as you relax your jaw . . . Stretch your neck muscles, bending your head back . . . and then forward . . . Breathe in, count to three: . . . 1 . . . 2 . . . 3 . . . and say to yourself, "Relax now . . . . . ," as you relax your neck muscles . . .

Tighten your torso, including your buttocks and stomach muscles . . . Breathe in, count to three: . . . 1 . . . 2 . . . 3 . . . and repeat to yourself, "Relax now . . . . . ," as you relax your torso . . . Tighten your thigh muscles . . . Breathe in, count to three: . . . 1 . . . 2 . . . 3 . . . and say to yourself, "Relax now . . . . . ," as you relax your thighs . . . Enjoy the feeling of warmth and looseness flowing through your body, making you more and more relaxed . . . and at peace . . .

Tighten your calf muscles . . . Breathe in, count to three: . . . 1 . . . 2 . . . 3 . . . and say to yourself, "Relax now . . . . ." as you relax your calf muscles . . . Point your toes and stretch your feet . . . Breathe in, count to three: . . . 1 . . . 2 . . . 3 . . . and say to yourself, "Relax now . . . . .," as you relax your feet. Hold out your arms, tighten them . . . Breathe in, count to three: . . . 1 . . . 2 . . . 3 . . . and say to yourself, "Relax now . . . . .," as you relax your arms . . . Tighten your fists . . . Breathe in, count to three: . . . 1 . . . 2 . . . 3 . . . and say to yourself, "Relax now . . . . .," as you let your fists open . . .

Notice if any part of your body continues to feel tense or uncomfortable. If so, repeat the process for that part of your body, tightening that muscle, breathing in, relaxing and saying, "Relax now."

Guided Fantasy . . .

Now that you're in a relaxed state, all your muscles may feel soft and loose. Continuing to feel relaxed, recall your feelings when the person at work said or did something that caused an uncomfortable feeling. Stay with those feelings. Notice how your body feels.

Focus on each part of your body, being aware of the feeling in each. Let your mind go away to some restful place, and focus on your physical self . . .

Slowly drift back through your childhood, noticing anything you see and hear . . . . . as you feel childhood feelings, see and hear what you saw and heard as a child . . . . . smelling the smells of your childhood . . . . . Stay emotionally right inside that childhood experience . . . . . stay with it just as long as you want to . . . . . Let yourself feel all the feelings and cry or yell if you want to . . . . . be there with whatever you experience . . . . . Consider these questions:

How does my body feel? . . . . . what parts of it feel that way? . . . . . Staying with your childhood feelings, ask yourself: What is the world like to me as a child? . . . . . take as much time as you want to consider that question . . . . . Continue to relax, as you notice what answers come to you . . . . .

What am I like? . . . . . what am I wearing? . . . . . how does my body feel?.....how do I feel about myself?.....Take your time again.....Ask yourself.....What are the lessons I'm learning right now?.....I might be learning something about how to keep myself safe.....how to be cared for.....how to persuade people to react to me in certain ways.....or something entirely different from any of those possibilities.....

Let the answers to those questions drift into your consciousness, at whatever rate feels comfortable. If you want to stay with your memories, continue as long as it suits you.....

When you're ready to come back to the present time and place, let yourself drift back as slowly as you like.....You might feel unusual emotions as you re-enter the here and now. But whatever you feel is going to be all right because you have plenty of time to consider those feelings at your leisure.....Whenever you are ready to come back to the here and now, drift back as slowly as you like, counting slowly backwards from five: .....5.....4.....3.....2.....1....., then give yourself plenty of time to look around and re-orient yourself to this time and this place.....

After this exercise, don't rush off to work or visit people who make emotional demands on you. Allow yourself a transition period to consider the past and how it relates to the present. Then write in your notebook the feelings you experienced as you relived a childhood incident. Include answers to the questions you considered in the fantasy about how you, as a child, felt, what you saw, heard and thought and—if it fits—what you decided. When the time feels right, focus on the relationship between the past and your current reactions at work. Your answers to those questions may help you understand your feelings.

Whether consciously or not, you carry into adulthood the lessons learned as a child. "Never trust anyone." "You don't deserve better." "Don't tell." The messages might have been delivered directly and verbally by a family member. But one or more might remain housed in your body, never having been expressed verbally. Some of the early lessons we learn serve us well, but many do not.

People usually described Nettie as self-confident and aggressive. But whenever her boss, Cliff, reminded her of her limitations or criticized decisions she made, Nettie felt like crying. Her reaction, as much as the boss's insults, shook her self-esteem, since she thought of herself as a strong, tough woman. Cliff frequently asked loaded questions such as, "Can't you remember *anything*?" or "Do you really not know how to do that?" Nettie had come into the job as a sales representative trainee and expected some leeway while she learned her job. She had already told Cliff of her limited experience before he hired her. He was getting a great deal of work from her beyond that in her job description, and since he paid her a very low wage, Nettie felt confident he wouldn't fire her. So why, she asked herself, did she get "so unhinged"?

During a *Focus On Your Feelings* exercise Nettie relived a scene at age five in which she played with her older brother and other children. The youngest of the group by two or three years, she struggled to keep up with the others. While focusing on the feelings these events evoked, she cried and decided she would never measure up. During the exercise Nettie lamented, "I'm very small. I'll never get as big as they are. I'll never be able to do what they do. They'll kick me out. I can't keep up."

Later Nettie remembered that on her third day at work the boss had warned her, "If you can't keep up, don't expect me to prop you up." She had put that remark out of her mind, but it had its effect. Every time the boss made a scornful remark she *felt* five years old. She tried to reassure herself that he wouldn't fire her, but a powerful voice whispered, "They're going to kick you out." Once she realized this connection between her childhood and her current situation, Nettie began to handle her boss's belittling remarks more constructively. She reminded herself, "I'm an adult," that she probably would not be "kicked out" and that even if she were fired, she would survive just fine.

After doing the *Focus On Your Feelings* exercise several times, Nettie's fear of Cliff gradually diminished. When she gained control of her hopelessness and anxiety, she could remind the boss, "You know, I'm just a learner here, and I *do* forget things. You knew that when you hired me." The boss shouted more insults in response, but subsequently reduced his insults by about half.

As you explore childhood feelings, you may find that on the surface they seem very different from the emotions you experience as an adult. Yet even a mild insult in the present can re-stimulate the pain of extreme childhood rage or humiliation. Likewise, serious emotional assaults by co-workers may take you back in fantasy to seemingly minor slights in the past. Like Ruth and Nettie, you can separate current emotional assaults from those of your childhood. You may have to live with abuse at work until you find a safe way to counter it. But you needn't endure the consequences of childhood traumas for the rest of your life. Repeating this exercise a few times can reduce the intensity of your feelings. You may also relive different events each time. If memories become too unsettling to handle by yourself, consider enlisting the aid of a therapist who specializes in childhood abuse.

In the past, perhaps you couldn't stop your family from mistreating you. But now, if your parents have taken residence in your head, you can silence them. First, accept the fact that they are still very much with you. You began that process in the last chapter. Monitoring your negative thoughts might have helped clarify which are your parents' voices, which are co-workers' and which are your own. The second step involves recognizing—at the very moment the boss begins pounding the table and shouting insults—exactly who is occupying your mind. You can become aware of the "occupation forces," even while feeling eight years old.

Anger

Some people direct harsh self-criticism, rage or even abuse at themselves rather than toward people who mistreat them. If you've usually hidden or repressed your anger, or targeted innocent people, you may feel uneasy about expressing your anger at all. Not knowing exactly what might pop out of your mouth can unnerve you. You could endanger your position by expressing negative feelings directly to a co-worker who later retaliates. Some women have been pleasantly surprised when their unaccustomed expression of anger shocked an aggressive person to attention. But you may not want to risk even that type of surprise.

For anger or aggression to accomplish what you want, you

need to know, first, whether you're only a little irritated or just plain mad, and at whom. Letting yourself fully experience a frightening feeling does not necessarily mean expressing it to another person. But understanding the dimensions of anger can help you decide whether and how to expose it to someone else.

As you explore the depths of your feeling you might discover that hiding it from yourself has produced depression. You don't dare express yourself to powerful people so you turn the emotions inward. Or the suppression of resentment saps your energy and sabotages your will to change. Paradoxically, both expressing anger and holding it in can wear you out. But at least a full awareness of your indignation gives you a surge of energy to deal with the problem.

EXERCISE 8D: Writing Your Angry Self

If your potential anger frightens you, this exercise will enable you gradually to express it safely. When a co-worker tries to control you or customers insult you, you may suspect that rage lies somewhere within you. Yet you don't feel it. Writing about how someone offended you can break through denial of your emotional reaction. Whether you experience too much or too little of a particular feeling, bringing the emotional truth to the surface gets you in training to handle feelings about abuse in more satisfying ways. Set aside an hour and a half for this exercise. You'll need twenty or thirty minutes for the work itself and time afterwards to regain your emotional equilibrium. Pick a private place and a quiet time—a time when you won't have to cope with a difficult person immediately afterward. If you have young children or live in a house bustling with people, you may have to retreat to a deserted spot in the country, send the children to a long movie or borrow a friend's apartment for a few hours. If, during the exercise, you feel like crying or yelling, give yourself permission to do exactly that. You might arrange beforehand for a close friend to be present to listen to your feelings.

Title a page in your notebook, "What I Might Be Mad About." Then start writing something like, "If I *were* mad at Betty/ men/ the boss/ the night shift crew . . . ," and write for ten or twenty minutes. Don't expect to express rational ideas. What you write probably will differ significantly from what you would choose to say to another person. Your writing might contain language you wouldn't normally use. Indulge whatever exaggerations, self-pity or fantasies of vengeance give you release. You will probably use lots of generalizations. You'll remember that earlier we encouraged you to avoid those generalizations. But this exercise helps you *explore feelings*, rather than make rational judgments. The two skills serve different purposes. This exercise doesn't call for you to be objective, specific, charitable or sensible.

Continue writing without censorship until your feelings begin to surface. You may have buried your anger under self-criticism or depression for a long time. In that case, you might experiment with this exercise several times before the feelings come to life. The first few times you try it, as new feelings emerge, anxiety about the unknown may tempt you to end the experience right there. Do whatever seems best for you. But if you retreat in fear from what you might discover, admit that to yourself. Then start a sentence with "I'm afraid" and see what you learn from what follows.

Proceed slowly with this exercise if that feels right for you. But if you commit yourself to bringing out previously buried feelings, eventually you'll need the courage to explore those fears. You'll urge yourself to continue writing, as those unwelcome emotions begin to make themselves felt. Keep trying, and let yourself discover the depth of your anger or grief.

After you've succeeded in expressing anger, you might surprise yourself by sobbing. Or you might still feel angry. Or drained. Excess energy sometimes causes feelings of anxiety. Experiment with safe ways of emotional expression. You could just fling yourself on your bed and enjoy a good old-fashioned temper tantrum, complete with tears and yelling. Or you might luxuriate in a long nap. Do just what you want, as long as you don't harm anyone. If you feel the urge to smash something, turn on fast music and dance to it instead. Clean out a closet; scrub the woodwork. Go for a brisk walk. Shovel snow or pull up blackberry bushes. Play baseball. While you exercise, don't repeat angry words. Focus on the movement of your legs and arms, enjoying the movement for itself. If you do physical work, talk to yourself about how much you are accomplishing. Keep experimenting until you discover what helps you regain your emotional balance.

"How Dare They Treat Me That Way!"

You may be able to forget many kinds of emotional abuse on the job when you leave the worksite each day or even permanently if you resign. Yet if part of a co-worker's mistreatment relates to your status as Other, you could be faced with an additional problem. Abuse based on negative biases about some Other social trait may continue in different forms outside of work. People may reinforce negative messages you endured on the job even after you've left the worksite. In struggling for a way to handle bigotry, you might even oppress yourself with repetitions of society's messages, such as "Native Americans have no ambition" or "Old women have nothing to contribute," which you then translate into, "I'll never make it."

As a child or adolescent you may have heard messages about the uselessness of trying to break through the barriers of the dominant culture. There's no point in underestimating the obstacles to crossing those very real barriers. Despite the reality, however, privileged people don't *always* succeed in keeping people like you—whoever you are—at the back of the bus, as it were. But it does take a lot of energy to remain in control when several people mistreat you in a number of social situations. So if your messages from the past include dire negative predictions, either-or thinking or global words about your Other status, do the exercises in this chapter more than once. Concentrate especially on those automatic thoughts related to your status as Other.

Resentment toward privileged people can be a hazard for you, especially if you have kept it in long-term storage until now. When you have a volatile substance bottled up, it's dangerous to lift the lid suddenly, especially while someone stands next to you with match in hand. An unplanned angry outburst could put you at risk if you unleash it in the presence of privileged people. The particular way co-workers stereotype you as "Other" might offer special reasons for hesitancy in expressing your anger. A woman is seen as "too emotional." An African-American, a Jew or Latina is supposedly "too volatile" to handle crises. If you're disabled and you dare express anger at being mistreated, the boss who pats herself on the back for "giving you a break" may label you "not ready" to work with able-bodied people. Perhaps none of those judgments has anything to do with the issue that angers you, but they can be used to distract you from dealing with your legitimate complaint. You may feel that expressing your anger would only help bigoted people flesh out their stereotypes of you. So you remain silent. But letting people know how you feel can be done in many different ways. When you make the decision to "lift the lid" you'll do it carefully so you can control potential steam.

Valerie had no trouble letting her anger out, but she didn't want to control it, with the result that she often didn't get what she wanted. "But I don't *want* to stop being enraged at injustice," she shouted at her therapist. Valerie had begun to realize that her rage was backfiring, yet she couldn't accept her therapist's suggestion that she could give up her out-of-control rage in favor of manageable anger. A Jewish, feminist political activist and union organizer, Valerie had for years flung her fury at friends and colleagues. They often responded negatively and sometimes punitively. Those reactions then sent her spiraling into a higher cycle of rage; only rarely could she free herself of emotional turmoil. She felt her righteous anger was justified because it usually defended against anti-semitic, racist or sexist remarks or abusive language and unfair treatment of employees. Valerie wanted others to change, but after a painful scene with a colleague she realized her tactics were counterproductive.

She told her therapist she knew she would have to stop "blowing up" at people. When the therapist suggested ways to do that, however, Valerie reacted with fury. When she later examined her extreme reaction to the therapist's idea, Valerie realized how important it had become to hold on to her rage. She began to realize her volatility was strongly connected to her identity as a Jew. "'WASPs' always accuse Jews of being too loud or too emotional, so if I stop being passionate," she insisted, "that's just colluding with oppression." To her, gaining control over her expression of emotions equaled giving up control to others.

But Valerie couldn't maintain that view when she saw that in equating Jewishness with volatility she actually stereotyped Jews (and "WASPs") herself. In addition, she remembered how frightening her parents' rage had been to her as a child. "That really wasn't such a great environment," she realized. "I'm not so sure I want to hand that down to my kid." After thinking through these ideas for several months, Valerie experimented with new methods of handling potentially explosive situations. She learned nonaggressive, assertive responses to offensive language and action.

Valerie realizes she can still intentionally unleash her anger at someone once in a while, when she chooses to pay the price. More often, when she notices injustice, she asks for clarification and when necessary calmly but firmly states her objections. "You and I have different positions about that," she might say. "I think what you said to Sonia implied secretaries are inferior. That goes against our principles here." Her colleagues don't always agree to change, but at least they can hear what she's saying. She feels secure in her identity as a passionate Jewish woman who also maintains control of the expression of her feeling. Now she achieves more of what she wants.

The Grip of Depression

For lots of people mood control presents an enormous challenge. But some of those people haven't succeeded because they haven't yet tried in consistent, organized ways to modify how they respond to the world. The process of change may seem too much like work.

If hopelessness about the possibility of change has sapped your energy, you'll have little incentive to initiate what you need most: to get moving. Perhaps taking a walk or calling a friend represent the least attractive activities you could imagine. Nor would you want to hear upbeat music. Nevertheless, those activities help many people take the important first step toward action. Do a little personal research to find out what works best for you. If you experiment with different activities when you're just a little sad or irritated, you can come up with your own personal list of "mood elevators."

If you have bouts of the "blues," promise yourself that the next time they hit you, you'll force yourself to take some form of pre-planned action. You might listen to music. After years of working with women who are battered, Marylou has had problems with moods of discouragement. She says playing tapes of classical flute music or folk songs has an immediately positive effect on how she feels. When she's "way down there with the snakes and worms," she only needs to get herself across the room, pick up the cassette (always in a convenient place), put it in the tape deck and push the button. Four short moves. See what kind of plan you can create to overcome your bad times—a plan just as simple to carry out as Marylou's.

To Act or Not to Act?

Although it is wrong and possibly illegal for your co-workers or boss to mistreat, threaten or insult you, you alone can decide how to respond. Maybe you're saying to yourself, "I've decided to do nothing about it." Women told us they made that choice for short or long periods. But we discovered that many didn't really mean they did nothing. They chose not to confront abuse directly, but some found indirect ways of maneuvering around mistreatment. We describe some of their choices in the chapters that follow, and we discuss a variety of ways to handle abuse, beginning with a description of exactly what we mean by an assertive response.

Choosing Your Options

Chapter 9

Passivity, Aggression or Assertiveness

Speak up, but know you may pay a price.

Diane Fisher, tradeswoman

Now that you've gained insight and emotional control, you're ready to think about action. But what kind? Your individual goals, history and job or career will dictate what kind of risks you decide to take. An assertive response to abuse is our first choice in most situations. That means speaking to another person honestly, directly and with respect. This chapter focuses primarily on definitions of assertiveness. But first we discuss tactics that may be more familiar—passive and aggressive responses to abuse.

Passivity **is enduring or submitting without resistance.**

A passive response means you allow things to happen to you—and sometimes to others—as if the events do not concern you. You act as if nothing can prevent troublesome events from impinging on you. So why even notice? You agree to just about everything another person wants or seems to want.

You habitually second-guess other people, so they get what they want without even asking for it. This may work to prevent abuse at times. The problem is, you can never be sure when the method will help prevent a regularly abusive person from threatening or intimidating you, and when it won't help at all. If you've developed passive responses to various situations, you may lose sight of what you actually prefer. You may suppress strong desires, which eventually fade away. You fear others' reactions, or you assume their opinions and desires are more important than yours. You may not respect yourself enough to speak up about your feelings, thoughts or preferences. You probably don't get much of what you want. Ask a passive person whether she has time to do a task and she might shrug agreeably, beginning the job even as you talk. She smiles encouragingly and appears eager to do anything you want. Some passive people gain a sense of moral superiority by always submitting to others' desires.

Signs of Passivity
The passive person may:

- Listen much more than speak.
- Speak in a soft voice, sometimes hard to hear.
- Cast her eyes downward and hunch her shoulders, as if trying to hide.
- Habitually give up the best chair to someone else or rush to fill a water glass before it's empty.
- Defer to others' opinions and requests.
- Nod her head in agreement before the other person's statement has even been completed.
- Flatter.
- Smile continually, even when she feels put upon.

Situational Passivity

You may find yourself in a position where "situational passivity" seems the only safe stance to take. That is, although you you are usually assertive, you act passively in a certain situation. This could happen when your race, age, gender or ability makes you a minority of one at your worksite. When your boss and co-workers make it clear they'll welcome any opportunity to find fault with you, you might decide to comply passively with unreasonable demands. You may hold to that decision unless a particular issue arises that makes objections seem worthwhile. Many workers carefully pick their battles. Others accept abuse without complaint while quietly arranging to find other work.

Polly, a licensed practical nurse (LPN), "got written up" by her boss, who objected to how Polly positioned a patient's pillows. Then he added insult to the criticism: "Maybe we need to give you a class in positioning pillows for surgery." Polly's ability to respond was inhibited by her situation. "It hurt my professional ego," she says. "But I had to bite my tongue, because I had kids to support." She followed her supervisor's orders to the letter, even though they often didn't make sense. She hoped that until she was ready to resign from her job she could protect herself from mistreatment by carrying out all directives. This situational passivity may be the most common coping method for employees of intolerable bosses.

A different technique consists of appearing to accept an order, saying some version of "yes, sir!" and then carrying out the task as the employee chooses. Many workers choose this way to avoid confronting a tirade. They know their abusive bosses will soon get over their anger and even forget the orders they barked an hour earlier. We discuss this "passive aggressive" technique in Chapter 11 on alternatives to assertive confrontation.

You might work for someone who seems so important in your field or so talented, you're willing to endure whatever it takes, including abuse, to continue the association. He or she may be the brilliant vice-president of the company, the master machinist with whom you apprentice or the entrepreneur who gives you a break. You may see the abuse as a necessary price for the opportunity to bask in someone else's reflected light. You might believe the person's talent or position gives her so much power or influence, you don't dare object to her treatment because she can ruin you.

Traditional dance training requires arduous physical assaults on the body, as Agnes De Mille described in her biography of Martha Graham. Performers in Graham's company voluntarily endured "the constant pelvic drive, the hammering on the organs, [and] menstrual disturbances." But they paid an additional price for affiliating with this particular luminary. Perhaps they expected creative genius to display an artistic temperament, to be autocratic or even abusive. De Mille describes the great choreographer's temper tantrums before an opening night.

Forty-eight hours before the opening, she went into her usual hysterical frenzy . . . She screamed at the dancers and stamped off the stage, slamming the dressing room door . . . The cast stared at one another, white-

faced. Nobody moved. Nobody made the slightest effort to leave the theater or even the stage, or to go home, although they were shaking with fatigue . . . A few dancers started tentatively to dress; the others stood silently and waited. Finally [Graham's adviser and lover, Louis Horst] brought her back. She did not seem surprised that they were still there, that they were waiting, that no one had defected.

Graham made no mention of her outburst when she returned, nor did any of the performers. The dancers' patient response to Martha Graham's behavior illustrates passivity, which may have been situational for some of them.

Hazards of Passive Responses

You may feel so overpowered by a boss or co-worker's abusive control that passive acceptance seems your only choice. You might reasonably decide to put up with the treatment to stave off dangerous retaliation or prevent the loss of highly prized benefits. But that *is* a choice you make. If you persuade yourself passivity is your only option, you rob yourself of power.

A pattern of passive reactions takes its toll. After a period of consciously choosing passivity as a tactic, you may forget that you can, at any time, change your response. In addition, if you decide to submit to abuse you may have to tell yourself a few lies to make it tolerable. You might try to persuade yourself, "It will be better tomorrow," "He doesn't really mean it," "I can take it, it isn't such a big deal." Yet it often *isn't* better tomorrow. Maybe he does intend to be cruel. If you decide on passivity as the safest course, ask yourself from time to time whether that response is working for you and what price you may be paying for it. Be honest about whether your stress has increased and about other negative tolls passivity has taken on your relationships and how you feel.

Passive acceptance of abusive treatment often carries side effects. Sometimes a combination of inaction and suppression of angry feelings stimulates ulcers or other illnesses associated with stress. Or, without even realizing it, you develop indirect, underground methods of getting at least some of what you want. Or you burst out with an aggressive verbal assault—perhaps directed at the wrong person. No one is more surprised than you. We also discuss these problems in Chapter 11 on options.

If you suffered sexual, physical or emotional abuse as a child, you may have adopted passivity as your least dangerous response. You might have coped with feelings of fear, betrayal or humiliation by "going away," emotionally. Perhaps you've continued to deny the effects, or even the existence, of abuse. Yet the mistreatment affects how you value yourself. Denial of its impact serves you well as a short-term skill, but you might discover that it demands too high a price in the long run. Passivity can also cause you to feel like a martyr. After a day of letting other people have their way, you might expect your partner, friends or children to cater to you, to compensate for what you've been doing for other people. Then you bristle when family members point out that you chose to adapt to the abuse by quietly submitting, and that they should not have to pay for your job problem.

When you take on a passive stance but seethe inside with resentment, you might periodically surprise yourself with angry outbursts. They might occur at the wrong time, spill over on an innocent person or include language or accusations that you later regret.

Some women see aggression as the only feasable alternative to passivity.

Aggression is acting and speaking as you choose, regardless of the effect on others, and without respect for their rights. When you act aggressively you trample on the ideas, feelings, ego or body of the other person. We focus, here, on nonphysical forms of aggression.

Signs of Aggressiveness
The aggressive person may do any of the following:
- Speak nonstop in a loud voice.
- Refuse to listen to the other person.
- Interrupt frequently.
- Call the other person names.
- Close in on another person with his or her body, face or hands.
- Point or shake fingers.
- Threaten, slam doors, break objects, pound tables.

 • Roll eyes or grimace when others talk.
 • Mock the speech, manner, dress, class, ethnicity, religion or lifestyle of other people.
 • Make sarcastic remarks or otherwise attempt to humiliate another.

If you're normally not aggressive but adopt a new tactic to deal with an aggressive person, your unexpected strategic switch could shock him into changing his behavior at least for a while. After a long period of abuse by co-workers, tradeswoman Laura Pfandler relished the satisfaction of finally saying to them, "I've had enough of this shit!"

The insults and dangerous harassment endured by women in trades sometimes seem to require extreme measures. Even women intimidated by co-workers bury their fear long enough to confront abuse with sharp, aggressive remarks. This often fosters a boost in self-confidence, especially when the targeted woman responds quickly to insults with humorous comebacks and when she has the support of other women. She might feel richly rewarded when her aggressive comeback results in less abuse.

Some women feel guilty about the way they succeeded. They know how it feels to be targeted by aggressive people, and don't want to become aggressive themselves. They see themselves as trampling on someone else's dignity, which doesn't fit their ethical standards. Triumph can have a brief life, if the abusive person feels humiliated and retaliates. Deciding to use aggressive techniques depends on whether you think it will help you get the results you want, at the risk of both retaliation and possible compromise of your values.

If passive and aggressive ways of responding to abuse have so many problems, what can you do? No technique guarantees protection from punishment. But assertiveness holds few dangers and the possibility of rewards. It respects everyone involved and is more likely than the other two methods to get you what you want. Even if the strategy fails, you will probably feel positive about your part in the interaction.

Assertiveness is stating your opinion, how you feel and what you want, with respect for yourself and other people.

When you're assertive, you're willing to discuss, negotiate and compromise, balancing speaking and listening.

Signs of Assertiveness

The assertive person demonstrates the following traits:

- Uses give and take in conversation.
- Listens and talks.
- Speaks with moderate voice volume and tone.
- Looks the other person in the eye.
- Does not intrude into another's physical space, nor shrink away.

Since the early 1970s, assertiveness training has provided many women with a relatively new way to stand up for their rights. Most women who took these classes wanted to learn how to speak up for themselves. They thought they were too passive, too submissive or indirect. A smaller number wanted to curb their aggression. Many women had learned the lessons of tuning into other people's feelings and desires so well they no longer knew what they felt or wanted. But they did know they wanted a change.

Alana's supervisor at her first community-college teaching job had a reputation for sexually harassing women. Alana was shocked at the way he spoke to her in an early discussions and assertively addressed the problem:

> **Supervisor:** *"Honey, let's take a look at that . . . "*
> **Alana:** *"Wait. I'm sure I heard you say, 'Honey.' "*
> **Supervisor:** *"Oh, that's nothing. I use those phrases with my children."*
> **Alana:** *"It's important for you to remember I'm not one of your children."*
> *That was the last Alana heard of her boss' inappropriate language.*

Maybe Alana's style sounds abrasive to you. When you speak assertively for the first time, you may sound strident or shrill to yourself. You make a straightforward request and imagine it comes across as a rigid demand. Offering an opinion strikes you as pushy. But maybe you react in those ways because you, like most people, haven't grown accustomed to women speaking clearly and certainly about what they want. If you haven't often been assertive, you might need time to get used to hearing your new voice. Other people might need time to adapt to it, too.

Jessica, an East Indian hospital nurse, experienced discrimination and emotional abuse from several levels of management. Supervisors either failed to fulfill their responsibilities to her, made impossible demands or ordered Jessica to perform in ways she considered unprofessional. Jessica's status as a foreign employee put her at risk if she challenged authority, but she carefully confronted abusive mismanagement whenever it seemed reasonably safe.

Jessica's job description included making home visits, but one of her supervisors periodically insisted she remain in the hospital. At a staff meeting her supervisor, Babette, instructed her not to visit a patient, despite a doctor's order to do so. Jessica had consulted with her team, who all agreed on the necessity of the home visit.

Jessica: "I have a problem in not getting out to this case. If the family doesn't want any further services I'll certainly close the case."
Babette (angry): "I don't want you out there."
Jessica: "But there's a doctor's order. Have you been able to get back to him and inform him that a nurse is not going to the home? Or are you documenting very carefully? Because otherwise I have a problem with the role I have. Should the file ever be looked at by Medicare they might ask why a visit was never made, and I hope the documentation will reflect it."

The staff "just froze," Jessica says, because they wanted to be supportive of her, but were frightened. "They were like little kids. Really terrified."

Babette (angry): "Are you saying I'm doing something inappropriate?"
Jessica (very calm): "No, I'm only saying we need to document carefully that the out-patient services have not been brought in at this time."

Jessica did visit the patient, despite Babette's continued resistance. She felt pleased at her ability to ignore Babette's "need to get in a fight." She also was glad she had offered the alternative of documentation in case the supervisor chose not to follow the doctor's orders. She prides herself for having had her say, "definitely politely, but definitely clearly."

Hazards and Benefits of Assertive Techniques

Assertiveness carries some risks. If a boss or co-worker tries to undermine your self-esteem, your assertive response tells her the tactic won't work. She will recognize your self-respect as a sign that she can't control you. She may reward those who give in to her demands. She may escalate abuse when she meets an assertive response.

Jessica sees assertiveness as both her best and worst achievement. A major goal was to improve her professional situation by putting a stop to mistreatment by several supervisors. But she had an additional purpose: to maintain her self-respect. She wasn't willing to forgo either goal, and if necessary, she would pay the price for not choosing passivity. Ultimately she complained to the hospital director. But she could not bring herself to approach him "like a nice little lady," regardless of the risk:

> *I used a professional process. . . . Had I been much more sweet and "feminine" and played the game, I believe I would have gotten further with this guy. I* cannot *behave that way. I know psychologically I stayed healthy.*

Eventually Jessica was maneuvered out of her job, but she negotiated a sizable settlement from the hospital. You may not choose to make the same kinds of decisions. Will assertive techniques gain you what you want or not? You can't tell until you try them out. Consider these reasons for giving them a try:

1. Even habitually abusive people may surprise you by listening to direct, honest statements of your position.

2. For a variety of reasons abusive people sometimes choose not to challenge assertive actions. Some people only abuse others as long as they can easily get away with it. They don't respect people who don't respect themselves, who "let themselves be pushed around." So you may gain more respect when you're assertive. Aggression sometimes has a similar effect, but it keeps you playing their game.

3. Even if you customarily use passive or submissive strategies or have learned to "let things go," you may sometimes release your anger in ways you'd rather not. Assertiveness can act as a safety valve. Simply stating your opinion or asserting your

feelings once in a while can relieve some of the resentment resulting from demeaning or intimidating treatment.

4. When you speak or act directly, with honesty and respect,
the other person's abuse becomes more obvious by its contrast to
your respectful approach. This helps clear up any lingering
doubts you may have about whether the abusive person acts as
badly as you think.

5. Regardless of the outcome, you will probably feel better
about yourself for having been straightforward, honest and respectful of both yourself and the other person. The most important point for you could become how *you* act, the only aspect of
your life you can control.

6. Even if you never use assertive techniques to deal with
abuse, the skills add an alternative to your usual repertoire. You
may decide not to assert yourself in certain situations. For example, you may choose to act passively at work, but to speak up
to your lawyer, mentor or union representative. Making such a
decision on the basis of having a real, informed choice builds
your strength and sense of control. In the process of determining
whether to act assertively, you learn more about yourself. What
you want and don't want—and why.

Assertiveness Guidelines

Sometimes it's difficult to tell the difference between passive,
aggressive and assertive statements. The words may indicate one
thing and a tone of voice or body language another. The following checklist will help you recognize assertiveness in yourself and
others:

Assertiveness Checklist
• Keep steady eye contact.
• Speak with a firm voice, moderate volume and cooperative
tone.
• Use reasonable, precise words; no sarcasm or demeaning
language.
• State your feelings precisely—if you want to.
• Describe what you believe has happened.
• State your opinion.

• Describe as precisely as possible what you want to change.
• Give examples of the behavior you're asking the person to change.
• Stick with your agenda.
• Use "I" statements; avoid accusations, blaming, global words.
• Document interactions after each encounter.

If you don't want to act assertively because it's "just not me," that could mean it's not you, *at this time.* But the fact that you chose to read this book means you're willing to consider expanding your capacity to cope with problems. You've given yourself the opportunity to learn whether a partially new self-definition might include being assertive under certain circumstances.

As you experiment with assertive action, other people may label your behavior "aggressive" or "stubborn." That can indicate you haven't polished the techniques yet, or that the other person disapproves of your directness. People familiar with your previous passivity may not like adjusting to your new response. An abusive boss, for instance, probably prefers your former obedience, submissiveness and attempt at invisibility. He or she may choose to define assertiveness as "pushy," "abrasive" or "strident." All those words, commonly applied to women who stand up for themselves, constitute a form of name-calling often used to silence women.

Whether assertiveness is new to you or not, you may find that it feels threatening to some people. Speaking of other nurses' reactions to her assertiveness, Jessica says, "Nurses are used to being given orders. Some of them think I'm being rude or uppity. They think you're being defiant when you're actually discussing." At first, you might feel awkward speaking assertively because your comfort in silence no longer protects you. New ways of handling problems feel strange at first, but with time, practice and experience, they feel more like you. Before you make a decision, consider alternatives to assertiveness and the benefits and risks of each choice.

Chapter 10

Out on a Limb: Risks for You and Your Family

One time when I was raising my [four] kids I was changing jobs, and I was scared because I couldn't miss a payday. I was talking to [my father] about it and he said, "You know, Babe, for somebody who's bummed around as much as you have, you're gettin' awful goddamned cautious." I knew he was on my side all the way.

Peg Phillips, actor

Peg Phillips, 74, plays Ruth-Anne Miller, a spunky storekeeper on the television series, *Northern Exposure*. She longed for an acting career all her life—then began training for it at age 65. Even as a single mother of four children, she had taken many risks, including going back to school to become an accountant after her divorce. She found time to participate in community theater, always ready to grab an opportunity to act: "I always knew I loved it, and I always knew that's what I was going to do for a living one day. Her father encouraged her to take risks to follow her dream.

The very word "risk" gives some people butterflies in their stomachs and some a rush of pleasure. That queasy feeling may be interpreted as either anxiety or a potential thrill. For other people, almost any change seems risky and makes them uneasy. But for some, change means hope. How you think about the risk becomes a very individual matter. Taking risks to challenge your abusive work situation could change your family relationships in various ways, ranging from finances to family roles.

Risk-Taking: Danger and Opportunity

The Chinese word for crisis is represented by two characters. One sign means danger, the other opportunity. Risk can be viewed in the same way. Often women focus on the dangerous side of risk-taking, forgetting to look at the opportunity. No matter how bad the present situation is, we may prefer it because it seems familiar and secure. By contrast, change looms as dangerous, mainly because it represents the unknown. But even what seems to be known often contains surprises as the future unfolds. Would you rather risk the opportunities and potential danger of change or stay with the certainty of familiar stress, even recognizing its hazards?

It may be risky to tell the boss what you think about his mistreatment, or to make a report to your union agent, or to organize a caucus of disgruntled workers to plot action. It may also be dangerous to resign yourself to a miserable work environment, or to begin to look for other work. Each of these possibilities contains the potential of both positive and negative outcomes.

Any decisions you make will influence not only you but also your partner or family. We recommend that you consider, in some detail, how these changes might influence you and your family before you decide whether or not to take action about abuse on the job. For example, how would your sense of power and respect shift if you were fired, suspended or demoted as a result? We encourage you to think realistically about the best thing, as well as the worst, that can happen if you challenge abuse.

Are You a Risk-Taker?

You may underestimate the number of risks you've already taken in your life. Women have to be courageous to live in a world that is dangerous for them in many ways. This is especially true for those outside the white, middle-class, heterosexual norm, women who don't enjoy much privilege or status. A female African-American television producer laments that if a male producer comes into a story conference with a strong new point of view and wants to take a big risk, people view him as energetic and in charge. But if she has an exciting new idea and wants to go in a brand-new direction, especially if she has strong views about it, she's seen as a "bitch". So let's consider the enormous, uncounted and unacknowledged risks women often take:

- Having sex (Who gets pregnant?)
- Having babies
- Getting married (Single women are generally happier than married women; married men are generally happier than single men.)
- Talking about personal/family problems in therapy and with friends
- Expressing hurt feelings/vulnerability

EXERCISE 10A: Recognize Risks You've Taken

Describe two risks you have taken in the past, no matter how big or small. Try to think of examples you've usually not counted as risk-taking.

Examples:

Left school to get married

Had sex without contraception

Found and talked with counselor when pregnant at sixteen

1. _____

2. _____

Consider how you have handled high-risk situations in the past. List at least two personal traits that enabled you to do that well.

Examples:

Determination (even when afraid)

Curiosity

1. _____

2. _____

The difficult situation which required risks in the past might not differ greatly from your current work problem. For instance, perhaps you faced a serious illness. Maybe you wanted desperately to have a baby and had several miscarriages, or you may have had to live with an abusive parent.

When you didn't cope well, what prevented you? Perhaps you were young, inexperienced, or less educated than you are now, or perhaps you had no friends or family who understood how you felt. Has your personal situation changed since then?

If so, consider the differences. Have you developed some new interpersonal or coping skills? Do you have more information? More supportive friends? More choices? More power?

EXERCISE 10B: Learn From the Past

List some of the positive differences between now and your past.

Example: *I now know more about men.*

1. _____

2. _____

Remember times in the past when you were overwhelmed by blows to your ego or sense of financial security. How long did the worst period last? How did you recover? What helped? What can you do differently now? List some of the possibilities.

Example: *When I start to feel depressed, I tell friends and ask for help.*

1. _____

2. _____

If you immediately thought of risks that turned out badly, or those that you handled poorly, go back to the beginning of Exercise 10A. Remember risks that you handled.

Example: *After I flunked the computer class, I realized it wasn't right for me and stopped brooding about it.*

1. _____

2. _____

Your comfort with challenging abuse will also be influenced by whether you actually value taking risks. Maybe you'd like to be a person who takes more chances. Think for a minute about your heroines and heroes. Do they include people who create change and risk the unknown when it seems right, in spite of fear? Or do you have more peacemakers on your hero list, people who reassemble the pieces after someone else initiated change?

EXERCISE 10C: Take Your Risk-Taking Temperature

	Often	*Sometimes*	*Rarely*
1. How often do I take risks?	___	___	___
2. Do I value security?	___	___	___
3. Do I enjoy taking risks or find it exciting?	___	___	___
4. How often do I choose comfort and familiarity over risk?	___	___	___
5. Do I take risks when it seems right, even if it's uncomfortable?	___	___	___
6. How much do I value risk-taking?			

	Very Much	*Somewhat*	*Very Little*
a. In myself?	___	___	___
b. In others?	___	___	___

Notice any pattern that appears in your answers. Decide if you are satisfied with your approach to risk, or if you would like to push beyond your familiar limits.

What Do We Mean By a Family?

When we discuss the impact of risk on your "family," we use the term broadly. We mean the people who are most important in your life, the ones with whom you are emotionally, and perhaps financially, involved and committed. They might include the traditional nuclear family: you, a husband and a child or two—or five, or perhaps some of the youngsters are foster or step-children or you're their only parent. All of the people you care about, and feel connected to, could be your family as we're using the term here, including lesbian and gay couples with or without children.

Stereotypes about men and women may influence your current relationships and family decision-making. Some people might feel comfortable with conventional roles. In other families the same expectations may remain unspoken, increasing the potential for misunderstanding and resentment if you begin to take risks at work.

A cautious husband or partner may hate conflict and wish never to ask for a raise, while you may love a good fight, especially at work. If your ailing father depends on you for partial support, he may object to your taking risks at work, unlike Peg Phillips' supportive father quoted at the beginning of this chapter. If you're a single parent you may worry about how other family members, such as your mother or grandmother, feel about your challenging workplace abuse, particularly if they've been helping you financially or emotionally.

Before you take risks at work, consider how change might affect these significant people if you confront emotional abuse on the job. If you don't have a clear idea of your family's feelings, discuss with them the implications of your taking risks that affect them. See how well their ideas match your own attitudes about taking chances before you decide what to do. This doesn't mean you will do just what your family wants. But knowing their perspective tells you what some of the stakes will be. Taking a big risk will be much less frightening if you can count on your family for support.

What Will Change Mean to Your Family?

If you challenge abuse, you take the chance that you might be fired from your job, demoted, or experience such severe retaliation that you decide to resign. Being fired or quitting would mean loss of status and income. A clear look at your income and expenses, as well as who depends on your financial support, will influence how readily you risk your economic security.

Notice how financial responsibilities influence your feelings about changing jobs or challenging abusive behavior. Do you get a pain in your stomach or a catch in your throat when you consider these expenses? Or do you feel lighter, more free to take risks?

In addition to money and family expenses, other factors can affect your willingness to risk change at work. When Zoe was faced with abuse, she had to recognize the scarcity of social worker jobs for a deaf person. When she finally did resign, her abusive boss insisted Zoe would never get another job, warning her repeatedly about the competitive job market, especially for a deaf person. Zoe had a supportive partner, with whom she consulted as she made her decisions. She recalls, "Before I handed in my resignation, I called my partner and asked her, 'Will you support me if I quit?' " Her partner agreed and Zoe took a big chance, successfully starting her own agency.

EXERCISE 10D: Look for Financial Flexibility

Consider how the following factors influence your willingness to challenge abuse at work:

	Yes	*No*
1. Have I estimated how long it will take me to find another job?	____	____
2. Do I have enough savings to carry me over this uncertain period?	____	____
3. Can other family members increase their financial share if mine decreases?	____	____
4. Would my health insurance and retirement plans continue in some other form?	____	____
5. Could I reduce my on-going expenses to match lowered income?	____	____
6. Could I postpone big expenditures?	____	____
7. I could do without these extras: _____		

Other potential changes in your family may also influence your willingness to make changes on the job. As you think about the following issues, consider what impact they have on your attitude toward taking risks in the workplace.

Balancing Your Time

Challenging abuse at work will take time away from your present commitments. How much time and over how long a period will vary tremendously. But you can save yourself some anguish if you think about this issue beforehand.

Time with others may be affected, especially if you meet with other people to plan strategy. But this could last only for a short time; you might attend only one or two meetings before you decide to act as a group. Risking change individually may also take more time than you had predicted, especially if you discuss strategy and practice options, such as assertiveness, with friends. But again, maybe that time will be short. For example, you may rehearse only one time and then confront your boss.

Your time alone might also suffer, especially if the planning process becomes lengthy. There could be less time for reading, exercising, watching TV, and talking with friends in person or on the phone. Are you willing to give up any of this? Remember that you might feel much more sane if the abuse is challenged and stopped.

Remember, too, that if you've been worn down by abuse on the job, you may have more energy for your family after that situation improves. Your entire family might feel proud because you stood up to abuse. You would be showing your children the importance of respect and assertiveness. As you consider both short- and long-term effects of confronting abuse in various ways, also consider the effects of not confronting it.

Changes In Your Status

Change might influence other family dynamics. For example, if your partner has been staying home full- or part-time and you have been the primary provider, will she or he resent or welcome changes in responsibilities and schedules?

Rebecca decided to push for a more livable schedule at her secretarial job in a hospital after ten years of frequently changing hours. She is Jewish and had felt harassed for years by her anti-Semitic boss. So she was disappointed but not surprised when her reasonable request for a fixed schedule was denied and she was ridiculed yet again for "being a demanding shrew."

This time, however, she knew she could not continue her job. Her family had planned and saved carefully for this possibility; everyone wanted Rebecca to work in an environment of respect. So Rebecca quit and took a part-time secretarial job in an insurance firm. Regular hours allow her to arrive home with the children after school. Due to her extra time at home, she even enjoys cooking the evening meals, which were no fun before when she felt hassled and abused. Her husband, who was able to move from part- to full-time work in construction, now enjoys being the main breadwinner again, although he had previously liked the break from this responsibility. They have agreed to change this plan again in several years, although unsure what work Rebecca will seek in the future.

Reflect for a minute on various ways in which changing your situation at work could affect your role in the family. Is your sense of personal power dependent on your paycheck? If you quit or are fired, or if you take a lower paying job than your partner's, how would that change the division of power between you? Would you be expected to do all or most of the housework, child care, carpooling, elder care, or cooking? Would these tasks be agreed upon mutually, on the basis of skills and needs?

Money arrangements often indicate the division of power in relationships. If you changed to part-time work, worked in the home, or worked for less money or status, would you have more or less say on matters such as spending? Would your family collaborate to divide up the work, all of which is respected, as in Rebecca's family? Also consider how a change in your situation might influence involvement in community activities. Consider the importance to any family member of participating in community or neighborhood councils, church groups, unions, PTA or volunteering in schools, political parties or sports. Think about the importance of these activities. How might they change, if you risk your job by challenging the abuse?

Consider the status or roles that flow from your work or job title, including intangible benefits. How would your family respond to such losses? Perhaps you're the first lawyer in your family, and all the extended family members enjoy the reflection of your status when they visit the prestigious company where you work. Or you've been honored as the outstanding worker in your firm, despite the abuse you've experienced. Maybe the best hours of your life are spent representing workers' claims in your position as a labor union steward. Think carefully about whether you and your family are prepared to give up these aspects of your life if your work challenge doesn't succeed.

How Bad Can It Get?

You might be afraid the boss will punish any resistance by yelling even more insults at you than usual, or by reprimanding you in public. Perhaps you worry that your supervisor will take your most enjoyable responsibilities away from you, or that the abusive co-worker will humiliate you by starting office gossip about you if you speak up. You might be afraid of being demoted or even fired on the spot.

Some of those imagined consequences may be unlikely. On the other hand, perhaps the boss or co-worker has already used some of these tactics to intimidate other employees. In either case, try to think through each consequence in all its frightening detail. Consider how you would deal with these worst scenarios. Then you'll be prepared for whatever happens.

EXERCISE 10E: Consider the Consequences

As always, it is useful to call on a friend for help in considering the consequences of your options. Ask him or her to walk you through each of the most feared possibilities. Tell your friend to ask four questions about each of the consequences you're afraid of:

1. What will be the short-term effects?

---

2. What are the most likely long-term consequences?

_____

_____

3. How can I avoid the most difficult results of any negative reactions? (Include guarding against anything you might be tempted to do that might make things worse.)

_____

_____

4. Is this scenario really harder than putting up with the abuse?

_____

_____

Hannah, a corporate lawyer, hesitated to consult with other lawyers about her job dissatisfaction. Afraid of losing face, she also feared that all her clients would leave or that she would be fired immediately, if word got around that she was dissatisfied. But when she gathered her courage, she discovered the risks were negligible. She consulted discreetly with other lawyers, asking them to keep her concerns confidential, as she gathered information about other firms and job possibilities. Her boss never found out about her explorations.

Hannah received very useful tips on how to improve her situation. The more she learned of other firms, the more she appreciated her own. So instead of leaving, she took risks to change her situation. She spoke to the managing partners, with good results. Significant positive changes occurred in the kinds of cases she received and in increased responsibilities and pay. She decided to stay on, and has grown increasingly happy with her position.

What If You're Fired?

What would be the financial consequences to your family if you were fired? How could you recover financially and emotionally? How long would this recovery take? Can you save money now or create or find other work?

If you have a low-paying job and little or no savings, that

may scare you into thinking you can't take any risks. But many low-paying jobs have high turnover, making it easier to find another one. When Belinda was fired from her waitressing job, she felt both scared and very sad. Her boyfriend helped her begin making contacts, and she was soon making more money working as a hostess in an exclusive restaurant where she also received more respect. She concludes:

> *Being fired turned out to be helpful, though it was a shock at the time. It forced me to look around and improve my situation. I had more choices than I thought.*

If you imagine you would be disgraced in the eyes of other people if you were fired, ask yourself, "Exactly who are these people?" If you know people who were fired from a job, ask what helped them recover. What was it like at the beginning? How do they feel now about the experience? Consider which aspects of their situation resemble yours and which differ. Is there any way you can make your situation closer to the positive aspects of theirs? If they had alternative skills, maybe you'll decide this is the time to develop one or two yourself.

Maybe You're Not Stuck

Imagining what it would be like to move to another area or town can also expand your options. Or you might think about moving if you live in a financially depressed area. Moving to another place might seem difficult or too expensive. But at least consider what a move would actually involve. Then, if you decide against it, you'll know staying in your town or city is partly your choice. And you still have the option of changing your mind later.

Gearing Up for Job Hunting

If you plan a confrontation that puts your job on the line, you need a work alternative. You could search the market long before it becomes necessary. Act as if you are serious about finding a new job. Consider a new field if appropriate. The more flexible you are, the better your prospects.

Investigating the job market for information about job possibilities can diminish your fears. You might develop ideas about new fields to explore. When you think about looking for a job, you might scare yourself with very broad threats, such as: "I'll never find another job"; "I'll never find a job that pays this well"; "This job is the only way my family can survive"; "I'm too old (or unskilled, uneducated, stupid, hard to get along with)." Don't listen to internal messages that terrify you with the specter of being jobless forever. Change those messages to facts or realistic predictions.

Interview people about your situation, your possibilities, new opportunities and retraining. Update your resume. Talk to union representatives about contacts that might be useful. Talk to friends about whether people are needed where they work. Get information about training at a community college or trade school. Of course, you will want to do all this with discretion.

If you fear exploring options because your boss or co-worker might retaliate, that's just one more indication that he controls more of your life than is acceptable. You do have a right to look for the best opportunities for yourself. When you have done that, and made contingency plans for you and your family, you will be much more confident in confronting your boss or co-workers. You have a plan.

When There's Abuse in Your Family

Many women face abuse not only at work but also at home. That dangerous situation can escalate risks. Physical abuse is usually accompanied by emotional, and often sexual, abuse. Together these kinds of abuse weave a treacherous web, a kind of reign of terror. Emotional abuse may occur without physical or sexual abuse and can be especially difficult to identify. Over time abuse tends to escalate and can result in homicide or suicide in the most severe cases.

Double abuse forms the complicated and dangerous reality of too many women's lives. If, in addition, you have limited status and privilege, or if you must also deal daily with racism, you might feel overwhelmed changing any part of your life. But seeing the pervasiveness of abuse in your life might also make you angry enough to fight back in one area or more.

Realizing the danger and extent of the abuse in your family

will help you decide what steps to take. When you're immediately besieged by abuse, it's hard to recognize its severity. If abuse at home becomes dangerous or frequent, and especially if it becomes life-threatening, take steps immediately to keep yourself, and any children, safe. Others can help you make this assessment and plan your own safety. Groups for abused women, individual therapy with a trained therapist, or self-help books could save your life. Challenging work abuse may need to wait until after you feel safe at home.

Beryl had worked as a computer analyst for five years when she became depressed. Her job was extremely demanding, both physically and emotionally. She often worked evenings and weekends to meet deadlines. But she received little thanks or money in return. One male boss criticized her work almost daily.

Even after she identified the pattern of abuse at work and its contribution to her present depression, she couldn't imagine leaving. She believed no one else would hire her, despite good written work evaluations and previous ease in changing jobs.

Beryl gradually realized she had also been emotionally abused by her partner, Lisa, for six years. Beryl found the idea of separating from Lisa very difficult. She knew she needed to leave to protect herself but worried whether she would be allowed to maintain contact with Lisa's son, whom she had helped raise for 6 years. These seemed like intolerable losses.

So Beryl tried to make changes in the relationship. Lisa, however, refused to enter couples therapy and declined to cooperate in any other changes, blaming Beryl entirely for their difficulties. Screaming and name-calling became more frequent and more intense. Still, Beryl thought she could endure. But on the day Lisa yelled at her for a steady thirty minutes, Beryl reached her breaking point. Whatever the cost, she had to leave. Only much later, after Beryl left their home and grieved for her many losses, could she challenge the abuse at work.

Nancy, an advertising executive, felt exhausted and demeaned by her husband's sarcastic remarks and constant cutting criticisms. She insisted that Mark move out when she realized how devastated she was by his chronic verbal abuse. Because he was not making much money as an architect, however, they felt a financial strain in maintaining two households. Both cared for each other, so they stretched their finances even farther to include marital therapy. This provided them with better skills and understanding of each other. Nancy's therapist supported her efforts to become more assertive with Mark, while he learned anger management skills. He also became more responsible financially. After months of hard work, they reunited successfully.

Then Nancy began using similar assertive skills to confront workplace abuse, but met with less success. Her partners didn't want to change their work demands or corporate culture. She recognized that the risks were high regardless of what she decided. When Mark demonstrated that he had changed significantly, she concluded that leaving her job represented the most acceptable choice. Mark proved himself by supporting her financially and emotionally during her time of transition into a more friendly, democratic work situation.

If, in contrast to Beryl's and Nancy's situations, the abuse at your home remains mild, you might decide it's safer, or more important, to challenge abuse in the workplace first. Success there might embolden you to challenge or leave the abuse at home.

Sexual Harassment and Risk-Taking

Your partner's and family's responses may intensify if the abuse you experience includes sexual harassment. It may seem both more important and yet more difficult to confront this kind of abuse. The risk of retaliation may appear especially great.

Family members may also share the widespread belief that the victim is somehow responsible for sexual harassment, as we discussed in Chapter 3. If you sense this, you may be hesitant to tell other family members about the problem, leaving you without the crucial family support you need.

All these issues may intensify the responses of your family to sexual mistreatment and the possibility of confrontation. As a result, you'll need to listen carefully to your own inner voice as you examine the risks to you and your family when you consider confronting sexual harassment. If you've thought through the consequences for you and your family, they should seem less of a threat now. Once you clearly understand the risks for yourself and your family, you can examine a variety of options.

Chapter 11

Going It Alone: Other Individual Choices

When I see things around me that are inappropriate, I need to decide whether I want to fight this battle. How important is this to me? Is this one I want to go to the mat on? Or is this one I can let ride? Or collude with for whatever reason?

Gwen, corporate administrator

Gwen, an African-American administrator for a large corporation, can act assertively when she chooses. But she also has a large repertoire of other behavior, including waiting passively for a storm to blow over, working behind the scenes with others for change, or waiting for some future time to act. This wide range of options has helped her survive and advance in a predominantly white, male institution.

Perhaps, like Gwen, you have tried some of these approaches to dealing with abuse without naming them as specific strategies. Or maybe these options for coping on your own seem new to you. In any case, you may want to review all your choices before you select a response to abuse. Your decisions may also vary over time.

You might decide the timing isn't good now to fight back because of your personal life or trends in society. Anita Hill had not originally wanted to expose the sexual harassment she experienced while working for Clarence Thomas. Many years later, when he became a Supreme Court nominee, she came forward reluctantly with her story. Public exposure of abuse of women ultimately pushes women's rights forward when, as now, people are ready to listen. We owe a large debt to those women who

177

take these risks and absorb the personal consequences. Each woman makes her own decision in her own time.

Your cultural and ethnic heritage, religion and personal style will also influence what kind of risks you take. Only you can determine how these aspects of your background interact with your economic and personal life. Self-image may also determine what behavior seems suited to you at any particular time.

Considering a wide range of options before you make a decision helps you feel more in control, even in a bad situation. A conscious choice feels more powerful than just reacting to others, and knowing why you make that choice gives you more strength and confidence. Whether the situation gets more difficult, improves or stays the same, you can remind yourself that "I chose this, out of all the options I saw" and that "I did the best I could."

Changing Yourself

Perhaps the abuse on your job remains one circumstance where you think that trying to change others won't work. Maybe you prefer to change yourself rather than working to stop the abuse, or perhaps you see self-change as the necessary first step before considering other options. If this approach appeals to you, refer to Exercise 2D, "Take Your Self-Inventory" and to the exercises in Chapter 7 on changing thoughts and in Chapter 8 on focusing on your feelings.

The obvious advantage of this approach is that you have most control over yourself. Since you pick the desired changes, you control the timing and approach. Of course, there remains a negative aspect. Your personal changes probably won't alter the person who abuses you.

Daphne struggled for years as the only woman partner in a large architectural firm. Although she brought in the most money, her ideas and requests were seldom taken seriously. The partners frequently ignored her opinions, and then accepted them from each other. But the managing partner's explosive temper posed her largest problem.

Rich would pace outside her office, then burst in yelling about finances or demanding that she take on yet another project. He phoned her at home in the evening and on weekends, ranting for hours about firm and personal business and ignoring her comments. He physically loomed over her and women staff in threatening ways. Several staff members quit and one filed a harassment suit that the firm settled quietly, out of court.

Yet Daphne wanted to stay with the firm for many reasons. She enjoyed the prestige and financial rewards of her position. She felt a desire and responsibility to bring at least one of the firm's talented women into the partnership, a goal she eventually accomplished. She valued her role as a mentor to many of the young architects, giving career advice and showing them the political ropes in the firm. And she assumed that all firms would similarly discriminate against strong, successful women architects.

So Daphne talked with friends, both inside and outside the firm, for support. She lobbied hard to get her office moved to a different floor than Rich's, which reduced the frequency of his tirades in her office. She looked for additional ways to change herself, telling friends, "I know my boss is either crazy or sadistic, but I want to stay at my job. So I want to find ways to react differently." First she worked to reduce her growing depression and sadness and isolation and to gain some control over her overeating. She changed her statements to herself of hopelessness and despair to reminders of all she was doing to make the situation manageable.

After her depression lifted, she had to deal with her anxiety about when Rich would pounce next, combining assertive moves with reminders that she had survived so far. She looked for patterns in her life of being the caretaker of others at her own expense. She then shifted her relationships with family and friends to be more mutually satisfying. These personal changes required hard work but increased her energy and hopefulness.

Yet Rich continued to explode periodically in anger, wreaking havoc throughout the firm. So Daphne built an alliance with other partners and confronted Rich about his behavior. This risky move resulted in small changes which satisfied the others. But Daphne found herself unwilling to accept the level of anxiety and abuse she and other women felt, as they awaited Rich's next angry outburst. Satisfied that she had done everything possible to change herself and her situation, she then found herself willing to look for other work. After discreetly interviewing with other firms, she decided to build a small practice with six other women.

Consider whether it will it be enough just to change yourself in your particular situation. If not, self-improvement strategies may prove to be only a single step in the long process of stopping the abuse.

Defusing Abuse

Like other groups outside the power structure, women have often found it safer to be polite and agreeable, looking for ways to succeed circuitously rather than by direct means. Many women have been taught to cushion requests with pleading looks or downcast eyes and to make others think they are smarter. Playful, circuitous ways of making requests allow others to feel comfortable. Although women sometimes give away power with these tactics, at other times these methods help obtain the desired results.

Jo likes her current position directing the child-care program affiliated with an elementary school. Yet for several years she has felt abused by her controlling and unpredictably moody boss. She describes her boss's reactions as irrational, but acknowledges that "part of it was that I was unwilling to play the game." If Jo made a suggestion in a staff meeting, the boss would often ignore it, later making the same suggestion as if she had invented it herself. At first Jo demanded recognition for her ideas. This proved ineffective and threatened her job security, so Jo became less aggressive.

> *Over the years I found ways to work around her. I found it was not in my best interest to be so confrontive because I was too exhausted and pissed off all the time.*

With experience, Jo found it more effective to bypass confrontation at times. If she simply agreed with her boss, she was often able to accomplish things the way she wanted. Aware of her decision not to confront the boss or demand credit, she did not suffer a lessening of self-esteem as might have happened had she simply reacted passively to her boss. She reminded herself that she and all the other staff knew the idea originated with her and viewed the boss as childish for not giving her credit.

Acting Aggressively

Leah, a computer programmer, describes one of the directors as being especially disrespectful toward the secretaries. He frequently shouted orders and criticized them publicly, using demeaning language. Even though Leah herself wasn't the direct target of his tirades, she found it draining to work in this hostile atmosphere.

A reasonable woman, Leah seldom screamed at people to get their attention. But she had been told that yelling was the best way to get this man to listen. Out of frustration, she tried it, and was surprised at the result: "I started screaming at him. But as [my yelling] escalated and escalated, he began to listen." Leah was surprised that this strategy succeeded in this instance.

Other kinds of aggressive behavior may also convince others that you're serious, especially when calm words haven't convinced them. Laura Pfandler, an apprentice pipefitter, spoke up when her male co-workers referred to women as "bitches" and "cunts." She says:

> *That led to me getting the nickname of Hothead. It meant they couldn't tease me in that way and that I'd call them on a lot of their shit. As a helper you don't have a whole lot of power, but some things have to be dealt with.*

Laura often felt offended by the sexist language and magazines of her male co-workers. When calm requests didn't get results, she burned a center foldout and got their attention. As new members joined her crew, others would tell them what she'd done, sparing her more sexist jokes and language. "I didn't have to deal with a lot of that afterwards," she says.

You might not choose to correct your co-workers' language, shout at your boss or burn magazine centerfolds. Perhaps there is something you'd like to do or say but have been afraid it wouldn't work. Instead of dismissing it outright, you might discuss your rage and fantasy with trusted friends or co-workers.

They might encourage you to try it after all, and maybe it will work.

Since men are often more comfortable with aggression than most women, they might respect action or words that would frighten or disgust many women. Of course, this behavior is risky. The abusive person's actions might escalate. You could become the target of even more abuse, or punishment by being fired, "written up," or demoted. Lashing out could feel good; you may even develop a habit of it. You might decide later, however, that you don't like being aggressive or hostile. Consider negative as well as positive results before you decide whether to try out aggressive techniques.

Kate, an investment company vice-president, finally reacted angrily to her boss's temper and obscene language after a long period of abuse. She knew the risks involved. In fact, she had consulted an attorney about her rights.

> *Why did I snap? I just knew I had had enough. I had some sense of feeling safe because I knew from my attorney that I didn't have to put up with it. When he [the boss] had his final "go" at me, I just lost my temper quite naturally.*

Her apprehension about the risks proved realistic. Although fired on the spot, she received a hefty sum in severance pay. These funds will carry her through a transition period and she feels good about being out of the abusive situation. Her skills and professional reputation have brought her the support of many people, and she has now started her own investment firm.

Going Through the Back Door: Indirect Aggression

Indirect, or passive, aggression disguises covert aggression with passivity. You try indirectly to get what you want without taking responsibility for going after your goal openly. You may make complaints and then retract or reinterpret then, implying that everything is fine after all. You may look not at all self-interested. You may pretend to be eager to give up your right, comforts, convenience or opportunities. You maintain an outstandingly cheerful attitude, despite implied self-sacrifice.

Other people might express gratitude for your kindness at first, impressed by your generosity. But sooner or later they discover that they've given you some kind of payoff. Then they grow angry without being sure why. They had no idea they would receive a bill for your sacrifices, nor what form it would take. Perhaps you didn't either.

Indirect, or passive, aggressive strategies may buy you time or help you accomplish short-term goals. But eventually others may feel resentment or that they were tricked into doing what you wanted.

Using Manipulation

When it's dangerous to confront someone, workers sometimes devise indirect ways to get what they want. They may use other people to carry messages for them or maneuver others to challenge the abuse. When you don't take direct action or act openly, you may be manipulating others. But many women believe they have no other choice.

Marva, the new director of a group home for runaway young women, summarily fired many staff members soon after her appointment. The staff feared she would ruin the agency and jeopardize services to the young women clients. Both individually and collectively, staff members tried direct approaches with Marva, which failed.

So they decided to involve other people in fighting their battle. They called colleagues in community social agencies who routinely referred young women to them, and inquired if these colleagues were aware of what was happening at the agency. Did they realize that the phone was being answered only part of the day? Did they know that a majority of the staff had been fired and that needed services had been drastically cut? Were they aware that these changes had come about since Marva had been appointed director?

Staff members made similar calls to the offices that funded the agency's services. They hoped these outside people would force a showdown with Marva. After much uncertainty and hard work, they knew they had succeeded when the board asked

Marva to resign.

Sometimes, key people may be manipulated into carrying messages. For example, an abused employee might go to the personal secretary of an abusive boss if she is unable to tell the boss directly that his treatment of her and of others threatens morale. She also knows that several women in the office plan to leave, so she thinks it especially important to alert the secretary.

So she invites the secretary out to lunch. She plants a seed, indirectly bringing the mistreatment into the conversation. Maybe she says other administrators have harmed their own reputations by mistreating employees. This strategy is tricky and must be done carefully. She manipulates the secretary's thinking and hopes this will stop the boss from intimidating or threatening employees.

A strategy of avoiding the situation means that you don't involve other people but manipulate your own situation to reduce contact with the abuser. For example, Daphne, the architect, maneuvered behind the scenes to move her office to another floor, reducing her contact with Rich, the explosive managing partner. A survey of more than 400 nurses found that their first response to verbal abuse was assertiveness. But when that tactic didn't succeed, they then began avoiding the abuser to decrease mistreatment.

Calling The Abusive Person's Bluff

Kate, the investment company vice-president, called the bluff of her abusive boss. She says:

He took me out on one occasion ostensibly to talk about company policy. In fact, what he told me was that I was a problem for the entire company (because I was so experienced and confident!) and that nobody could work with me. I threw that one out by telling him I would check that out with my colleagues and I did. It called his bluff and embarrassed him and he never tried it again. I don't think it occurred to him for one moment that I would do anything else but accept his claims.

Kate knew her boss's derogatory statements were false. She might have told him that directly. Instead, she feigned concern and called his bluff. She successfully manipulated the situation and stopped that particular abusive behavior.

How About Humor?

Since humor often acts as a respectable mask for angry feelings, some women use it to challenge abusive people. At some workplaces, such as in surgical operating rooms or on construction sites, employees relieve boredom or stress with almost continual bantering. Often biting humor suits this environment.

Jane, a tradeswoman, shared such a sharp, direct response in the "Comebacks" column of *Tradeswomen* magazine. Male co-workers were discussing photographic equipment.

> *One of the guys turned to me and said, "We could use Joe's camera and take nude pictures of you and use Tom's enlarger to blow them up!" I replied, "I have a better idea, we'll take nude pictures of you, then there'll be a real need for an enlarger!"*

A woman truck driver collecting a signature for receipt of goods came face-to-face with numerous pornographic pictures of nude women embedded under glass on a male dispatcher's desk. Thinking quickly, the driver congratulated the dispatcher on his fine-looking "family," adding that they photographed extremely well. No doubt taken aback, he made no further comment.

Christine Craft, a TV anchorwoman, was surprised when the general manager of her station told her to wear a bikini for her next weather forecast, ostensibly to cheer up farmers worried about their crops during a heat spell. Shocked and numb, she nodded agreement, arriving to work the next day in a trench coat. At the moment of truth, she announced her intentions to her viewers, then opened the coat to reveal a rented turn-of-the-century bathing costume, complete with bloomers, ruffles and bows. She concludes,

> *That done, I proceeded to give the weather information with a perfectly straight face and demeanor. Everyone, especially the general manager, seemed to get a kick out of it. For years after that I believed the best way to deal with sexism was with humor.*

Her sense of humor wore thin as harassment escalated at a subsequent assignment at another station in Sacramento, California. She later filed a sexual harassment lawsuit when she was taken off the air after managers decided she was, as her book title suggests, *Too Old, Too Ugly, and Not Deferential to Men.* So humor's effectiveness varies, as does its appropriateness and tenor. But its importance cannot be denied. Professor of literature Regina Barreca states that women in higher level positions must use humor because it "appears as evidence of intelligence, personal strength, and quick thinking." She also reminds us of the power of women's humor to challenge social conventions:

> *Much of women's humor is directed at the supposedly unchanging and unchangeable institutions of our culture. Many of these sacred cows have their feeding groups in the corporate world. It is no wonder, then, that it's in the interests of the men who maintain these institutions to be particularly wary of women's humor and to discourage it whenever possible. . . . The man who fears the laughter of women is the man who fears the power of women. . . . The only way to make such a man happy is to sink back into the typing pool, permanently.*

Alliances With Co-Workers

Sometimes these individual strategies will not succeed against abuse. Confrontation won't work for other reasons. Often women reach out to co-workers to try to change their situation indirectly.

Jo, the child-care director, has expanded her use of indirect and nonconfrontational strategies for keeping her job and her dignity. She lines up support from parents or staff before she proposes an idea to the director. Jo reports, "So now I've found ways around . . . to keep my sanity. I do everything through the department heads who are so supportive of me."

Leah, the computer programmer, learned the usefulness of building alliances with co-workers. The section manager wanted to be democratic and developed a policy stating that each person's job was equally important. He set aside such ideals, however, when he needed something typed immediately. Then his deadlines took preference over the needs of the staff, even to eat or to get home on time. At such times he would shout orders to the secretaries and word processors.

Leah made a concerted effort to get to know the other women staff, even though they performed different kinds of tasks. "I wanted to know who they were as people outside of work and wanted to know what they thought of their work," she says. Leah discovered that others felt as discontented as she did. She organized the group to hold meetings where "we would talk about being treated disrespectfully for the work we were doing." Although the group met only a few times and was not ready to confront management, the meetings reduced everyone's isolation. Each member realized her co-workers had similar concerns. They let off steam and strengthened their alliances. They also gathered new information about the manager's resistance to criticism or change, despite his democratic ideals.

The support of co-workers or other groups has helped many women survive abuse. Meeting regularly with other women who do similar work at different locations has proved a lifesaver for many a woman plumber or office worker. With isolation diminished, the support generated has enabled the women to challenge abuse and survive it.

Alliances With Mentors

The phrase "the old boys' network" indicates the power of alliances, both on and off the work scene. Women have traditionally been excluded from avenues of friendship and power on the job, simply by virtue of their gender. These male networks have proved difficult to infiltrate. They are formed on sports fields, in bars, at private schools and clubs, in fraternities or in bowling leagues. Everywhere they are reinforced by male camaraderie and language. Race, class and income level can also exclude certain men from these networks.

Women began to discuss these male alliances publicly in the 1970s. Then they developed alternative networks, such as organizations of women in business and the trades. They encouraged each other to seek mentors—or become them for other women. Finding such mentors can be slow going though, with so few women in powerful positions. Most women find they need the support of both men and women to advance, or even to maintain their positions, especially in economically uncertain times. If your workplace is abusive, you may decide you need alliances with powerful people to protect you. Forming and nurturing these connections is another common form of indirect action in the face of abuse and harassment. Sometimes you also need large numbers of supporters. As one nurse commented, "It takes a whole room of women to overthrow one sleazeball man."

Many women in administrative and management positions agree with Gwen, the corporate administrator quoted at the opening of this chapter who says, "You don't go in there and try to slay the dragon without some armor." She uses people in powerful positions as her armor, and points out that they are especially needed when you choose risky public moves against abuse.

Postponing Action

In whatever you decide to do, timing and circumstances will play an important role. If you have been on the job a long time and believe the risk of being fired is slight, you might be ready to confront the person mistreating you. If you are newly hired, the situation can be far too risky. When family illness complicates your situation, you may seek support of others to survive abuse, instead of confronting it. Changing circumstances make a big difference. Many people alternate between direct and indirect action, according to the risks, their confidence and the situation.

Gwen recounts a time when changes in her personal situation caused her not to act on a serious issue. Her two most important mentors had both recently taken early retirement. She asked herself, "Who's going to support you?" She concluded, "There's nobody there to help you fight this fight." Like many workers, she decided to sidestep or postpone a confrontation that she couldn't win. Her support was too weak and her resources stretched too thin. She might have decided to act at another time, when her support was stronger.

For any number of personal, economic or political reasons, you may decide not to take any overt action now. Remember that doesn't exclude future action. Nor does it mean you're a coward or a failure. This could represent a very smart, practical decision. A conscious choice to postpone action often represents an honorable choice.

Your Parting Shot

Even if you decide you can't take on the abusive person, that doesn't mean you can't encourage someone else to confront her or him. This strategy can work even if you've decided to quit.

Helen, a hospital physical therapist, took pride in her work and cared deeply that patients received good care. She says, "I thrive on providing a high standard of care." Helen was deeply offended by the unprofessional and incompetent actions of an alcoholic co-worker who didn't provide good patient care and made obscene sexual gestures to all women staff. But since he did this in a somewhat comical manner he was never confronted, leaving the staff fearful and tense. Helen reported his behavior to his supervisor, who ignored her complaints: "I did not feel supported by the management. Medical hierarchies are male power. . . . And the union was too young to be effective yet." Unsupported, she faced what she considered one of the worst possible examples of the old boys' network: ignoring addictive behavior and providing protection solely on the basis of gender, not merit.

When assertive action failed to improve her situation, Helen tried various back-door approaches and stalling tactics. She also talked with co-workers in confidence. She kept careful notes of his behavior, accumulating concrete evidence over ten years.

Finally she found the situation intolerable. Because of her unwillingness to ignore the co-worker's bad patient care and the harassment of staff, she knew she would eventually be fired or quit. She decided that quitting was preferable. Her letter of resignation to several superiors included very detailed examples from her notes about the co-worker's behavior, which eventually led to his being fired. Although she couldn't get rid of him herself, her documentation and willingness to complain publicly in her resignation letter provided the necessary information for more powerful people to act. She says, "I never regretted my action because he was a real sleazeball. Everyone slips sometimes so you can't be petty. But it was powerful to see and document real abuse."

What Helen was able to accomplish contrasts sharply with

her powerlessness at an earlier time. In her early twenties, she worked as a nurse's aide in a nursing home with high staff turnover. She worked very hard but liked the work and felt quite competent. So she was flabbergasted to be unexpectedly fired over the phone on the basis of what she knew to be untrue stories. Later she discovered another co-worker had apparently trumped up charges against her. No matter how she tried to defend herself, the supervisor wouldn't listen to her or believe her. Looking back years later, she is sure she was fired for being a lesbian. At the time, however, she was young and inexperienced, in an era when fear and hatred of gays and lesbians was socially sanctioned. She didn't understand that her boss fired her because of her sexual identity. Of that firing she now says, "Being fired opened my eyes and lowered my trust and naivete. . . . It made me more cautious, which had both good and bad points." Years later, she could fight back more effectively.

Lynn, a librarian, was emotionally and sexually harassed at a large university. Her actions, both direct and indirect, led nowhere. She finally went to someone in the personnel department and told her story. This person broke confidentiality and phoned Lynn's boss, who angrily confronted Lynn as soon as she returned to her desk. Lynn decided to resign. But in a last-ditch attempt to save others from abuse, she sent a copy of her resignation letter to the Board of Regents. The person who abused her was subsequently fired. Proud of contributing to change, she wonders whether she could have retained her job if she had gone to the board earlier.

Creative and resourceful women have developed a wide range of strategies for dealing individually with workplace abuse. You may want to change yourself in some important way in order to improve your work relationships, or make alliances with co-workers. Perhaps you'll decide instead you don't want to do anything now, but realize you may need to later on. Expand your sense of choice and explore all options. Before you make up your mind about whether you want to take any kind of action you may want to examine closely the power arrangements, both subtle and obvious, in your workplace. Let's examine how your boss and the whole organization really operate.

SECTION V

Knowing Your Workplace

Chapter 12

Your Boss and Power

My boss walked up to my desk where there were reporters and editors around. He threw down our competitor's newspaper on my desk and yelled, "You don't have the report on that government investigation in this morning's paper! Why don't you have this in this morning's paper?" He quickly turned his back on me and walked away. I wasn't even given an opportunity to explain my position. Even though he later defended my position about the story in public, I never got an apology.

Ruth, newspaper editor

Getting in training to handle abuse requires the kind of personal awareness we discussed in previous chapters, but that's far from enough. You also need to analyze how people use power where you work, though the person in power may act more subtly than Ruth's boss did. So now we focus on the power structure that surrounds you. Knowing as much as you can about how your workplace functions increases your personal power, your power to act—and your power to cope with abuse.

To help you choose the best strategies, we first suggest sorting out systemic injustice from emotional abuse, and legitimate power from illegitimate power. Then, if you've determined the boss has crossed over the boundaries of what's fair, examining managerial styles can also help you to decide what to do.

As you consider the ideas in this chapter, you may want to bring to mind the discussion in Chapter 4 on the effects of privilege. The interaction between you and your boss might be affected by your ideas about his status and his ideas about yours.

Injustice and Abuse: What's The Difference?

Maria, a Latina packager in a food-processing plant, stands all day feeding the machine that wraps food in plastic. She receives the minimum wage for her work.

In this typical plant, the plant manager is a white man. He sets the pace of the packaging assembly line and expects the women wrappers, most of them Latinas, to keep up with that pace. Once in a while, one of the women gets distracted and loses the rhythm. Then the line foreman might scold them all, as if they were children. The foreman has humiliated Maria in front of her co-workers a number of times. She has learned from the men in her family, who work in a different part of the factory, that the male workers have fewer restrictions than the women and the foreman treats them with more respect.

Maria's situation illustrates several of the ways in which the world of work is often unjust. Most of the time, white, Anglo men give orders at Maria's plant. It's unfair that most of the people taking those orders are men of color and women. Nor is it right that Maria and her co-workers receive very low wages. It also isn't fair that women are treated differently from men at work. These represent examples of systemic injustice.

Systemic injustice and emotional abuse do not always fit neatly into separate categories; sometimes they overlap. But in general, systemic injustice in the work world stems from company, industry-wide or national policies that view workers as profit-making units. At Maria's plant, the owner believes that a hierarchical organization maximizes profits. The owner tells the foreman to control work on the food-packaging line. But the foreman oversteps that power. When he humiliates Maria in public, he moves from carrying out systemic injustice to being emotionally abusive.

Focusing solely on the most cost-effective method to produce profits often results in unjust treatment of both men and women. Some business owners think safety measures for workers, even in physically dangerous occupations, cost too much. Too many managers ignore workers' individual capacities and individual stress, treating them like machines. A warehouse packer says: "Faster, faster is all they care about."

The food-packaging industry in which Maria works reflects

the common practice of dividing work along racial or ethnic lines. As another example, the electronics industry generally employs white people as managers and people of color and women as production workers. Like many women of color, Maria works in an unjust system that is sexist and racist.

These unjust practices throughout an industry have a serious impact on many workers. Such practices affect women and men in ways that are as important as emotional abuse. But each type of unfairness requires a different approach.

People in power carry out unjust policies even when the profit motive doesn't influence work arrangements. Doris works as a nurse's aide in a large nonprofit public hospital. Managers there don't have to show a profit for stockholders, but they still have to live within their budgets. To keep costs down, they hire the fewest number of workers possible to do the work.

Doris realizes that women provide most of the hands-on work with patients. And those giving the greatest proportion of interpersonal care are the worst paid of all the staff—the licensed practical nurses (LPNs) and the nurses' aides. The farther the worker is from close contact with patients, the more that person earns, and the more likely that person is to be male and white. The workers who are farthest away from the patients have the most control over decisions about patient care. Understaffing, poor pay, close monitoring of work tasks and the sexist and racist division of work add up to systemically unjust treatment.

Often the supervisory nurse makes unreasonable demands on Doris to work overtime. She gives orders at the last minute and sometimes accompanies them with a threat such as: "If you don't need this job, go on home." She yells at Doris: "Can't you see these patients need their breakfast now? Do those beds later." Doris rolls her eyes at the other aides, but quietly does as she is told. Then, ten minutes later, the supervisor snaps: "I told you to do those beds and then feed Mrs. Collins!" The supervisor's put-downs and on-and-off orders are examples of emotional abuse. Let's summarize these two kinds of mistreatment:

SYSTEMIC ABUSE	**EMOTIONAL ABUSE**
• *Low wages*	• *Humiliation*
• *Sex discrimination*	• *Unreasonable demands*

SYSTEMIC ABUSE	**EMOTIONAL ABUSE**
• *Race discrimination*	• *Name-calling, yelling*
• *Electronic monitoring*	• *Isolation from other workers*
• *Chemical poisoning*	• *Exhaustion/debilitation*
• *Physical hazards*	• *Sexual harassment*
• *Lack of grievance procedures*	• *Threats*
• *Fragmented robot-like tasks*	• *Abuse of power*
• *Privacy invasions (urinalyses, psychological tests)*	• *"Crazy-making" behavior*

A continual "sorting out" process enables you to think clearly about mistreatment at work. If you experience systemic injustice, there may be no point in confronting your immediate supervisor about it. Instead, you may want to think about organizing for legislative action or joining or starting a union. You could look for a workplace with more fair employment practices or, if you have the resources, start your own business. However, even if the system is fair, individual people in charge can still misuse their power.

The Exercise and the Abuse of Power

When the boss says "Do this now," like most employees, you probably stop your current work and start the newly assigned task. The boss has the power to cause you to shift your task because of his position and his "power over" you as an employee. We define power or control as the ability to change the way a person acts, thinks or feels.

Some people handle power so adeptly that it doesn't feel oppressive to their employees. A manager says, "Please," "Would you mind," and "Let's do this next," creating a smooth and pleasant working atmosphere. This style may indicate good management. It can also mask the reality of who's in charge. In this kind of situation, you may feel good about pleasing the boss. If the boss sometimes acts abusively or unjustly, this seems overshadowed by his usual "nice" manner, making it difficult for employees to object to mistreatment when it occurs.

Understanding the difference between legitimate and illegitimate power can be difficult. Let's say the boss hides his own errors and disorganization by telling lies about your work to other staff members. He keeps you from explaining the truth to co-workers by insisting you not have lunch or breaks with any of them. When you object, he yells at you and slams doors. None of this is his legitimate right. It is abusive.

Then, one day, while you are still stung by his abuse, he says to you: "I want you to stop that project and deliver this to Mr. Harrington." With your attention focused on finishing that project he asked you to rush this morning, you feel irritated that he has changed his mind. You feel particularly angry about leaving the project at this moment. The boss acts inefficiently and is disorganized. But the power he exercises in asking you to shift gears is legitimate.

If you had felt angry all week (or all year) about the boss's illegitimate use of power, this sudden change of orders could seem like just part of the whole abusive pattern. For a long time, you have held your temper in check, hoping he would change. But now you explode at him when he instructs you to switch tasks. Or you decide to report him to his supervisor. In either case, you might reel off a long list of all his irritating habits, tossing his legitimate orders in with his abusive actions that are the illegitimate uses of power.

In this situation, neither he nor his boss will likely hear your complaints about abuse of power. Probably they will focus on defending the boss's right to exercise the legitimate aspects of his power, such as assigning tasks. They will ignore what you said about the lies and door-slamming and yelling. Eventually you will have to admit that he does have the right to control what project you work on at what time.

You can avoid that kind of frustration and confusion by recognizing the differences between these two kinds of power. You recognize your boss's right to organize your work (even inefficiently) but not to insult you or lie about you. You don't have to accept personal belittling or capricious demands or intrusions on your private life, but if you want to keep your job, you probably have to accept legitimate orders.

Now, let's assume you've decided that you face emotional abuse and not systemic injustice. Let's assume the perpetrator of the abuse is your boss or supervisor and that he wields illegitimate power. Knowing something about the range of managerial styles can help you consider what approach you'll take to stop the mistreatment.

When the Boss Abuses You

How you approach your boss depends, in part, on that boss's usual behavior. Managers are as unpredictable as anyone else and don't fit neatly into perfect categories. Nevertheless, certain tendencies stand out. The shorthand terms we use to describe different managers—the dictator, the admiral and so on—stand for their predominant way of acting. They may not engage in this behavior all the time.

The Dictator

People with a dictatorial style of management believe they can motivate by orders and punishment. They focus on the product, whether turning out a car, winning a case, curing a patient or selling encyclopedias. They view you as a means to that end. A typical response to complaints or suggestions may be: "If you don't like it here, get out." Or, as a supervisor in a nursing home said to the LPNs: "You're all dispensable."

The description that Muriel, a government accountant, gives of her boss, Bernice, illustrates this type of manager:

I believe that Bernice is motivated entirely by the desire of power over others. . . . Those reporting to her have a choice of total subjection and adoration or marginalization, and in my case, destruction.

This kind of boss doesn't usually understand the problem of mistreatment of employees. If you want her to change, you may need additional clout from outside the organization or support from someone higher up. But in some situations, you might persuade her that the organization can be more effective if she stops intimidating workers and shouting orders.

The Admiral

The admiral wants things "shipshape." Neatness and an uncluttered desk reflect his highest priorities. He may be able to convince the stockholders, the company's president or the owner that his style produces super-efficiency. Such a boss is likely to be more concerned with a superficial image of efficiency than with how your work environment affects you.

Even if the manager's focus on image repels you, you can use it to your benefit. If a customer witnesses abuse, you can point out to the admiral that this interaction "looks bad for the company." You can hint, or overtly threaten, to disclose the problem to a monitoring body such as a union or better business bureau. If the admiral can be persuaded that his ship is running aground, he may decide to act on the problem. You have to be careful. He may blame you for bringing the message.

The Manipulator

Another kind of manager wants to hide his errors. He may look for people to take the blame for his miscalculations or forgetfulness. You find him hard to confront because he refuses to take responsibility for his actions. He manipulates you into cleaning up his unfinished details. And he might simply lie about your separate responsibilities.

Dealing with this type of manipulator poses problems, because he doesn't want you to expose the mess he attempts to cover up. He denies his own mistreatment of employees or may look the other way when co-workers under his supervision act abusively.

Bosses and supervisors can manipulate in other ways. Jessica, the nurse from India, expected her supervisor to complete a fairly routine Immigration and Naturalization Service form so that Jessica could obtain resident status. For months, her supervisor delayed doing this. When Jessica inquired, her supervisor gave no reason for postponing action.

> *I told her I needed to have the process completed. I might get a deportation order (which later did happen to me). She had no apology. She just "shooed" me off. I was shattered.*

Dire consequences for Jessica and her family would result if she didn't get resident status. She felt scared and powerless, like a puppet in her supervisor's hands. Jessica felt reluctant to challenge other kinds of abuse because of her supervisor's control of her immigration status.

You might not experience such a dramatic example of manipulation. But some supervisors seek out your vulnerable areas. They then exploit that knowledge and may stop you from complaining about mistreatment.

The Democratic—or Pseudo Democratic—Boss

At the opposite end of the spectrum from dictators and admirals sit democratic managers. Ideally they listen to employees, delegate authority freely and motivate mainly through rewards. When this type of manager harasses you, you might feel bewildered. He may value a democratic process. But when his insecurity takes over, when he races for a deadline or he's harassed by *his* boss, he suddenly switches personality and abuses you. This is so confusing that you might find yourself reluctant to criticize or complain about him, or even to report co-workers' abuse to him. But even if the boss treats you well some of the time, a pattern of abuse that occurs still may harm you.

If the boss truly values a collegial relationship with employees, you don't do him any favors by tip-toeing around him. He may play the dictator role at times but may still see himself as the democratic and caring boss. When you make a justifiable complaint about abuse, you may redirect him to the democratic course.

Some bosses who act democratically really just want to be liked. Such a boss will try to treat the group working under him like one big happy family. You may be tempted to believe this family fantasy. Then if you bring a charge of abuse, the boss might claim injured feelings. "How can you talk that way when I treat you like a daughter (or a sister)?"

You may decide it works better to join with co-workers and confront this boss as a group. Then everyone hears the same information at the same time. When you get vague promises that the abuse "will be taken care of," a few of you can take turns asking, "Can you tell us exactly what will be done?" or "Will you give us a schedule now, so we'll know when to expect changes?" These questions may need to be asked several times. If you're the only one doing it, however, you can sound like an annoying broken record. But in his effort to be liked, he may not want to show a whole group of his employees that he doesn't care what happens to them, so he may respond with the results you need.

The Unpredictable or "Crazy" Boss

When you can't predict the boss's reaction from one moment to the next, it becomes extremely difficult to know how to approach her. She praises your work and promises you a raise soon, so you choose this time to respond first with appropriate positive comments but then you raise a problem. "Sometimes when you're upset, you yell and call me names and..." You get just that far and she starts yelling and calling you names. Maybe you shout back in fury, not because you planned it, but because you "lost it." (Employees are sometimes unpredictable too.) To your amazement, she instantly mellows out.

Barbara's boss, Helen, exemplifies one of those unpredictable types. Sometimes Helen praises Barbara for her secretarial work; at other times she humiliates her in front of others. Both can happen on the same day. Sometimes Helen includes Barbara in decision-making; at other times arbitrary rules arrive in memos from Helen's desk. This unpredictability adds to Barbara's tension at work. When Barbara confronts Helen about her actions, Helen sometimes seems to listen and talk of change; at other times she gets increasingly angry.

Barbara hadn't considered leaving this job before, because she's a single parent and she needs the job. "I had to stick it out for at least a year. I have to support myself and my daughter." But the emotional toll from this unpredictable boss's behavior has become too high. Someone else in Barbara's office has brought a complaint against Helen to the company's president. Barbara has decided that if Helen stays on, she will leave her job.

The Crisis Manager

Your boss may be the kind of manager who goes from crisis to crisis. He may never seem receptive to a calm and thoughtful discussion of your problem of abuse. If he does listen, you worry that he will just give a hurried response. Then, before you know it, another crisis consumes him. Crisis bosses show up anywhere but some workplaces seem tailor-made for them.

Daily newspapers, for example, operate under constant pressure, and staff must respond to continually changing circumstances. Ruth describes how the privileged male newspaper editors add to that confusion:

> *They knee jerk, it's all crisis management.... There's nothing organized or planned. Everything is so haphazard and so last-minute.... There's no consistency in how to deal with situations.*

In the flurry of one "crisis"—the one described in the beginning of this chapter—Ruth was charged with not having a story ready. In fact, she did have it completed but the editorial group had already decided not to run it. Nevertheless, she was criticized in public about her "error."

> *They know they're out of line. They sometimes come back and apologize. But they always do* that *in private.*

Ruth gets no help from higher-ups to develop a more reasoned way to handle workload. This has made confronting her boss about ongoing abuse even harder. Even if you don't work on a newspaper, you may be dealing with this kind of crisis-oriented worksite and management. You too may worry about approaching a hassled boss about the mistreatment you suffer.

The Combination Boss

Organizational analysts have identified additional managerial types. We've focused on the few that seemed the most applicable here. Keep in mind that your boss's behavior may vary from one situation to the other. Your boss's managerial style might be a combination of several types.

At a group home for runaway girls, the director, Marva, acted like a classic dictator. She reacted to employees' attempts to discuss complaints by refusing to allow meetings of more than two people. She also acted in admiral fashion to make everything look splendidly efficient to outsiders. In addition, she blamed the staff for her own contradictory orders. She manipulated the board of directors by lying to them and distorting her plans. She manipulated staff by promising new people they would soon take over responsibilities of the old staff *before* she told the experienced staff she was unhappy with them.

Marva made a pretense of democratic management by telling workers she wanted to hear their ideas. Tina, a staff member, recalls:

> *She called us to her office one by one and asked what we liked about our job and what we wanted from her. People got excited about that. But after the first sentence we said to her, we were deluged with what she wanted to do. She didn't really take the temperature of the agency.*

Marva's staff members never did have a chance to express their opinions. She had wide mood swings, and made erratic plans and proposals. Many factors and styles combined to make Marva a confusing, as well as an abusive, administrator. But bad management does not necessarily mean abuse. A manager can be very disorganized, indecisive or emotionally volatile and can make you feel crazy. But if she doesn't insult or take advantage of you, her bad management doesn't add up to mistreatment.

In later chapters we suggest strategies for acting assertively about abuse. As you consider those tactics, you may want to check back on the styles discussed in this chapter. You can then see whether specific alternatives we suggest are likely to be successful with your particular boss.

Women Bosses Are Different—Or Are They?

"Women bosses are harder on their employees than men bosses."

"Men won't work for women bosses."

"Women hate to work for women bosses."

So goes the mythology. We call them myths because studies don't substantiate such beliefs, and some research contradicts them. Some women say they don't want to work for female bosses, believing that male bosses have more status. Many workers become more positive about women bosses after they have the experience of working for one. Other women like the idea of women bosses because they feel more comfortable with them and want to see women get ahead.

Whatever your attitude toward women supervisors, you may also know from experience that some women managers, like men managers, bully, intimidate, insult and manipulate employees. Unfortunately, women bosses were among the most abusive supervisors reported to us. And men, as well as women, can be the brunt of women bosses's abuse.

Sometimes, abuse reflects a woman boss's own approach to management—women vary as much as men in personality and supervisory styles. At other times, your woman boss may be caught between two management styles, hers and her boss's. Although your woman boss may want to work with her employees in a more democratic and collegial way, she must also consider what her own boss expects of her. He may assume the only right way to supervise is from an authoritarian stance. In either case, you can hold her accountable for her abusive actions.

Because of women's history of being excluded from managerial positions, women who reach the management level face particular problems. They may endure special scrutiny, they may receive insufficient training, get little support and even be considered incompetent. In addition, they may be reluctant to ask for information, believing that a request for help will be interpreted as evidence of inadequacy. Those fears aren't manufactured out of whole cloth. Some male executives look for excuses to fire female managers. They believe that such "evidence" will give them license to stop hiring women, because "women don't work out on the job."

But Women Should Be Better Bosses, Shouldn't They?

You may have accepted the false but common idea that women don't perform as good managers and that women can't get along well together. If you believe that, you may notice every small irritating interaction with a woman, even those you might ignore with a man. If so, your hypersensitivity makes the boss appear worse than she is. Setting aside those minor irritations helps you evaluate and concentrate on the more serious mistreatment.

You might expect a woman to help you up the career ladder or listen to your personal troubles. If she acts in a strictly business manner and doesn't respond, that's disappointing but not abuse. Give some thought to how you'd react if a man treated you in the same way. Then decide on a fair way to evaluate the boss's treatment.

If your boss has a more personal touch, you might expect her to nurture you or listen to your emotional problems. You might anticipate more attention than she is willing to provide. If she mistreats you or doesn't respond to your concerns about a co-worker's threats or harassment, you might be doubly troubled. "And she's a woman! How dare she treat me this way? I'd be better off working for some man!"

You may feel angry at your boss mainly because you expect better of a woman, but you could be compounding your difficulties. Understanding your woman boss's position doesn't mean you have no right to complain about abuse. But when you understand your own attitudes, as well as the pressures your boss endures, you can make a more successful complaint.

The Limits of Sisterhood

On the other hand, you may have extra empathy toward your woman boss, especially if she appears harassed or specially scrutinized by her male supervisors. You might minimize her abuse of you, forgive her too readily or just refuse to see it. "I don't think she's that bad, considering what men are like." "Look at all the stress she's under—how can she help taking it out on us?" "I don't want to get her into trouble, so I'll just let it go."

Zoe felt pleased to be hired as the first deaf supervisor in a counseling agency for people with hearing disabilities. She considered it a special bonus to work for a woman boss. When the boss, Terry, began to act in erratic, bad-tempered, unreasonably demanding and manipulative ways, Zoe found herself making excuses for her, refusing to see how Terry manipulated her. Zoe recalls: "It was hard because she was a woman. I wanted her to be good. She was the first woman boss I ever had." Only when an agency consultant recognized and described Terry's mistreatment did Zoe recognize the full implications of her boss's abuse.

You might feel caught between your own emotional survival and concern for your boss's career. Maybe you worry about lost opportunities for other women, if this woman "fails." That's a valid concern. You may want to act on that concern if you can manage that without doing a disservice to yourself. Making sacrifices for someone who abuses you can jeopardize your self-respect. No one has the right to abuse you, even if she is a woman like yourself.

Analyzing your workplace extends beyond your interaction with your boss. The official organizational chart of any workplace may hide subtle and complex uses of informal power. That hidden, informal source of power, to which we turn now, plays a dynamic role in the workplace, and can hinder or help your challenges to abuse.

Chapter 13

Shadow Organizations

We began our usual meeting of all the managers by reviewing decisions left over from the previous week. As we talked these over, I realized that the "drinkers' caucus" had already made these important decisions when they went to the bar after work the day before.

Janice, computer company supervisor

A close look at the formal structure of your organization and your boss's style may still leave you with important unanswered questions. Co-workers who mistreat you have no official power, so why are they so intimidating? The problem may originate in the "shadow organization," that is, the informal, practical power structure. The abuse you experience may be related more to informal relationships than the official chain of command.

Certain people use the "shadow organization" to gain power for themselves. Their position of privilege may not be found among the items in our Privileged/Other chart in Chapter 4. But your co-workers may gain higher status through their connections to individuals and groups who have the formal power. For example, in certain organizations, a coterie of workers and managers who go drinking together have the inside track to power, while the outsiders—the Others—are those who decline the two-martini lunch or the trip to the bar after work. You need to look at the shadow organization for the power that co-workers appear to have when they become abusive.

Look at how your boss and each of your co-workers fit into the real power structure at work. Janice, quoted above, realized the group which frequented the bars after work made crucial decisions there. You may see that the floor manager at your chain restaurant bypasses the branch manager's authority. He goes right to the owner of the company with ideas and complaints. If you're a hairdresser, you notice that your co-worker at the next booth has the owner's ear. You're puzzled about that until you find out her husband plays golf with the boss. When the junior partner is the senior partner's girlfriend, the two of them probably don't exactly follow the written rules of office management. Knowing about these unofficial connections can give you clues as to how people achieve informal power. Those clues can also suggest the best person to hear your complaint about mistreatment.

Participants in the informal or shadow organization can be just two or three people but often involve larger groups. They develop their own set of unwritten rules, expectations and accepted values. They may make decisions informally among themselves about who gets promoted or fired, who gets opportunities for training and who gets transferred to another department. They may socialize outside the workplace. The co-worker who abuses you could be a part of that shadow organization. In "old boys" or "old white folks" networks, their common position of privilege translates into power. If your co-worker can influence your boss and actually cause you to be fired or demoted, that represents real power. If he gets away with abusing you because of his membership in your boss's informal network, he exercises unfair power over you.

Take a look at who spends social time together and who seems to get inside information first. Try asking questions of people you trust. Sometimes you can ask these questions directly; sometimes you have to be more subtle. You can answer some of these questions yourself.

EXERCISE 13A: Assessing the Informal Organization

1. What does it take to get ahead here?

---

2. How do you stay out of trouble at this place?

_____

_____

_____

3. Who are the employees who seem to get the "news" first?

_____

_____

_____

Old-timers at the office or plant can provide good information. They can tell you about the people in control in earlier times as well as now, and how they got there. You don't have to announce that you want to examine the power structure. You can just ask about what changes have occurred and what the job used to be like in the old days. You can also pick up clues about who gets rewarded and for what. Rewards may or may not have anything to do with production. The "golden one" may be the person who provides the fifty-yard-line tickets to the Big Game or the one who covers for the boss in an emergency.

You may find, surprisingly, that some people on the lower end of the job ladder have more influence than you would predict from their formal job titles. Those in power may like them. Perhaps you are one of those people. Do you have informal access to a higher-up? If not, can you identify someone else who has such influence? Maybe you can enlist that person to help you think through what will get your boss or your co-workers to stop their abuse.

If abusive co-workers play golf with the boss, you have a difficult problem. You might want to consult with another co-worker who also socializes with the boss but who wants to support you. That co-worker could give you ideas about how to approach the boss, or even do it for you. Ruth, the news editor mentioned in previous chapters, confides in Mort and occasionally asks his intervention with the top boss. She doesn't entirely trust him, but she says she has to talk to someone. If she carefully chooses what she wants him to know, he can be useful.

He supports her up to a point and definitely has the ear of the boss.

A Dangerous Mixture: Addictions and Shadow Organizations

Abuse hurts whether it comes from an addicted person or not. But mistreatment becomes more difficult to address when alcohol or drug abuse permeates a shadow organization.

If many workers are addicted and react in similar ways, a certain tolerance for inappropriate behavior can develop. A group of addicted men may have a raunchy style of "banter" that insults women. If people miss work because of hangovers, other addicts cover for them and offer excuses. If the boss becomes part of this group, the situation can be deadly for a nonaddicted worker.

EXERCISE 13B: Addictions at Work

Consider the following possibilities and *check* those that hold true for your workplace. Do you find:

____ 1. *that social functions center on alcohol or other drugs?*

____ 2. *that those who don't join in get ridiculed or teased?*

____ 3. *that alcohol or other drugs serve as frequent rewards at work? (For example, are bottles of wine or champagne given to reward "The Salesperson of the Week"?)*

____ 4. *that drinking and other drug use are encouraged off the premises? (For example, do important meetings, formal or informal, take place at a bar or lounge?)*

____ 5. *that important decisions come out of informal talk in bars or lounges, and exclude those who don't drink?*

____ 6. *that those who don't drink or use drugs find themselves excluded from positions of power or from promotions?*

____ 7. *that management protects addicted employees from accountability for their addiction-related mistakes?*

_____ *8. that no one will talk directly about the employee's or employer's drinking or drug use?*

_____ *9. that employees who share their manager's or boss's addiction receive special privileges?*

If you have checked several items, addictions to alcohol or drugs are complications at your workplace. Notice how many of these questions point up the existence of the informal, shadow organization. Notice also how many involve co-workers as well as bosses.

Janice, the supervisor mentioned earlier, noticed gradually over ten years of working at the computer company that decisions were often made without her input. She noticed that the people included in the decision-making routinely went drinking with the boss, even on company time. So Janice tried going to bars with them in an effort to become part of the decision-making. But it upset her to see that heavy drinkers made policies about hiring, promotions and salary increases while they drank. She stopped going out for drinks with the group. They then ridiculed her and excluded her from power once again.

She discussed her experience with her nondrinking co-workers as a reality check. Eventually she realized that alcohol addiction affected the entire organization, not just the steady drinkers. She also learned that two very powerful company officials used alcohol heavily, making it less likely they would support her if she spoke up about how misuse of alcohol affected everyone's work. If your workplace looks like Janice's and you suffer emotional mistreatment by one of the members of the addicted group, you know the difficulty of a confrontation with that perpetrator or his boss.

Janice worked with the personnel department to bring in speakers about addiction. She built solid alliances with nondrinking co-workers. She felt good about having tried to educate the rest of the staff, but the addicted shadow organization continued as before. Janice began job-hunting, preparing to resign when, for reasons unrelated to the addiction issue, the company hired a new director. The power balance then began to shift toward people who made responsible, sober decisions.

Confronting the Shadow Organization

If some of your co-workers worry about the impact of addictions, and especially if alcohol or drug abuse complicate your challenge to emotional abuse, you might form a group to approach management. If you know that the managers you appeal to suffer from addictions themselves, be prepared for defensiveness and anger. A group of addicts who act abusively and support each other will present formidable opposition to your complaints. So before any confrontation, you might line up some person or organization to help. You and your co-workers would then have more power behind you.

Your company may have policies in place for dealing with addiction problems. Employee Assistance Programs in some businesses help workers find treatment for their addictions. Before you consult with the staff of such a program, find out if your confidentiality will be completely protected. This is particularly important if the addict occupies a superior position to yours. If he has mistreated you, prepare for the possibility his abusive behavior may increase when he feels threatened or exposed.

Confronting addiction can be tricky. If the abusive individual enters an alcohol or drug treatment program, he may feel anxious or irritable while on the way to sobriety. He may look for a scapegoat—an outlet for his anger, guilt or anxiety. But if he completes treatment successfully, his increased self-awareness may ultimately cause him to treat others better, including you.

If you confront addiction and related abuse on the job, you may get punished for rocking the comfortable, if dysfunctional, boat. Many individuals have decided to quit rather than try to change the organization. Prepare yourself for all possibilities.

What Buttons Does Addiction Push?

Addictions at work can be harder to spot and take seriously if any of the following holds true of you:

> • As you grew up, members of your family had alcohol or drug addictions.
>> • You have a problem with alcohol or drugs.
>> • Your current partner is addicted.

You may find it hard to see and confront your own addiction or that of others close to you. But recognizing those problems becomes crucial if you intend to cope effectively with workplace mistreatment complicated by addictions.

An alcoholic supervisor emotionally abused Edith, a buyer at a department store. As Edith considered how to handle her supervisor, she recalled the trauma of her father's alcoholism. Yet she didn't want to recognize her own drinking problem. She finally realized that to confront the abusive boss, she had to do something about her own drinking first. She felt in a bind. She needed to keep her job and she had to make work tolerable. In desperation, she went to Alcoholics Anonymous and quit drinking with the help of that organization. She then felt on firmer ground in complaining to the store manager about the abusive supervisor. She also decided she would find another job if the abuse continued.

Sexual Harassment and the Shadow Structure

The shadow organization often plays a powerful role in keeping sexual harassment alive and well. Sadie, an attorney, describes the office lunch ritual:

It was unbelievable. The men would do nothing but gross out women. The language was not to be believed. I expressed my displeasure and explained how destructive it was. I stopped going [to the lunches] when they wouldn't stop.

The only woman attorney in the office, Sadie believes that the prevalence of sexual harassment had driven out other women previously. Eventually two more women attorneys were hired and subjected to the same abuse. They decided to retaliate. Sadie recalls:

One day when a man walked by in real tight pants, one of these women exclaimed: "Wow, look at that basket!" She was just retaliating... but the men went crazy. They couldn't see it at all and came down on her real hard for being unladylike. She left after a year and I'm sure one of the reasons was this sex thing.

Men who harass co-workers use their informal power to reinforce each other in these illegal acts. When a co-worker perpetrates the harassment and the boss does little or nothing to stop it, the shadow organization perpetuates the offensive sexual behavior. A personnel manager told a woman factory worker that he knew the foreman used his position to force his attentions on many women, yet he asked her not to "make trouble."

Risking Your Job Ratings

In Chapter 10, we described the potential dangers of taking action against abuse. We now add another hazard to that list. Challenging abuse may adversely affect your evaluations for promotion, higher salary or a transfer you want. The informal organization can play a part here as well. Many people, both men and women, decide not to challenge abuse because they fear punishment for causing trouble, for being called "uncooperative," "a whistle blower," or "not a team player." If you protest mistreatment, those labels can plague you the next time your evaluation comes due.

Anything you can learn about how employees are informally evaluated by higher-ups will help you. Find out how others were treated if they complained about abuse. If regulations on your job clearly describe and control the evaluation process, this provides some protection. But many places don't have written procedures. Your supervisor might judge you on the basis of your race, gender, age or sexual orientation, rather than your work. Judgments may be based on whether you operate in the informal organization and whether you "play the game." If you question abuse, you might receive the label of "troublemaker," not a friendly and cooperative worker. Your actions may then result in demotion, further harassment or firing. Do you think this could happen to you?

Rana, a manager in an insurance office, refused her new supervisor's attempt to force her out of her job with no real justification. He then gave her a poor job evaluation in retaliation. She had to file a formal grievance to protest his action.

To fight serious abuse you may very well decide to take the risk of receiving a poor evaluation. Many women have taken that risk.

Increasingly, employees say their most serious complaints focus not on salary but on their right to be treated fairly. They want respect at work. As you become more aware of the abuse you experience, you may be joining a growing number of workers determined to demand respect and to carry on the struggle for better work conditions.

A Shadow Organization of Your Own

Many shadow organizations act as support groups to employees abusing power. But you can start your own informal organization at work to support you in challenging mistreatment. One common denominator stands out in all our interviews of women abused in the workplace. No matter what their job, their personality or their strategies, the women emphasized the importance of support during times of stress. Co-workers who share your values and concerns can help you set your goals, make decisions and practice strategies. They'll also provide a cheering section when you carry out any part of your plan.

Even if you decide not to confront the abuser, co-workers can lend you their support to help you as you survive what comes next or as you make plans to leave the job. The people standing behind you can provide warmth, validate your perceptions and help with strategies.

The support I had was that the other women had experienced the same things and would say, "Yeah, everything you say is correct." I had that outside validation that I wasn't a complainer. I wasn't crazy.

Leah, computer programmer

I met with the black caucus and prepared a response. They formed a committee and confronted my boss on his manner and demanded a rationale for his charges against me.

Alana, community college teacher

If it weren't for the faculty I wouldn't be here. I've often gone into the teachers' room crying and said, "What is it with her, that she treats me this way?" All the women say, "I've been in your shoes. Here's some strategy."

Jo, child-care administrator

You can be quite purposeful about getting the support you need. For example, you can think ahead as you consider telling someone at work that you plan either to confront or not to confront the abusive person, or that you have decided to resign. Do you think she will be angry about your decision? Disappointed or hurt? If co-workers don't approve your plan, will they leave you out in left field? Or will they support your decision regardless of whether they agree with it? Knowing what to expect from co-workers could affect what you do.

The more you know about the probable consequences of your action, including whom you can rely on, the more successful your plans. Sometimes people can't predict how they will respond to a suggested plan of action. By asking co-workers what they think they can do, you give them a chance to think about their responses. Using the workplace analysis in this chapter and the previous one, think about those you can count on to stand by you.

Most women find support by talking informally to co-workers. Women workers are likely to offer comfort spontaneously, suggest strategies and give examples of their own experiences of abuse. Some empathetic co-workers stick by their abused friends, regardless of the consequences. However, when faced with threats from the boss or strife among co-workers, some will decide not to align themselves with you. They may have more at stake than they realized or simply lack the courage they thought they had. So you need to ask exactly what people are willing to do. You could give your co-worker an idea of what you'd like from her and, at the same time, provide her an out if she wants it.

You: "If I confront Fred about his abuse, I can imagine he'll try to scare you about losing your job just because you have coffee and lunch with me. I'd like you in my corner, but if you're not sure what you'd do, I'd rather know it now." Ask your co-worker to think about it, to imagine it. Would it affect her own security on the job? Would she think you reckless to take the risk? Tell her you'll get back to her in a couple of days for her answer and remind her to keep this confidential, at least for now.

The Others Join Forces

The question of where to look for support can pose special

problems if co-workers consider you "different" or Other, as we discussed earlier in the book. Even if only one or two Others share your difference from the majority, their understanding and support can bolster you.

People who mistreat Others at work sometimes succeed in playing off two women defined as Other against each other. Maybe nothing you can do will stop that from happening if the second woman plays into their attempt.

Time and social progress may offer the best hope. When three or four additional people considered Other begin working at your job site, the majority may become used to your presence on the job and accept it as "normal." At that point a minority caucus can develop in an informal or formal way. This group can provide support as you struggle against abusive treatment, as the black caucus did for Alana, the community college teacher. They can pool information about similarities in abusive treatment. They might compare or develop strategies to solve common problems. But don't just assume, without checking it out, that those you perceive as "your kind" will stand by you. One purpose of joining a caucus may be to determine your differences from other members, as well as what you have in common.

If you are Other, don't dismiss the possibility of getting feedback and encouragement from those who form the majority. If one or more seem friendly to you, they can lend an important perspective, even though their understanding of your situation might be limited.

You might also form a coalition or support team with people who are vulnerable because of different kinds of "Otherness." Laura Pfandler, the pipefitter mentioned in previous chapters, made alliances with men of color, as have other women in trades. Heterosexual women and gay men, and heterosexual women and lesbians can sometimes work together to confront abuse.

Don't Forget Family and Friends

You'll probably want to know you can count on family and friends outside of work to stand by you. Friends can offer a special kind of support because they have no reason to be threatened by fear of retaliation or other complex work-related interactions. They can provide a cheering section and helpful doses of empathy.

Even people close to you won't always know what kind of help you want from them, so you might have to tell them. For instance, if you just need a listening ear, you might be disappointed by a problem-solving response. "Why don't you just tell him what you think?" "Well, I'd just quit." "You better not say anything, there's a recession, you know." Even with the best of intentions, your friends, family or colleagues may offer advice that doesn't help. A simple clarification can help them give you what you want.

First, be clear about what you need. At times you might welcome problem-solving ideas—suggestions, advice or brainstorming on how to change the situation or how to make a decision. Sometimes you would just like emotional support: you need to talk about your feelings while your friend listens and to be appreciated for how you feel without judgment or solutions. You can ask for what you want and say when you want it.

Some friends and family members turn up whenever you most need them, sensing your troubles and offering the coffee, fun, company or good crying partner that you want. Sometimes they give you what you want even before you realize it. Rana, the insurance office manager, was in the midst of a lengthy legal suit against her abusive boss and under extreme stress. Her family helped to keep her going.

> *My husband never said anything when we had to put a second mortgage on the house [for legal fees], but continued to support me. My family made sure I got out for fun. I remember thinking I didn't want to get out of bed. But my family kept calling.*

If you don't have people who offer a sounding board and encouragement, consider seeing a therapist. At the very least, you'll then have someone to listen to your thoughts and feelings. She might also help you figure out how to form a support system, either at work or among friends or family, by pointing out possibilities you've overlooked. If you can't afford individual therapy, think about the less expensive or free alternatives: women's support groups, union committees, professional, political or feminist organizations, Alcoholics Anoymous or Women for Sobriety, if appropriate.

If you believe addictions are part of your boss's problem or infecting your entire workplace, try Al-Anon, which is designed to help people involved with alcoholics or drug addicts. Some cities have support groups for women who have been sexually harassed. Don't rule out a class in aerobics, meditation, dance or assertiveness training. You might meet someone you can talk to about the abuse, but even if you don't, taking the class can still make you feel better.

If the abuse has had a negative effect on how you feel about yourself, you may not feel you can trust anyone, especially a collection of strangers. But try not to dismiss the idea out of hand. You might find it easier to talk to strangers in a structured situation than to good friends. No one enduring emotional abuse should go it alone.

Now you know what you need to consider about yourself, your workplace and the larger society so that you can make the best possible decision about confronting abuse. These topics create a framework for the rest of the book: how to carry out direct action—both individual and collective—to stop abuse.

Taking Individual Action to Stop Abuse at Work

Chapter 14

Target Your Goal

You have to be very deliberate about your goals and what you want to happen and don't want to happen. What I wanted was for the behavior to stop.
Alana, community college teacher

Goals are essential, but cannot be set in concrete. Patty, a bartender turned nurse whose story we told in Chapter 8, originally set a goal of taking a new job. She tried two new types of work before she zeroed in on the goal of working for a nursing degree. Jessica, also mentioned in earlier chapters, at first aimed to stop the abuse, then to get her "green card." Still later her goal changed to getting a financial settlement. Each time you purposefully shift a goal, you exercise personal power.

Set Your Assertiveness Goal

Even if your commitment to confront abuse directly wavers from time to time, complete the following exercises *as if* nothing will deter you from the goal you set. Acting as if you will follow through with a plan helps you evaluate your feelings about both the plan and the probable results. If you take the exercises seriously, and later decide assertiveness doesn't suit your needs, then you can explore another path.

Because assertive confrontations are usually spoken rather than acted out, most of our examples demonstrate verbal responses to abuse. Later in the chapter we briefly discuss action that doesn't include speech. Such a method might include leaving an area whenever another person treats you in an unacceptable way or removing offensive material from a bulletin board. Women often choose to use both responses together. Both types of action operate most effectively when guided by the principles described in Chapter 9 on assertiveness.

You may know, beyond all doubt, that a co-worker or boss demeans, disrespects or threatens you. But the person responsible may not understand how the actions affect you, or may pretend ignorance. To contend effectively with either situation, your goal must include a description of exactly what behavior you find objectionable.

Choose a goal that requires a brief interaction with an abusive person, or a mentor, supervisor or union representative. An assertive confrontation might include one or more of these goals for an interaction with a privileged or powerful person:

1. Make a statement about what you observe or think, how you feel or what you plan to do.

2. Obtain information from the person or make your feelings, thoughts or plans understood by the other person.

3. State what you want another person to change.

4. Take action yourself for change.

Goal One: To Describe Observations, Thoughts or Feelings

Most assertive acts include making a statement which describes feelings or observations of a problem and its effect on you, the job or other people. When you add a plan of action to your assertion, you may imply an "or else," to persuade someone to change. You can, however, make an honest declaration of your intentions, one that simply provides information for the other person without implying a threat. Declaring out loud that you intend to make a certain change might well increase your resolve to follow through. You could explain, "I don't like your yelling at me, and I'm going to leave the office if you do it again." You could add: "Then when you've calmed down I'll come back and we can continue. I'm letting you know so you won't think I'm just walking out in a huff." Your explanation may have a different impact than saying, "If you don't quit yelling, I'm leaving."

Goal 1A: To State Thoughts and Describe Observations

When you make a statement that describes to a boss or co-worker his or her unacceptable conduct, use factual, objective words and focus on specific behavior, rather than using global descriptions. If you use words like "abusive," "rude," "sexist" or "racist," the other person may not even know what behavior you object to. Then you're likely to get an offensive response, in both senses of the term. If your statement results in a verbal attack, you may never get a chance to finish what you want to say.

Specific, Objective Statements

You: "You said on March 3rd that you would speak to the men on the factory floor about whistling and calling me names. This is April 4th and nothing has changed."

You: "When you give my reports/ restaurant tables/ clients to others without telling me, I have trouble giving good service. When I don't know who's responsible for which tasks it slows my production."

You: "When you require several reports from me in a day, as you did yesterday and when you ask for exact descriptions of how I respond to each customer, as you did this morning, I think you don't trust my judgment. I'm being paid for that judgment."

Ruth found it helpful to let off steam by describing her male newspaper colleagues to friends as "tyrannizing" and "tailgating." But if she had used those words in confronting the other managers, she undoubtedly would have inflamed the very people she wanted to change. She probably would have undermined her goals.

Say straight out how the boss behaved toward you and how it affected you. But avoid global and emotionally loaded phrases, such as "You look over my shoulder all the time." If the boss tries to present a reasonable image, your specific language may keep him focused on what he's done. If he makes no pretense of fair treatment, you will at least know you haven't stooped to his level. Your ability to be objective will give you credibility if later you appeal to a third party for help.

EXERCISE 14A: Specific, Objective Descriptions

Describe, specifically and objectively, the offensive behavior.

Example: *You told me last Tuesday I could head this project. But Mel says you had already told him he could take it over. These contradictory statements cause confusion and make it hard to get the work done well.*

   The guidelines for clear thinking in Chapter 8 can help you remove global words and other nonrational language from your statement. In the example above, the boss made promises to two employees, creating conflict between them. A boss's contradictory directives may seem like links in a manipulative chain that squelches all rational response. Added to innuendos and erratic decisions, they can sorely test your capacity to name exactly what has been done. You may just want to shout, "I feel manipulated!" But the difficulty of pinpointing what offends you makes it especially important to describe the acts precisely. It won't work to say, "I hate it when you play us against each other."

Goal 1B: To State Feelings

   Some abusive people are thoughtless or ignorant rather than cruel. They think their "wisecracks" are funny or that you ought to know they're "just blowing off steam." Supervisors and co-workers don't always recognize racist or sexist comments. Others, insecure about their jobs or narrowly focused on production, don't notice the emotional effects of their demands on workers. For example, a usually considerate man can unwittingly drift into group "hazing" of a woman worker.

   Spelling out how you feel when you're mistreated might make a difference in how another person receives your complaint. Fear of vulnerability argues against that choice for many women, however. To assess the risk, you have to balance the possible advantage of increased understanding against giving a punitive person additional ammunition to use against you.

If you decide to express or describe your feelings, ask yourself what you hope to gain. If you can't easily answer that question, consider how you react when someone ignores how you feel. Maybe you interpret abuse as an indication the person doesn't care that you feel hurt, worthless, angry or incompetent. Then, because of what you assume to be a lack of caring, you feel even more hurt or devalued. So you might hope that if you describe your emotions, the other person will show concern about them. You might expect a change in behavior to follow. You may want the abusive person to accept guilt or responsibility for how you feel. Maybe you hope to banish your reactions of helplessness, isolation or another painful emotion.

Keep trying to bring the vulnerable feelings to the surface. Will expressing your feelings to the abusive person help dispel or change them or might they increase? How will you feel if you're not able to make your feelings understood, no matter how well you articulate them? When you understand exactly what you want and have set the goal of expressing your emotions to the boss or co-worker, practice how you will do it.

You: "Mr. O'Neill, when you give me conflicting orders, as you did this morning, I have trouble deciding which of them to follow. It seems that any one of them might be considered a mistake. Then I feel helpless and even hopeless about doing what you require."

Ruth says her male editor colleagues typically respond to such personal statements with "the one line: 'You're just taking it too personally, you're just too sensitive; [example of abuse] happened to me, and I didn't worry about it.' " Ruth's response: "You should have. I am."

Such a direct response may hold too many risks for you. If using the word "helpless" seems too threatening, experiment with others like "confused," "frustrated," "bewildered." This may be a situation in which you prefer to compromise an assertiveness principle by using general words. But if your goal is to tell the boss exactly how you feel, those words won't help you. Regardless of the specific word you use, your boss or co-worker will probably hear more of your statement if you speak of *your* feelings than if you call attention to his failure to comprehend.

In spite of some hazards, describing your emotions can carry a powerful impact. Even an aggressive, disdainful person may be chagrined to learn her behavior affects others negatively. Embarrassment might lead her to try persuading you that you "shouldn't" feel that way, that she "didn't mean it." Then you can explain that her intentions are not as important as the consequences. Regardless of whether you should have felt that way, you *did* feel that way. She might recognize her responsibility in the interaction.

Trying unsuccessfully to hide angry or hurt feelings sometimes backfires by increasing the intensity of the emotion. In this type of situation, directly stating emotions can give you a sense of control. Because the words you've deliberately chosen match your expression of feelings, you won't feel that you've unintentionally exposed your vulnerability. When you couple an admission of vulnerability with a statement of your intention to act, you strengthen yourself. For instance:

You: "I feel humiliated, but that won't drive me off the job."

You: "I'm hurt and I intend to report you."

Hazards of Expressing Feelings

When someone victimizes you, you may be awash in a mix of feelings difficult to name. Anger may take over, momentarily drowning out fear, hurt, helplessness or humiliation, which might be more threatening to you. Because anger masks so many feelings of vulnerability, you may find yourself crying if you unleash your rage. There's nothing wrong with that so long as you've thought through the possible consequences, but crying unexpectedly puts you in an unnecessarily vulnerable position. Anticipating what feelings might emerge along with your anger helps prevent embarrassing surprises.

On the other hand if you deny your rage, you may sound resentful when you express your hurt or humiliation. Your unintended accusations could spark a negative reaction. Ignoring your feelings can keep you from achieving your goal.

If you decide to express your emotions, separate them from accusations. First, describe specific, objective examples of offensive conduct. Then state your feelings separately. Make sure they really are feelings. To keep emotions and thoughts straight, start with "I feel." Then put a name to what you experience: "sad," "hurt," "humiliated," "hopeless." Do not start with "you," especially "you make," or continue the sentence with "like" or "you." Those words will probably lead you straight into accusations: "I feel like you take advantage of me." "You make me feel like I'm stupid." "I feel you despise me." These statements do not describe emotions. They present conclusions about other people's flaws or your projections of their attitudes. Keep your eye on the two parts of your goal: (1) to describe the other person's actions and (2) to state separately your feelings about them. Avoid blame and interpretations of others' actions.

Keep revising your statement until you can separate the other person's actions from your emotional reaction and can state each specifically:

You: "I agreed to work a double shift on short notice once. But for the past five weeks you've assigned me a double each time someone else didn't show up. I feel angry about it."

You: "When you call me stupid in front of customers I feel humiliated and angry."

An abusive person may try to get you off track even when you've clearly expressed your sentiments. By giving him the word, "feel," you may have made it easier for him to shift the subject away from what he's done to you. He may insist you're just "too sensitive," or attribute your emotions to your gender: "Oh, you women, you can't take it. You all want roses on your desk every day." If you let him distract you into explaining that you're not too emotional or you lecture him about sexism, you lose your point about his offensive acts. If someone mocks your feelings or denies their validity you can move on to a topic that puts you in control. For example:

You: "It's a waste of time for us to discuss how sensitive is too sensitive. Let's go on to the major issue. What you're doing interferes with my best work. If you agree to make the changes I've asked for, it opens the way for us to work successfully together."

You: "Not roses, just respect. That means . . ."

EXERCISE 14B: Describe an Abusive Action and Your Feelings

Describe an offensive behavior and—separately—your feelings about it. Start with two separate sentences, which can later be put together, if you want to make a direct connection.

Example: *Touching me like that is harassment. I'm angry about it.*

_____

_____

_____

_____

Goal 1C: To State an Action Plan

You may include in your statement what you plan to do. "I just want to let you know that since you continue to insist that I answer your personal questions, I've decided to take the problem to the boss this afternoon." This statement differs from a threat, since your action will not depend on the other person's response. You just want to let him know what to expect. Most people reserve this tactic for situations in which repeated objections to mistreatment have been ignored.

Suppose, as an office manager, you promised yourself that you would no longer work unpaid, unplanned overtime. You've already told the boss you object, but after murmuring sympathetically he continues to ignore your requests for overtime pay and notice of upcoming unscheduled hours. You've decided to back up your verbal complaint by leaving each day at the time stated in your contract. But you want the boss to realize this is your *intention,* not a move to get him to change. If you forewarn him of your new plan and explain the reason for it, he might understand your unprecedented behavior when it occurs. Your initial explanatory statement might include a reference to your feelings and take a conversational tone, rather than an overtly adversarial one:

You: "Mr. Washington, I recognize you're under a lot of

pressure, but when you ask me at the last minute to stay late, I feel anxious about my children. I've managed to comply with what you ask, so far, because I've been afraid to say I couldn't. But I can't fulfull my obligations outside of work unless I can plan ahead. From now on, I'm not going to stay after five unless you give me at least 24 hours' notice and pay me overtime. Even so, I'm only available for a real emergency." If Mr. Washington agrees, but then "forgets" after a week or two, your next statement can be much more brief. Your plan is specific.

You: "As we discussed last week, I'm not going to work overtime, even in emergencies, unless you give me 24 hours' notice. And you agreed to overtime pay. Since you didn't do those things, I'll be leaving at five o'clock."

Or even more crisp:

You: "As I explained last week I'll be leaving at five."

You can handle sexual harassment in similar ways:

You: "When you give me the title of secretary, but direct me to flirt with customers, I feel humiliated. I've decided to treat all customers in a completely professional way from now on."

A fine line separates making a threat from warning someone of a planned new response. In these examples your plan will be carried out regardless of what the other person does. You will leave at your scheduled hour. You will limit your tasks to business. By contrast, a threat implies a contingency. If you do X, I will follow it with Y. You had better make a change *or else* I will take a certain action. We discuss threats later in this chapter.

Before you state your intenions, think about exceptions that could interfere with your plan. If anything at all could stop you from carrying it out, mention it. Furthermore don't announce a plan until you're certain you can carry it out.

You: "I'm only willing to stay after five if auditors show up unexpectedly."

EXERCISE 14C: State a Complaint and a Plan

Describe to your boss or co-worker a behavior you object to and your plan to handle it if it isn't changed.

Example: *When you say I look "sexy" and want to know what I'm wear-*

ing underneath, I'm insulted. I'm going to leave your office any time you comment on my appearance.

Goal Two: To Be Understood

When you state your observations, feelings or intentions, you control what you want to do. Unless the person you're addressing walks away or verbally drowns you out, you can carry out your plan. But now you set a new goal of gaining the other person's understanding of your views. Even if you articulate what you want with great clarity, you cannot control the other person's response.

A person who frequently dictates orders and insults others may have only a murky picture of what constitutes an insult and of how much he dictates. Even if he seems to want to learn, his lack of insight may block progress. Or he may not choose to understand what triggers your negative reactions, preferring to argue about details of your statement. He may focus on a minor irrelevant error you've made or claim you imagined his treatment of you. Try to predict ahead of time how long you will persist in struggling to get your points across and how you will know if you've been heard. At what point will you withdraw and form a new goal?

Did Your Message Arrive Undistorted?

You've made your statement. Next you need to determine if the other person understands what he's done to offend you and how you feel about it. You want to be sure he won't be surprised if you carry out the plan you warned him about. To find out whether he truly heard both parts of your statement, ask directly:

You: "Do you realize you're undercutting my professionalism when you focus your attention on my appearance?"

You: "Do you understand that I feel humiliated when you take over my meetings and describe my flaws in front of the staff?"

You: "Do you know I feel afraid when you shout and pound the desk?"

You: "Do you understand that I'm absolutely serious about resigning/ reporting you/ leaving the room, if you continue yelling insults at me?"

You may have good reason to feel unnerved in asking such questions, especially if a boss or someone in a higher position intimidates you. Co-workers may resent your acting "bossy" or "uppity" when you ask if they've really heard you. Such questions often come across in the tone of a school teacher, parent or therapist—a tone that others resent as inappropriate. You may need quite a bit of practice to get just the right words and tone.

If your anger is palpable it may drown out the meaning of your question. The listener will hear only that you're furious, and may respond in kind. A calm, controlled tone of voice provides the best possibility of being heard and getting the information you want. However, even when you do control your emotions, an aggressive, defensive person, or someone in authority may hear your question as an attack or a challenge.

Maybe you've said something like this: "You've directed me to do X instead of Y, and then you've stated in your quarterly reports that I've done Y. This places me in the position of seeming dishonest." The boss looks like he couldn't care less. So you ask, "Do you know what it says here in the funders' contract about our compliance with Y? Do you understand that you're in violation of . . . regulations?" Because many people phrase verbal assaults as questions, the boss may hear your question as an attack or accusation. To avoid that, introduce the question with a statement explaining your intention:

You: "I want to be sure you remember what's in the contract, so we don't get into trouble with the funders."

You: "I really do want to know if you understand my feelings."

You: "Sometimes I think we understand each other, and later I find out I was misunderstood. I think I'd better check it out. What do you think my point is?"

You: "I don't want you to be surprised if I report you/ leave the room/ resign . . . so I'd like to know if I've made my intentions clear."

These statements somewhat soften the questions that follow them. The point is to be absolutely clear that you want an answer to your questions about whether you've been understood. Your aim in this situation is not to express your resentment. You might endure several moments of silence before the other person responds. Don't be tempted to fill the air with more words. Just wait. The other person might reply with blaming statements, explanations or excuses. Don't let yourself be drawn into a discussion of other subjects. Keep the focus on your question.

You: "I'd be glad to talk about those issues. But first it's essential for me to know if you understand my point so far."

You: "Those are important points, but before we go on to them, I need to know if you understand what I'm objecting to."

You: "I really need to know, first, if you get my point."

Even if the boss never does get it, at least you have done your part. You've spoken clearly about the specific treatment that troubles you. If you've been plagued by self-doubt, or if the offensive person is adept at "crazy-making," you may have been tempted to let him off the hook. Now that you've made a specific, concerted effort to get your point across, you can stop minimizing the behavior with excuses such as, "He just doesn't understand." "Maybe he doesn't realize how serious I am." Perhaps the abusive person has understood your objections and what you want, but derision and harassment continue. Knowing that the boss or co-worker sees the problem clearly, yet makes no move to change, brings you closer to a decision about your next step.

But what do you do if you still get no sign of whether you're understood? For instance, how many times will you say what you want or plan to do, if the boss interrupts and insults you without indicating whether he comprehends? Before you begin a confrontation, choose your own guidelines, such as how many times you'll repeat yourself. Your decision might depend on how you feel during the encounter. "If I feel like crying or screaming or insulting him, I'll stop trying." Your knowledge of the abusive person and yourself will help you to decide. Try to make your guidelines allow for all reasonable attempts to gain understanding, *if* the other person shows the motivation to try. This qualification is important because your next decision may depend on whether you believe you've "tried hard enough" to get your point across.

EXERCISE 14D: The Last Ditch Effort for an Answer

Write the question you want answered, including an introduction that indicates your seriousness about wanting an answer.

Example: *It's important for me to know whether I made myself clear when I described the lewd remarks the men in the payroll department made to me, and to know whether you agree that they are objectionable.*

Goal Three: State What You Want Another Person to Change

You've stated what you think and feel about how you're treated and your precise objections. You've checked whether you've been understood. Now you also want to state what you want changed. Your requests may be simple and immediate, beginning with a statement:

You: "I would like you to stop calling me names like 'Lame Brain' and 'Sweetheart.' "

You: "I want you to stop changing the settings on my machine when I'm out on a break."

You: "If you're going to change the report that goes out in both our names, I want you to consult me about it ahead of time."

Maybe you choose to allow for one more possibility of change before turning to an authority or resigning. Decide ahead of time whether you'll state your intention to take your complaint to a higher authority as an ultimatum. "If it happens again I'll report you immediately to the union/ boss/ board." A threat may add clout to your complaint, but don't underestimate its impact. Expect to make a threat only once. After that, if you don't act on it, it will lose its power.

Threats can be dangerous, too. Any corrective action will take time to implement, while you continue to work with someone who may retaliate. So unless you're willing to resign or take a leave of absence immediately after making a threat, plan carefully how to deal with repercussions.

Confronting Sexual Harassment

Some men will not tolerate sexual rejection without retaliating. Others really don't hear women, even when they say no in various ways. When objecting to sexual harassment you need to speak precisely and definitely. This may not be possible to do without the man interpreting your comment as an assault on his ego. But if you're determined to bring the harassment to an end, you have to take that risk. However, you can add a nonpersonal reason for turning down an invitation:

You: "You may not intend your talk of pornography to offend, but I don't want to hear it. Please don't bring up the topic again, or I will leave the room."

You: "I don't ever go out with anyone I work with. I don't think it's good for our working relationship to mix socializing. So I'm saying, 'No, thank you.' Will you please not ask me again?"

Asking "Are you willing to do what I ask?" gives the person harassing you two choices. He either agrees, or he gives you information that he has no intention of complying with your request. If he refuses to do as you ask, your notes will reflect that, which could be useful if you file a grievance. If he does agree, then the next time he repeats the behavior, you can remind him of his promise.

If the harassment consists of an unwelcome, clearly sexual touch, the person's intentions may be more hostile and call for a more blunt response:

You: "Please stop putting your hands on me. That means keep your hands off any part of my body, face or hair."

Some women can mix humor with their responses to harassment, but they risk the other person not taking them seriously, or their humor being interpreted as a "come-on." Most women find it difficult to think of humorous responses that don't seem either flirtatious or aggressive.

Changing Systems

Your requests to bring about change could reach beyond yourself to involve or affect all employees:

You: "I'm requesting that you institute training for all employees on how to treat people with respect, including people of color and women."

You: "This system is run on an unfair basis. Opportunities for advancement and specialized training have gone to Jim, Harry and Ben, who all go out drinking with the boss. None of us who choose not to drink have been offered such opportunities in the past twelve months. I'm asking you to bring in an outside consultant to change this situation." (A similar request might apply to an "in" group formed on racial, ethnic or gender lines, or just among old buddies.)

You might accompany a request for change with a statement of what you'll do if the other person doesn't agree to it. Keep in mind the difference between a plan and a threat.

The ability to make these kinds of assertive requests may seem beyond your skills or courage at this point. But learning assertiveness principles and practicing the techniques have helped many women stand up for themselves for the first time. Zoe and her colleagues at an agency for people with hearing disabilities persuaded their boss to hire a consultant to work with the entire staff and the director. The consultant didn't resolve all the problems with an emotionally abusive boss, but two important changes did result. The consultant encouraged staff members to speak straightforwardly to each other about their work and salaries. Soon the disparity between salaries of deaf staff and hearing workers became an employee issue. The deaf workers assertively complained to the board of directors and obtained significant raises. In addition, practicing assertiveness techniques with the consultant helped Zoe develop skills to confront the agency director about her mistreatment.

Goal Four: Taking Action, Yourself, For Change

In some situations you can take assertive action without saying a word. For instance, you may know that a co-worker or boss will soon get over a display of temper and will forget the series of orders that accompanied it. So you perform your job as you judge most effective, ignoring the orders. You know the person shows distorted judgment, so you act on your own and prepare to deal with the consequences later. You'll need to prepare for being punished, if your action is disapproved, but you may also receive congratulations if the person forgets his or her orders and approves of the results of your actions.

Ignoring or openly defying the orders of an abusive person puts you at risk of being fired or reprimanded for insubordination. But it also could offer the best alternative for dealing with someone who displays erratic behavior, and could even bring satisfactory results. Navy nurses simultaneously used words and actions to give a strong message to an abusive doctor. They added aggressive speech to assertive action:

> *One time, a doctor was doing a procedure and he started yelling at the nurses. They told him, "We don't talk that way around here. We'll come back when you clean up your act, when you can talk to us like an adult." Zoom! They were gone! The doctor was left trying to do a procedure by himself. You better believe the doctors quickly learned what was acceptable and what wasn't.*

EXERCISE 14E: Actions Speak Louder Than Words

List any action you could take to assert yourself.
Example: *Leave when he shouts at me. Walk out at 5 o'clock if I'm not given warning about overtime.*

Terese M. Floren, the only woman firefighter in her city fire department, said, "it was either appalling or funny what contortions they went through to avoid having to put me in the bunkroom." Special arrangements were made for her to have a rollaway bed in the firehouse TV room. But that interfered with the male firefighters' TV time and led to bad feelings toward Floren. She was prohibited from working at two of the most desirable stations because they lacked separate sleeping accommodations for her. The chief was adamant that she could work only in certain stations and had to sleep in a separate room. Floren thought such precautions unnecessary and destructive to the relationships she had with other workers. Eventually she decided simply to take action.

> *Without asking anyone's permission, I chose a bed in the bunk room and put my sheets on it. The lieutenant walked in and asked what I was doing. "Making my bed," I said firmly. "Oh." If I wasn't worried about it, neither was Jake. He watched me for a moment, then shrugged and wandered off. That was the end of it.*

In completing the exercises in this chapter, you've had an opportunity to plan what you'd like to say to a co-worker or boss who threatens, degrades or otherwise abuses you. As you thought about possible consequences, you may have decided not to spend time and energy trying to stop mistreatment at work. The women we interviewed gave many explanations for such decisions. Maybe you have good reason to expect the offensive person not to listen to you, no matter how well you speak. He may have warned you of a retaliation plan "if you cause any trouble." Perhaps you have too much at stake in this particular job or career; or you've decided to wait out a transfer or the appointment of a new manager. You may want to pursue some other tactics.

If you do decide to challenge abusive treatment assertively, the next two chapters will help you plan assertive acts and evaluate them each step of the way.

Chapter 15

The Nitty-Gritty of Assertive Confrontation

*I gradually became assertive with the boss, which both produced good re-
sults and left me feeling better. But it didn't always end positively and it
was always scary. It did leave me with my self-respect intact.*

Miranda, research assistant

Assertion isn't a matter of just speaking your piece at the vital
moment. To achieve your carefully chosen goals requires planning and practice. This means allowing for a variety of circumstances—including some surprises.

You may already know how to be aggressive or passive, but
unless you have taken a special course in how to be assertive, you
probably aren't familiar with its principles. So we devote the
next several chapters to describing how to assert yourself in work
situations and how to evaluate the results.

Choose the Person to Approach

You may have decided to confront someone who mistreats
you or who tolerates or encourages an abusive system. Or you've
chosen to report to someone who could intervene for you—a
third party such as a mentor, a union agent or human rights
worker. Recalling your analysis of your workplace from Chapters 12 and 13, determine the safest and most effective people to
approach.

EXERCISE 15A: Analyzing Possible Results of Confrontation

Answer these questions as a check on your decision.

If I confront someone who mistreats me:

1. In what ways could the person retaliate? Emotionally? Physically? Placing my job in jeopardy? Intervening in my career?

_____

2. How can I prevent or minimize negative effects of my assertive action?

_____

By support from influential people? _____ *Who?* _____

_____

From witnesses? _____ *Who?* _____

3. Exactly what benefits do I expect from the encounter? _____

_____

4. If I don't achieve what I want, what will I do next? _____

_____

For encounters with a third party:

1. Is the person able to do what I'm asking? _____

2. Have I seen her use her power effectively? How has it operated?

_____

3. How far can I trust his confidentiality? _____

_____

4. What dangers might I face if I have miscalculated and she tells the abusive person I've complained to her? _____

_____

5. If the perpetrator discovers I've gone over his head, how might he decide to punish me? _____

_____

6. Will the third party resent being asked to help? _____

Discuss your answers with a supportive person familiar with your situation. Try to enlist her help in practicing your assertive confrontation.

Third Party: Help or Hindrance?

Sometimes aid comes from unexpected sources when people with power offer to intervene. Using the questions we've suggested, you will need to decide whether to accept unsolicited assistance. Help offered by powerful people may be hazardous to your job.

As a newly hired co-administrator of a small social service agency, Priscilla suffered from the lies her co-administrator, Louise, told to her and the directors. Louise ignored Priscilla's assertive complaints and benefited from the confidence of the board of directors, who rubber-stamped her decisions. Agency staff also followed Louise's wishes without question. Priscilla felt outflanked. She hired an outside consultant for herself, just to get an objective ear. She discreetly talked to people in other agencies to learn how they handled similar situations. But she needed the help of someone in her own agency, and Louise appeared to have lined up all possible allies.

Priscilla sensed danger in approaching either board or staff for potential alliances. But a board member, Denise, surprised Priscilla by confiding her awareness of Louise's tactics. She offered to work with Priscilla to resolve agency problems. Priscilla didn't yet know the board members well enough to judge whether she could trust Denise. She would have had to answer most of our suggested questions with "I don't know." But she understood that none of her available choices would be completely safe.

She accepted Denise's offer to keep her informed of board decisions and to advise her about timing and tactics in relation to the board. Since Denise also lacked allies, she could not intervene directly for Priscilla with Louise or the board. Nevertheless the alliance proved invaluable, and during the next year the two women recruited new board members who eventually shifted the power base away from Louise. She resigned and Priscilla, having demonstrated her value to the agency, advanced to the position of sole director.

Such alliances, however, should be approached with caution. Frances, a high-level administrator in Alana's community college, suggested that Alana help her in maneuvering, so that Alana's immediate supervisor, a man who had harassed Alana and her staff would have to leave. Alana describes the dilemma:

> *First Frances asked, "Would it be better if he were not your supervisor?" I said, "If you're choosing to reorganize the department, whether with him or without him, I can work with it." Frances spoke cautiously, but she said, "He's getting complaints, grievances, and he has difficulties in his interpersonal style." She asked me if I'd think about some ways that I could assist her in dealing with him. I remember taking that with me over two or three weeks, and decided not to do it. I thought, "That's not my job, that's her job." I told her I couldn't come up with anything that would be helpful. I didn't have a real trust of her. You start giving that information to a superintendent, and the result could be that she'd act on it and it would make me look bad.*

Practice Assertiveness

Before beginning to practice assertiveness, you may want to review the definitions and guidelines in Chapter 9 and the specific goals in the exercises of Chapter 14. Make notes of what you want to say to the person you plan to address. Include phrases that will keep you on the right track: "I have observed that...I feel...What I'd like to know...What I would like to have changed...When you...I." Next, rehearse what you want to say, speaking into a mirror or tape recorder. If you don't like what you see in the mirror or hear on the tape, remind yourself that you will improve as you practice. What you actually say in your confrontation won't be exactly what you rehearse. But going over and over the message clarifies your intentions, helps you focus on central points and calms your emotions.

Ask a friend or co-worker to rehearse with you and give you feedback on how you sound. Begin by asking her to play you, while you take the part of the person you plan to confront. After listening to the abusive boss or co-worker at his worst for months or years—and maybe sometimes at his best—you know better than anyone the range of his possible reactions. You can act out a clear picture of his manner when he evades, rages, insults or seems to capitulate. As you listen to your friend playing you, you'll get ideas about how you do or do not want to come across. Then switch roles and play yourself.

How to Evaluate the Role-Playing

When you've acted your own part, check the Assertiveness Guidelines from Chapter 9 and say out loud which ones you followed well. Always start with positive comments. Then choose one or two points you would like to improve. Next, ask your friend to begin her feedback by telling you which guidelines you succeeded in following. When she notes what you handled well, don't contradict her. Just make a mental note of what you want to continue doing. Next, she can suggest ways to improve your assertive speech or body language. Ask for special feedback on anything you worry about, such as sounding angry or submissive. Don't try to improve all errors at once. If you're new at role-playing or assertiveness, give yourself time to get over anxiety, so you can play your part seriously.

As you rehearse, periodically review your goals and experiment with new phrases and tones. As you play your part with more assurance, have the "boss" or "co-worker" played by your friend increase the challenge by responding in purposefully vague or confusing ways. Or she can offer an unacceptable compromise, so you can practice saying no. Next, have her enact the kind of treatment you might face if your adversary lashes out in her worst possible style. Practicing these roles gives you a chance to try responses to a variety of challenging situations. If you plan to confront a man, ask a male friend to play him for you.

As long as you're just rehearsing, allow yourself some bursts of nervous laughter and the freedom to play around with responses that may seem silly at first. Sometimes ideas that seem outrageous at first turn out to be useful. Shouting, "I could show you how to run this place!" in a practice session might evolve into a serious request: "Rudy, why don't you let me take over the stockroom problem and see what I can do with it?" Maybe you never dared consider such a suggestion before. Yes, the boss might consider it out of the question, but he might agree, if only because he imagines you'll fail. Maybe you can surprise him.

At some point, though, take your role as seriously as possible. Practice helps you decide what to say and to gain confidence. In addition, you'll learn more about reactions to power—the abusive person's and your own. Those attitudes toward power and control may reflect potent feelings from childhood or ideas about status.

Anxiety Sends You a Signal

During your role-playing, a surprisingly intense level of fear might result from a view of yourself as extremely disadvantaged compared to your boss or co-workers. You may feel intimidated by their privilege and perceive them as holding a stacked deck. Yet no one person holds all the power. Your lively sense of humor, intelligence, skills or courage may enable you to affect change more readily than someone who enjoys many social privilege but lacks personal capabilities. You also might compensate for lack of privilege by "borrowing" power from a lawyer, mentor, affirmative action officer or other agency advocate.

Anxiety about speaking up may stem from thoughts and feelings about your status as Other. Earlier experiences of bias and vilification based on your religion, physical condition, race or sexual orientation may have taken a high toll. Your fear or rage, reactivated by the current situation, has probably stemmed from real and threatening experiences. But you need to decide whether you'll let feelings from the past interfere with advocating for yourself now. If, in your practice sessions, you become overwhelmed with tears or too afraid to speak, you can explore the origins of those feelings by repeating the Focus on Your Feelings exercise in Chapter 8.

In order to modify your reaction to people in power or to bigotry, try talking and role-playing with a friend who shares your Other status. Then see if you can trust someone of the dominant group enough to discuss the possible effects of your encounter with the powerful person. If you can afford it, or your community offers low-cost counseling, look for a therapist who can help. See if a class is available that will help. None of these possibilities solves the basic problem of abuse or cultural discrimination. But control and understanding of your feelings, plus maximum support, will enable you to work toward constructive long-range change. They will also get you through a short-term confrontation with the least possible pain. For instance, Ruth reduced her fear of speaking up in newspaper management meetings by joining Toastmasters, an organization that teaches public speaking.

Try to predict all the things that can go wrong—and right— in your encounter and decide how to handle them. When you've practiced responses to the most difficult challenges, you've laid the groundwork for success.

Plan the Action

Although the examples that follow suggest ways to confront an abusive person directly, most of them apply to meetings with a third party as well. Carefully choosing the time and place of the confrontation sets the stage for maximum gains.

Choosing the Time

To the extent you control the time of the encounter, choose an hour, day, week or month when you tend to be at your best. Try also to pick a time when the other person is most likely to be unhurried, in a tolerable mood and generally most receptive. Such opportunities may seem to you either nonexistent or impossible to predict. But if you pay close attention, certain hours or days might emerge as more promising than others.

If at all possible, don't try to catch the boss in the hall, even to ask for a meeting time. A simple request could result in a rude response or involve you in a public discussion of the problem. When you ask to set up a meeting, the boss might say, "Go ahead, tell me about it now," while he stands at the water cooler or the cash register. You know that's not what you want to do. But refusing to comply on the spot might feel awkward, as if you're making too big a deal of the issue. Remind yourself it *is* a big deal. Don't be coerced into a conversation on public ground or at a time you haven't chosen. Your response needs to be assertive:

You: "The issue I want to discuss is complicated and I'd like plenty of time to discuss it in private. When is a good time, when we won't be interrupted?"

If you give in to the boss's insistence on discussing the issue right there in the typing pool, the board room or at the construction site, you'll find yourself in the midst of a public confrontation. To avoid this possibility, consider writing a note that suggests possible times and offers an estimate of how long the meeting will take. At some worksites, putting anything in writing to the boss or co-workers is "just not done." Try to predict whether such a deviation from custom will start your meeting on an unnecessarily negative footing—or whether breaking that custom will do everyone a favor.

We think private space gives you the most control and spares you a potential problem of the other person "grandstanding" to other workers. However, some workers prefer a public confrontation. One woman was frustrated that no one else had witnessed her boss's abusive treatment and she deliberately provoked him in public so that she would have validation of what she wanted to report.

Make a realistic prediction of how long you'll need. Use your practice sessions to make a reasonable estimate. Then add fifteen minutes just in case. It might take only five or ten minutes to explain what you want. But unless you're determined to simply say your piece and leave, allow for the boss's response, and then yours and possibly a complex discussion. You won't do the boss or yourself a favor by underestimating the period that's necessary. Having more time than you expect to need will help you relax.

You: "I have three things to discuss, and I think they will take no more than forty minutes. When is the best time for you?"

If your boss meets with you regularly for supervision, discussion of your work or formal evaluations, you might suggest at the beginning of such a meeting, "I'd like to discuss some other items before we get to our regular schedule for today." The boss might insist her supervisory issues take precedence, and you'll then have to insist that she recognize your issue as a priority. You may want to assure your supervisor that it's in her interest to take your item first by adding a comment like, "It will help our work if we can get this other item taken care of first."

Not everything can be planned or predicted. But the more you think ahead, the more your confidence will rise. Jessica wanted to meet with her hospital administrator, Dave, about various kinds of on-the-job mistreatment. She planned to make the appointment after she returned from vacation. But an encounter with Dave on a hospital ward gave her an unanticipated opening when he asked, "How are things going?" "Not very good," Jessica admitted. "I'd like a few moments with you when I come back from my trip." But Dave replied, "Let's talk now. Come into my office." It was in Jessica's interests to meet with Dave immediately and his office was an acceptable place. Fortunately, she had thought carefully about what she wanted to say or she might have been in the awkward position of declining Dave's invitation to discuss the problem immediately.

Choose Your Arena

If you feel intimidated in the boss's office, try to meet in a neutral place or on your own territory. That may not be possible if the boss assumes underlings should come to her. Still, it might not hurt to ask, "Would you be willing to come to my office?" If conditions related to your work space will help you illustrate a point, mention them as reasons for asking the boss to meet there. For instance, you might want to show her the inadequate lighting over your computer, the dangerous condition of machinery or where your colleagues have put threatening messages.

In some circumstances, meeting in your own space increases the boss's opportunity for vilification. Janine's junior high school principal mistreated her and other teachers. Whenever he came into Janine's classroom, he found new faults to criticize and excuses to insult or threaten her. So she offered to meet in his office, which he took as a sign of her compliance with his authority.

Set Your Limits

Let's suppose your boss, Elliot, has tried to intimidate you by publicly shouting orders and racial slurs. During the first year you worked for him you periodically asked him to stop both types of behavior. He gave vague replies about the pressure he suffered, and nothing changed. You've tried to ignore his treatment, but now the stress threatens your emotional balance.

You've about decided to report Elliot to Mr. Barner, the general manager, but first you want to give him fair warning of your plan and one more opportunity to change. You hope to state your complaints to Elliot in person. But you know he can refuse to let you finish itemizing them, so you're prepared, as a last resort, to leave a written list with him to review later.

You mention at the beginning of the interview that you brought notes to keep you focused. If Elliot tries to distract you from your goal, or your feelings of hurt or anger threaten to take over, you may forget the most important information you want to convey. Any time you lose sight of your agenda, you can refer to the notes you've already said you would use. Referring to notes does not indicate weakness, but shows you are well organized.

You: "Elliot, I want to talk to you about several concerns. I've got some notes here to help me keep track of each item. They go back a ways, but they form a pattern that I consider important. I also have suggestions for resolving them."

On the chance Elliot will respond positively, you present concerns, not complaints; solutions, not trouble. You can't control his responses or even predict what he'll do, but you can increase the odds of achieving your goal. If Elliot decides to take a negative stance, whatever approach you choose entails some degree of risk. If you leave solutions entirely in the boss's hands, he may dismiss you as an irresponsible crank. But if you suggest improvements he can accuse you of overstepping your role. A careful introduction to your topic might arouse his impatience. Yet if you dive right in to your complaints, he may view that as "pushy." Your knowledge of Elliot will point to the most promising approach, and his unpredictability may argue for playing the scene by ear.

Suppose, as you enter his office, Elliot starts tapping his fingers on the desk, checks his watch and announces that he can spare you only ten minutes. Don't let him coerce you into trying to explain in ten minutes what you've planned to discuss in half an hour or more. The boss's reluctance to meet for the time agreed upon may mean that he doesn't intend to hear you at all. Planning the limits you want to set will help you evaluate the significance of his switch to a ten-minute meeting. You may have decided that any stalling or negativity on Elliot's part would signal that it's time to withdraw.

You: "I have my list of concerns right here, so rather than try to spell them out too briefly, I'll leave them with you. If you'd like to talk about any of them, please let me know. In any case, I'll be giving the list to Mr. Barner."

If you believe an unavoidable conflict did come up for Elliot at the last minute, you might take a more optimistic stance:

You: "I could spell out the issues quickly, but I wouldn't be able to explain them well enough. We agreed to a forty-minute meeting, and I think it will take that long. When can we schedule a new appointment so you'll be sure to have enough time?"

If Elliot makes a new agreement to allow sufficient time, you re-check your limits. Since you have several requests of him, you'll need to decide ahead of time what to do if the boss agrees to one or two, but stalls on or refuses others. At your next meeting, if Elliot doesn't grant your minimal requests, you explain that you'll report the problems to Mr. Barner unless Elliot provides concrete, specific plans to implement the rest of what you've asked for right away. This is the contingency, or threat, we discussed in Chapter 14.

You: "I would prefer to work this out between the two of us, but if you're not willing to do that I'll take these concerns to Mr. Barner, so he can decide what steps to take."

Witnesses and Record Keeping

Maintain a record of exactly what the offending person has said and done during each of these interchanges. You may need precise information later for litigation or workers' compensation, for your own sanity, or for the next supervisor up the ladder. Kate, an investment counselor, advises:

If there are no witnesses, write it all down in full detail. Your record will one day impress someone and you will not suffer [because of] memory lapses. However acute the experience, it's surprising how quickly one forgets the detail.

Even if you can't imagine ever forgetting one bit of what you've endured, take Kate's advice. Many women we interviewed urged note-taking, and commented on the temptation to forget situations that might arouse fear or anger. Act as if you could wind up in court, whether you want to or not. Play it safe even if you don't believe it could happen. For example, you could get fired for standing up to abuse. The perpetrator might try to prevent you from collecting workers' compensation, which may cause you to respond legally even though you would rather not become involved with the law. When you challenge someone who bullies, intimidates or plays dishonest games, prepare for her to retaliate. If she does, you'll need those notes.

Keep copies of all correspondence, including minor office memos between you and the person you're contending with. Your letter requesting an appointment supplies you with one document of your efforts to "go through proper channels." The reply gives you another. If you don't receive a response, then a second letter noting the failure to answer still provides you with an additional document.

After each meeting or interaction with the troublesome co-worker or boss, send a note confirming what took place. Include a description of insults or intimidating tactics used by the other person or promises for reform, refusals to change, arrangements for further meetings or progress reports. When you say in your note, "I'm sending this letter to confirm," the onus is then on the other person to contradict your interpretation. If he doesn't respond, your note may stand as the record. If he does answer with his own interpretation, you can send still another note agreeing or disagreeing. This builds a record that will impress any third party you appeal to later.

Tape recorders and witnesses can both be useful. But if you want to tape a meeting, think about whether there's anything *you* might say that you wouldn't want recorded. One woman abused at work strongly advised against taping, because the tape might be turned against you. If you decide to take that risk, give the other person notice beforehand that you plan to tape the session or to bring someone with you. Your boss might try to persuade you that he can't permit a witness or tape recording. Check with your union or a lawyer on that.

Rana, an insurance office manager, lost ground early in her

case because she didn't know her rights and attended a human rights hearing without the lawyer she was entitled to. Jessica learned too late that she had a right to union representation when she confronted the hospital administration. Later a friend advised her not to go into a meeting with supervisors without a lawyer, warning that the hospital's actions were illegal. Jessica's first response was, "They wouldn't do it, if it were illegal." But her friend prevailed on her to get advice from a lawyer, who not only validated her friend's opinion but accompanied Jessica to the meeting. Her friend's suggestion turned out to be important, since at that meeting her boss tried to force her onto "administrative leave."

Serving unequivocal notice that you won't endure more abuse clarifies your position. Once you and the other person recognize that you've moved into a clearly adversarial relationship, setting limits may come more easily to you than when you were attempting to be more accommodating. For example, you might decline to meet with a supervisor until you can arrange for a witness or representative to attend. These principles apply to meetings with union people, human rights officers and anyone else you appeal to for help. Women who have experienced harassment or abuse suggest you declare, "If this meeting might lead to my termination, I must have a witness."

Confronting the Boss in Public Territory

If you can't arrange a private meeting, you can still manage some control over the environment where you meet. Maybe the boss uses a corner of the supply room or an employee pass-through area as an office. Pick the time most likely to be fairly private or when your most supportive co-workers will make themselves useful by leaving you alone with the boss for ten minutes during a break. You could also enlist the co-workers to distract the office gossips most likely to enjoy overhearing your talk with the boss.

Let's suppose the boss barks orders, riddled with insulting obscenities, at top volume. When you complain she insists, "It's just my way." Her only other response takes the form of an increased workload. You worry that she has retaliated by setting you up to fail. You're going to present her with a detailed plan for distributing the workload fairly, because you need that to reduce your stress. But you hope the boss's response will also reveal whether she purposely discriminated against you to make you look incompetent. You've picked a time when you hope not to be interrupted for about five minutes. You get right to the point and talk fast:

You: "Heidi, I've got too many assignments to do at once, but I have a solution to propose. I wrote out some suggestions on how you can distribute our assignments evenly."

To which Heidi might respond:

Heidi: "If you can't keep up with the work, there are people who can."

Hazel, viewed as the "company gossip," zips cheerfully into the room.

Heidi: "What do you think, Hazel? You don't have too much work, do you?"

You: "Hazel, would you give us five minutes alone to finish?" You wait until she leaves before continuing. If she stalls, you continue anyway. You would prefer privacy, but your planning allowed for interruptions and a possible audience.

You: "Heidi, I didn't come in here to discuss this with anyone but you. I've stated what it is I want, and I'm wondering if you understand my point."

Heidi: "Sure. You're bitching about too much work."

You: "It's not that simple. It's that I get more than my fair share of assignments. Then when I don't finish I look bad. I don't like the unfairness of this treatment. I have a plan here that I think will work, and I need to know if you're willing to use it or some other method to see that we each get the same amount of work. Are you willing to do that?"

Heidi: "Well, now, don't get all hot under the collar. I'll look into it and see what I can do . . . "

You: "I'd like you to respond tomorrow with a specific plan, Heidi."

You have pushed Heidi about as far as you can expect to and if she explodes, swears at you or dismisses you, at least you have an answer. She will not give you a reasonable workload.

But she may respond differently:

Heidi: "Oh, hell, I'm tired of your pestering. I'll do it. I'll revise the schedule tomorrow."

Take time to enjoy this victory. And if she doesn't come up

with a plan by the next day, be sure to remind her of her promise. If she puts you off, you can turn to the follow-through guidelines we describe in Chapter 16.

Confronting a Co-Worker

Most of the principles illustrated in this chapter apply equally to confronting either a co-worker or a boss. But in dealing with a co-worker, writing a note or suggesting a meeting may seem too formal. Your co-worker might interpret your request as a sign you think you're a cut above the usual, casual exchanges. That could put him on the defensive. But a formal approach could alert him to the fact that you won't let him slide away from this serious matter which warrants special attention.

The Short, Snappy Comeback

A short, assertive statement that directly follows an offensive act can make a dramatic impact. The immediacy of your reaction offers little opportunity for denial, contradiction of facts or other mental gymnastics that occur when objections come long after offensive behavior takes place. In addition, if you later decide to report what happened, someone in a position of power will probably ask if you objected to the behavior at the time. A few authorities have begun to understand that women—and men too—typically resist objecting to mistreatment on the spot. But many people in power still believe if you didn't protest at the time, then nothing happened. Or what happened didn't matter. If you speak up immediately and record what was done to you, including your response, you increase the odds that a judge, human rights officer or lawyer will take you seriously.

Two other situations favor an immediate response to abuse. Even though it's obvious to you that someone's words have demeaned or threatened you, he may not see it that way. In some settings insults masquerade as jokes, kidding or friendly banter. Workers defend "hazing" as fun: "We've all been through it. Now it's your turn." Some verbal "hazing" takes the form of insults based on Other status. If you clearly state your objections to such comments at the moment they arise, the other person may learn something new about the effect of his or her words.

You may not choose to educate the abusive person about the offensiveness of slurs against people of color or those who are old, disabled or gay, for instance. But you might find it useful to state, once, what you object to. Then if he continues to use language that stereotypes, excludes or insults certain groups, you have a better case for whatever you decide to do next:

You: "When you refer to me in court as a girl it demeans my position."

You: "You just said someone Jewed you down, which implies all Jews are out to get as much money as possible. That kind of stereotyping is offensive to me."

An immediate response doesn't always provide the best opportunity to achieve your goals. If an offensive comment comes in the middle of an important job, you may not choose to interrupt the task to protest it. You may know your objection will lead to a long discussion. Any of the following circumstances might argue against an immediate, short statement:

• You want to explain a complex interaction.
• You have reason to believe the abusive person will have trouble understanding your complaint.
• You have a long list of grievances.
• The offensive person frequently makes long, discursive, distracting statements or grandstands to other workers.

If you decide that the next time a co-worker insults you, you're going to object immediately, you don't have to know exactly what you'll say. You can still plan various responses to typical comments. Molly Martin, editor of *Tradeswomen Magazine,* says tradeswomen collect "comebacks," because similar types of harassment, "hazing" and insults occur frequently at certain jobs. "For me," she says, "it helps to practice. We pass around jokes, comebacks, that we use all the time."

Women employees need research that indicates what works in particular job environments. Martin says, "If you can keep your cool and have a good comeback that's the best," but sometimes she becomes impatient with that tactic. "I get tired of thinking of comebacks, you should just be able to tell them to fuck off." Martin's favorite comeback story is this:

Twenty guys are in an elevator and one says to another about the one woman on the elevator who is also the one woman on the construction site, "I'd sure like to get in her pants." She says, "I've already got one asshole in here, and no room for another." The guys all laugh at the guy. This is the best. You're using humor and putting him down. And he has to stand there while you get to the 20th floor. You're playing their game in a way. They respect you.

Martin explains this technique further: "It's not the same as being one of the boys. It's also putting them down at the same time." In a way you're being accepted, in a way you're being respected. A woman may not use a practiced comeback the first or second time she plans to, but eventually she does, and feels good about it."

Many of the tradeswomen's responses are aggressive, as well as humorous. Since we favor assertive responses we offer some straightforward comments you might use in a variety of situations:

Boss: "Didn't they teach you anything in school?"

You: "Yes, as a matter of fact: patience and fortitude in the face of criticism."

A man in a construction area, referring to a woman worker, suggests:

Worker: "Get that little girl over there to do it."

You(with innocent surprise): "Wow! If there are children here we'd better get them out. This is a dangerous place for kids."

Worker: "What in hell are you talkin' about?"

You(looking around): "Well, you said there was a little girl here somewhere. I'm trying to figure out where she is."

If you've been insulted or harassed several times at the same job, you know more or less what to expect. Decide how to answer each type of insult or uninvited sexual innuendo and practice how you might use it in various settings. Ask a partner to give you responses, including interruptions or reactions of other co-workers who might be nearby. A decision to respond immediately to the objectionable treatment may require a public confrontation.

Confrontation in a Fishbowl

Maybe you work at a construction site, restaurant, factory or a large office that has no private cubicles. Everyone works in the middle of a stream of traffic. In order to set up a private discussion, suggest a walk, a cup of coffee off the grounds, or a meeting right after work when everyone else has left. If the other person declines or begins another verbal assault with the audience of co-workers hanging on her words, you have few choices. A similar situation can arise if a co-worker unexpectedly confronts you in public work space. In each instance you can choose to remain and possibly subject yourself to a tirade, or you can leave. Although in some circumstances you may "talk down" the other person, you could wind up in a public shouting match instead.

Suppose your co-worker, Mattie, encounters you in the staff room, where various people take breaks or use the copy machine.

Mattie, pounding table, red in face, shouting: "Can't the idiots in your department get it straight even one time?"

You, turning to leave: "I've decided not to listen to your shouting and name-calling any more. Let me know when you want to discuss the next step in the project."

Mattie: "Where do you think you're going? You can't walk out like that, I'm talking to you."

You continue silently moving out the door.

Or you repeat, in a normal voice even though Mattie can't hear unless she stops screaming:

"I've decided not to listen to you shout any more."

Another situation might work something like this:

George comes by and leans over you to get a file from a shelf. He unnecessarily rubs his hips against you and, smiling, mutters, "Sexy, nigger bitch." He's done this before.

You, loudly: "George, if you touch me like that, or call me a sexy, nigger bitch one more time, I'll report you to the union." George may deny what he's done or try to make you sound paranoid, but your comment could also make him wary of repeating his action. If he fires off an even more insulting remark that can be heard by your co-workers, you now have witnesses to his verbal abuse. But an audience can sometimes worsen the problem. If you're the only woman on a crew with men who like to harass, this scenario can backfire. George might get a big laugh at your expense, which will egg him on.

The Open Wound of Other Status

Some verbal assaults penetrate your self-image with devastating force. You may know that a personal insult has been used against you because the perpetrator believes a certain word or phrase will demolish your ego. If you feel sure that "fat," "ugly" or "crazy" do not describe you, you can shrug off these words. But maybe you believe you *are* a little crazy, ugly or fat, and have accepted society's ideas that such traits are shameful. An emotional reaction might wipe your agenda right out of your mind. Of course, even if you were fat, ugly or crazy, that would hardly be a reason for anyone to hurl insults at you. But most of us can't respond rationally enough to think of that when we feel humiliated. In addition, abusive people often zero in with unerring accuracy on other peoples' most tender spots and fears of inadequacy.

If a verbal sling comes right at your most sensitive wound from family or social abuse, first take a deep breath. Remind yourself the comment illustrates the speaker's problem rather than yours. Then tell the person that you won't discuss your physical, mental or other personal traits, which are not job related:

You: "Whether you consider me fat or crazy has nothing to do with our job. Even if I agreed with those comments, that wouldn't entitle you to insult me."

You've given the other person an important straightforward message, but also reminded yourself of those same points. If you're shaken, use your notes to get back on track:

You: "I've written a list of topics I want to address, and I see I haven't finished stating my first point yet. I'd like to continue."

When you challenge a bullying, vengeful or extremely controlling person, he or she may pull out all stops and focus on your presumed vulnerabilities. So rehearse responses you want to make in situations where you confront slurs about your Other status. Maybe you're handling your feelings just fine until an aggressive, abusive co-worker gets to your racial or ethnic heritage, sexual orientation or age.

Sam: "Ever since affirmative action came alone, you blacks—or is it "African-American" you want to be called this week—you think you can just make a complaint, and everything will come your way. Well, let me tell you something, until you get off your black asses and start putting in some serious work. . . . "

You have a serious choice here, but one which you've anticipated in your role rehearsals. Your feelings may charge right up the Richter scale. You might feel like leaping over the desk to provide this person with a quick lesson in race relations. Or you might struggle against tears of rage, frustration or sorrow. Your response may be the same if Sam has used words like "chink," "dyke" or "little old lady in tennis shoes." Maybe this co-worker has exacerbated your anger by acting as if he can boss you around, though he has no such authority. You muster control and assert yourself:

You: "Sam, those comments clearly indicate race (gender/age) discrimination. The best way for me to answer them is to file a complaint."

You: "I won't continue listening to you call people 'chink' or 'dyke,' which I consider racial slurs and anti-gay. I'm leaving." (When you get back to your workplace you decide what step to take next. If this happens on your own work territory, you can still leave, hide out in the bathroom and hope the offender has left when you return.)

You: "You have hit below the belt, using racial slurs like 'Squaw.' I'm angry and I'm hurt. Do you realize the effect those words have on me?"

You can think of other assertive responses. If the other person uses a variety of tactics to intimidate and control, you might have difficulty deciding which to challenge first. You might decide to temporarily ignore a co-worker's enforcement of trivial demands or efforts to isolate you in order to deal, first, with sex harassment or racist comments. You choose your own issue on the basis of its importance or your ability to handle it most effectively.

If your boss, Al, frequently calls attention to your white hair and "older woman" status, you could just smile, pointedly address Al as "sonny boy" and see what happens. Depending on your relationship with Al and your tone, the statement could be a friendly amusing instruction or an aggressive crack. Or you could assert yourself in a more straightforward way, taking an educational approach, especially if the affront is subtle or presented in the guise of "helping."

You: "Al, do you realize that calling me 'Granny' is insulting? I think you might intend it to be affectionate, but it calls attention to my age as if I am a sweet, domestic little thing, not likely to be efficient. I want to be treated as the competent professional I am and called by my name."

When Harriet hired Jo, a white woman, as a child-care worker, Jo told her she was a lesbian. Harriet assured her she needn't worry about discrimination. Jo worked at the school for several years, receiving favorable work reviews and promotions. Then Harriet assigned Edna, an African-American woman, to work under Jo's supervision. Edna spread stories about Jo among the staff. Jo might have appealed to Edna on the basis of their shared status of Other, allowing for their differences. Jo knew that institutions and their representatives sometimes pit Others against each other to compete for privileges. She didn't want to view Edna as her adversary. But Edna flatly declared she would not cooperate with Jo and would never accept a lesbian as a supervisor. She then "reported" to Harriet on Jo's sexual orientation, as if she had discovered a dirty secret.

When Jo learned what Edna had done, she immediately told Harriet she expected her to stop Edna's homophobic and insubordinate behavior. Harriet tried to dismiss Edna's behavior as unimportant. But Jo responded, "No way can you let this go, Harriet. This is clear insubordination and homophobia, which is against the city ordinance. If you don't tell Edna to treat me with the respect I deserve, I'm out of here. For good." The director instructed Edna to stop making remarks that were hostile and anti-lesbian and to accept Jo's supervision. With occasional prodding from Jo, Harriet regularly reminded Edna of what was required. Edna soon resigned and Jo remains on the job. Jo saved her job by her persistence in confronting Harriet when she stalled in dealing with Edna.

The boss who, like Harriet, agrees to make changes and then

waffles, presents problems that are common and difficult to handle. To get results requires continual follow-through and an ability to regularly evaluate your own actions as well as the promises you're given. The subject we take up next presents ideas on how to do that.

Chapter 16

Evaluation and Follow-Through

I yelled at him, "What's going on?" . . . I wanted to know what changes had been ordered. He wouldn't answer, so I got a bit flustered and asked again. He still wouldn't answer. I kept probing, and he kept not answering. Finally I said, "I'm talking to you. I want a response." . . . Finally he answered me and explained there was a change in plans, not any mistake. I could see he was a little taken aback and I felt so good. I had won something.

Elaine Canfield, carpenter

You don't evaluate your assertive action just once. You don't give yourself an "A" or "C" grade when you complete a planned confrontation, and then retire from the action. If Elaine had judged herself on whether she succeeded or failed after her co-worker's first refusal to give her information, she would surely have given up. Instead she viewed her persistent requests for an answer as a process, and followed through until she reached her goal.

Each step may take you closer to achieving what you want. Evaluations along the way comprise an important part of the process. So we've distributed evaluation questions throughout this chapter to emphasize the importance of regularly checking out your progress. They will help you judge whether another person heard and understood your message, and show you how to follow through on resulting promises. Use the questions as tools for planning your next step; then use them again when you've completed the action.

Evaluating a Confrontation

Immediately after each step of your assertive action, notice what you did well. After you've focused on the positive, consider what you might have done more effectively. If old habits of global self-criticism threaten to intrude on your thoughts, ask a friend to help you regain a more balanced perspective. She asks you, "What did you do right?" And keeps asking until you give her several clear and positive answers. Maybe "I kept eye contact" is the best you can come up with at first. "Well, at least I didn't run screaming from the room." With practice you can do better than that. Refer to the Assertiveness Guidelines in Chapter 9 to recall your goals. Keep trying to remember each thing you did well, no matter how minor it seems.

Evaluations guide you toward further practice, special classes or therapy—whatever helps you develop skills for handling difficult situations. Self-improvement programs will then either encourage you to assert your rights anew or help you modify your reactions to intimidating or infuriating people at work.

The evaluation questions, especially in Exercise 16A, can help you decide on next steps at each point in your process. You might want to use them after rehearsing for a confrontation, after checking back to see if promised changes were made or after any assertive action, no matter how small it seems. (If you tend to postpone an action, or feel anxious about it, it probably isn't small.)

EXERCISE 16A: How Did I Do?

This first set of questions refers to an encounter in which your main purpose was to make a statement. *Write* the answers to: What part of my plan did I carry out the way I wanted to?

	Some of the Time	*Most of the Time*	*All of the Time*
1. Kept eye contact?	___	___	___
2. Controlled my tone of voice?	___	___	___
3. Clearly described what I observed?	___	___	___

	Some of the Time	*Most of the Time*	*All of the Time*
4. *Expressed my opinions?*	⸺	⸺	⸺
5. *Described my feelings?*	⸺	⸺	⸺
6. *Listened carefully to abusive person's response?*	⸺	⸺	⸺

Mark the following yes or no, and add pertinent comments:

	Yes	*No*
7. *Did not apologize for what I didn't do.*	⸺	⸺
8. *Expressed anger with respect.*	⸺	⸺
9. *Expressed vulnerable feelings with respect for myself.*	⸺	⸺
10. *Kept in mind alternative steps if this didn't go well.*	⸺	⸺
11. *Kept thoughts to specifics; didn't scare myself with global negative predictions or self-criticisms.*	⸺	⸺
12. *Met with a supportive person afterward.*	⸺	⸺
13. *Started a new plan for the next step.*	⸺	⸺

Now we look at how to discover whether the other person understands what points you're making.

Did The Person Understand?

Determining whether your message has been understood challenges your persistence, sensitivity and resourcefulness. Sometimes even direct questions result in only evasive comments or a change of subject. Then you have to follow up with more questions to discover what the responses really mean.

At the center for deaf and hearing impaired people, about half of the employees, including Zoe, were deaf and the other half, including the director, Terry, were hearing people. Terry frequently took visitors to Zoe's office and announced to them that Zoe had "been using ASL (American Sign Language) all her life." Zoe says:

> *I felt like a five-year old, dressed up so she could impress people. The truth is I didn't sign until I was eighteen, and I was mad that she didn't remember my story. I told her to stop because it bothered me. "Oh, yeah, yeah," she would say, "I forgot." Then she would do it again.*

Zoe made one last attempt to be explicit about how strongly she objected and to extract a specific commitment for change. In evaluating the results of her clear statement, she could only say her *words* were understood. To find out if Terry understood her meaning, she would have to wait to see how she acted. It didn't take long to find out. Once more the boss introduced her with the same words she had always used, and Zoe knew she had received her answer. Terry's unspoken but real answer was, "No, I didn't really get your meaning." Or "Yes, but I don't care enough to alter my ways." Shortly after that Zoe resigned.

EXERCISE 16B: Did I Do My Part?

Although you can't control whether the other person thoroughly grasped your words or meaning, the following questions enable you to check whether you did everything appropriate to help your boss or co-worker understand.

A. Did I do my part to clarify my goals and to determine whether the other person understood them?

Did I ask:	*No*	*Sometimes*	*Frequently*
1. if the other person understood what I said?	____	____	____

2. for specific illustrations that I was   No   Sometimes Frequently

heard?   _____   _____   _____

The next set of questions refers only to whether the person you addressed understood your observations or request. Only the other person can control his part of the interaction. However, your answers will indicate what path you might explore next.

B. What did the other person do to let me know he understood me?

1. Was he able to repeat back the sense of what I said? Yes _____ *No* _____

*2. Did she indicate understanding of the signifiance of
what I said?*   *Yes* _____ *No* _____

How?

_____

_____

3. If I still question whether the meaning of my words or feelings was absorbed, how will I determine if they were? _____

_____

If you didn't directly ask whether the person understood your words and meaning, or if you accepted a vague response, you can still confront him again and ask exactly what he thought you were trying to convey. Returning to ask the question when you've already completed your initial interaction could feel awkward, but the rewards may be worth it. You will gain useful information and probably you will never again forget to ask for specifics. You also provide yourself with another chance to practice setting up an appointment and asking difficult questions. Next time it will be easier.

If you expect the other person to resist making an additional appointment for clarification, try to avoid stating the specific reason for the meeting. Otherwise, she might involve you in a full discussion of the issues on the spot, rather than at a place and time you choose. When you do meet with her again push for verification of whether you were heard:

You: "I've been thinking about our conversation the other day, and I'm not sure I got my point across. Will you tell me what you thought I said?"

You: "I know you heard my words when we talked on Friday, but I'm not sure you understand what my complaint/ request is really about. Would you tell me your understanding of my reasons for my request, so we can be sure we're on the same track?"

Press For An Answer

Let's suppose you have a request, or a series of related demands for an end to abuse. You present them to the boss or coworker, who agrees to make immediate changes. The answer seems completely out of character, and you're at a loss to interpret it. Many irritable, disdainful people respond unpredictably to pressure. Even someone who frequently jeers, taunts or disregards you may switch tactics once he understands that you're serious and ready to follow through on what you want.

Suppose your supervisor has been on his job as department manager for just three weeks. You describe his actions to him:

You: "Paul, you've done several things in the few weeks you've been here that have caused problems for me. You said, in our initial talk, that you'd welcome information about how this department has been managed in the past. But when I explained to you that staff is used to being regularly consulted about important shifts in the work flow, you shouted and slammed the door to your office. You did that on three occasions this week alone. Calling Sybil 'stupid,' as you did yesterday or me a 'space case' the way you did this morning lowers morale.

"In addition, I've just heard that you offered my job to Mildred and told her I'd be leaving. I need to know if that is true. I want to know that the yelling, door slamming and name-calling will stop and that if you're dissatisfied with my work you'll give me fair notice of that, so we can try to work out the problem together."

At this point you breathe a sigh of surprised relief that you actually got through the list. Paul makes sympathetic noises, even takes a few notes. Then he speaks, syrup in his voice.

Paul: "I'll be glad to consider what you said. I've been thinking that I'd better calm down. You know I'm such a perfectionist, I just want everything to go smoothly, so we can give the best possible service."

You expected Paul to blast you with a windy defense of his actions. The lack of wind has collapsed your sails. You're reluctant to escalate the conflict by flatly declaring you don't believe him, but you also aren't willing to leave without getting details about action to match Paul's words. It's time to repeat your requests:

You: "I'm glad you recognize there's a problem. But my requests are quite specific and I'd like an answer to each. I want to know that you'll stop referring to me as a 'space case' or by any other derogatory names and stop shouting and slamming doors. Can you promise me that?"

Paul's neck has turned bright red and his veins are protruding as they often do when he's about to shout, pound a desk or slam a door. But his effort to control himself is successful:

Paul: "Well. That's quite a list. You really shouldn't take my kidding so seriously, but if it makes you feel better I can knock off the names. I just get excited, you know? Got to get some of this pressure off. Which reminds me you better get back to that report."

Your task now is to determine whether Paul is serious about giving up his name-calling. You will probably want to let him know you heard his statement as an agreement with your request, and that you want more information about exactly how much he understands of the word, "name-calling." If you ask him to paraphrase what you said, he may interpret the request as hostile, insubordinate or demanding. Although you want to show respect for him, maybe you don't feel so respectful right now, so it's doubtful whether you can ask, "Do you understand?" without an edge to your voice. Since you've just been dismissed from his office, he might also take offense if you refuse to leave. But it's important to make sure he understands your message, and he might interpret your offer to clarify as an indication of good intentions:

You: "I'm relieved to know that you're willing to stop calling the staff names. And I want to make sure we agree about what that means. The first couple of weeks you were here, sometimes I thought I was clear in what I said to you, but later I realized you didn't understand me. I think you do now, but I'm not sure. I suggest we go over what we each think I've just said."

Paul: "Well, I said I'd go along with no names. Isn't that enough for now? What do you want, blood? You know I count on you for a cooperative attitude, which I really need while I'm still new at this job."

You: "No, I don't want blood. And if I can count on no more name-calling that will help a lot. But I'm not absolutely sure you know what I consider insulting names, and it would help if you could give me some examples of what you think I mean. Also you didn't respond to each of my additional points and I'm reluctant to leave without assurance that you understand exactly what my complaints are. But, first, let's be sure we understand each other on the name-calling. If I haven't been clear, how can I clarify what I mean?"

The suggestions we've made here illustrate a pretty high degree of articulation and "cool." You may be able to come close to this type of response after a few rehearsals. But if you don't, give yourself credit for having the courage to try. The more you confront abusive people the easier it will become.

If you're worn out or convinced that Paul won't provide guarantees about other issues, you might consider his sarcastic response, "What do you want, blood?" discouraging. But by agreeing to stop calling you names Paul *has* given you something. You have to decide whether you've achieved enough to leave the struggle for today. At this point it could make sense to make another appointment soon to deal with the other grievances. You won't know until the next meeting what Paul truly intends to do.

You: "I have other issues to discuss, but I'd like to leave this list of them with you to discuss later. I'm asking you to look them over and to talk again next Thursday, in case some things aren't clear."

A Promise Is a Promise, Not an Action

Some of the abusive bosses of the world escape reform because others accept their promises and don't check back on performance. At times Paul may want desperately to please. So he persuades himself, as well as you, that he can manage an overnight about-face of long-held habits. He easily convinces you of his sorrow, sincerity and good intentions because he believes in them himself. If his "syrupy" facade becomes mixed with a bit of acid, you can take it as a reminder of what lies beneath the surface. But often the opposite occurs. You want to keep the syrup flowing. You forget for the moment how mean-spirited this person can be. You empathize with his problems in doing a tough new job. You may even fear that questioning this suddenly warm-hearted, agreeable person will hurt his feelings. Paul can present himself as so vulnerable you believe you're the only one who understands him. You have the urge to protect the person who abuses you.

You might distrust someone's promises without being able to name the reason. Trust your doubts enough to put a "caution" sign in your mind. Your co-worker or boss may have agreed to whatever you asked in hopes you'll forget about your requests and leave him alone. To determine the truth, ask as many direct questions as necessary. Remind yourself you have reason to expect a clear answer. When you request commitment to action and the other person makes vague promises, you might feel like saying, "I've heard that song before." But you don't, not unless this is close to the last straw, or you've already written your resignation letter. Instead, begin with something positive, even if you're skeptical: "I'm glad you understand my problem. I wasn't sure you would." Then ask for a commitment: "When do you expect to speak to Charlie about this?" "Who will monitor progress?"

If the boss replies, "Don't worry, we'll take care of it," the "we" tips you off that the problem probably won't be resolved unless you push for a specific person to take on the task at a particular time. "It would help me to know exactly who will do it. What is a reasonable time to expect it to be done?" Or try something like: "How can I help expedite it?" "What are the first steps you'll take to begin the process?" "Shall I remind you of your decision/our agreement on Tuesday?"

If someone who frequently mocked or belittled your ideas now accompanies vague promises with offers of minor favors, look out. You might want to review the section on Occasional Indulgences in Chapter 2, "Naming Emotional Abuse." It could save you from a painful, repetitive cycle of abuse.

Lay the Groundwork for Checking Back

Your boss may answer your question about who will make the desired modifications in this way:

Boss: "I'll have Joe take it up."

You: "When will he begin?"

Boss: "As soon as he can."

You: "Will you give me a date for that?"

If your pen is poised to take notes on the answer, the boss may take you seriously. To avoid the awkwardness of firing out a series of questions, try an introductory statement about what you want and the reasons for it:

You: "Since things sometimes slip through the cracks, I'd like to work out a plan with you, spelling out exactly what will be done, and when. Then I'd like to set up an appointment for mutual feedback about how the changes are going."

You: "You've said before you'd take care of this. But it hasn't happened. Once you did tell Luke and Ben not to call me sexist names, but they only stopped for two weeks. This time I want to make sure it's permanent. Would it help if I let you know each week how it's going, so you can get to them immediately if they start again?"

You: "I think you really want to do this, but you've got a lot of things on your mind. And this might take more time to get in place than we can predict right now. How about letting me come up with a detailed plan and then carry it out, checking back with you every couple of weeks?"

Any of those statements could set the stage for asking a series of questions, now legitimate: "Who will do what?" "When?" "How?" "What is your standard of success?"

Play with phrases that feel natural after some practice. Keep trying for language that offers at least some possibility of being heard: "What procedures and channels would be most appropriate?" "Let's get this show on the road. Where shall we begin?"

EXERCISE 16C: How Did I Do on Follow-Through?

If the person you ask to make a change is usually cooperative, and says he will take care of it, you might want to assume that he means exactly what he says. The exercises that follow are designed to facilitate your encounters with abusive people or those who have already demonstrated a tendency to stall and make empty promises. To get commitments from such people, you need to be persistent and to insist on responses that in other situations might seem unreasonable. Like many other women you may find it difficult to ask, "Are you going to do it?" "All of it?" "When?" "How?" And it's tough to keep asking until you get answers or you're sure it's counterproductive to pursue the issues further. Don't be too hard on yourself as you do this evaluation, especially if this is a new process for you.

	Yes	No
1. I asked how, when and who would follow through.	——	——
2. I asked for specific answers to those questions.	——	——
3. I asked for a time commitment.	——	——
4. I asked for a time to check back.	——	——
5. I took notes during the interview.	——	——
6. I took more detailed notes after the interview.	——	——
7. I sent a note later to confirm agreements, note our disagreements, expectations and the time line.	——	——
8. I did something special to reward myself for my efforts and for what I did well.	——	——
9. I met with a supportive person afterward.	——	——
10. I started a new plan for the next step.	——	——

The questions above evaluate only your part of the interaction. If you couldn't persuade the person to do what you wanted, that doesn't necessarily mean you didn't assert yourself well. Focus on the appropriate things you did carry out. We've suggested general guidelines, but you may have had good reasons for not following some of them. For example, you may have decided not to take notes during your meeting, because you knew that would seem more threatening than you wanted to appear. Maybe you didn't ask who would follow through, because the person had already made it clear she had no intention of doing anything you asked.

If there are things you wish you had said, think of a new plan to correct the situation. Then write it down. Decide whether you're willing to meet again to try for a better interaction. Practice what you want to say so you can improve your presentation while the interaction remains fresh in your mind. Even if the other person didn't comply with your request for action, consider the encounter at least a partial success if you gained a clear idea of the abusive person's intentions. Your new understanding will enable you to evaluate the next step with increased confidence.

Keep in mind your original goal. If you wanted to persuade an offensive person to treat you with respect or to obtain such a directive from her boss, the following set of questions helps you evaluate how well she responded to you. You've already looked at how well you did your part. Now you can judge how close you've come to reaching your stated goal of getting someone else to act. Be sure not to confuse your specific goal with how successful you are *as a person*. The outcome in relation to your goal is an evaluation of your situation, not your worth.

EXERCISE 16D: Keep Tabs on Promises

Before you answer these next questions, be sure you have completed those in Exercises 16A and 16B. Nothing guarantees a connection between how well you asserted yourself and the response you got. But knowing whether you have said what you wanted and have been heard will help you evaluate the answers you give below. Apply these questions to any interaction in which you're making a difficult request:

1. If the person I approached for change said she was willing to act, what exactly did she say she'd do? _____

---

2. When? _____

3. *Who will carry out the changes?* _____

4. *How?* _____

5. *Did he agree I should check back? When?* _____

6. *What will I do if she doesn't follow through?* _____

_____

7. *At what point will I decide that enough has been done?* _____

_____

8. *How will I know if he has completed the changes I asked for?* ____

_____

9. *If she does some of what I asked and not all, which of those actions will*

be enough for now? _____

_____

10. *What are my next steps?* _____

_____

Check Back

If your boss, co-worker or a third party promised to do some of what you requested, check back to see if it's been done. Suppose she agreed you could ask her in a week about her progress. That week has passed and you can't see any results. You know you have to confront her because you will lose ground if you let this opportunity slip by. Yet you might hesitate, fearing an unpleasant exchange. Your last session with her wore you out. But you judged this issue important enough to make that first appointment, and this follow-through meeting completes the action.

If you say you want a meeting to discuss progress on the plan agreed to, the other person might stall with a casual remark about "working on it" or say, "We've run into some snags. Let's wait till I have something definite to tell you."

Don't leave it at that.

You: "If you have problems completing the job, I'd like to

hear about them. If necessary, maybe we can renegotiate our agreement. In any case, I want to follow our plan to meet today."

You take a risk with this statement, since the abusive person may seize any opportunity to compromise your agreement. But this approach also gives you an opportunity to hear about what she considers "snags." That will tell you a lot about whether she's just stalling, or whether progress is out of her control at the moment. You could continue pushing her to keep the commitment to meet again or you could view her postponement as a passive way of saying she will not do what you asked.

Your reminder of the scheduled check-back session could bring about an immediate meeting. The same guidelines apply here as for the initial interview. Plan carefully what you'll say, where and when. Rehearse your statements, specific questions and how you'll answer probable and improbable responses. Decide ahead of time what to do if the other person waffles, excuses, delays or changes the terms of your original agreement.

Boss: "You know how hectic things have been this week with the annual report due and three new hires. I'll get to your problem next week for sure."

You respect the other person's rights; you don't raise your voice; you don't deride anyone. You listen carefully. *And* you're clear about what has to happen before you'll be satisfied. Still, it takes nerve to continue to press for what you and the boss or coworker agreed to. If you're convinced she's purposely evading action on your agreement, you might make a graceful retreat with a plan for different action later. When other people drag their heels over a period of time you may recognize two unwelcome choices: to continue insisting on immediate action, or to give up this particular struggle.

You may have succeeded in getting part of what you asked for. If you retreat now, you might lose ground in achieving the rest of what you want. On the other hand, you may feel drained by the struggle. You want a well-deserved rest before returning to the ring. If so, let the person know you're making the choice to withdraw for a time. Don't let her think you just forgot about the other issues or decided they're unimportant:

You: "I'm glad we got this part settled. I can live with this for a while. But I'll be back to talk to you about the other items before long."

EXERCISE 16E: How Did Your Boss Do?

This part of the evaluation includes questions about your commitment to yourself to keep checking on the other person's follow-through. Many women, especially those uncomfortable with power, find it burdensome to monitor other people's behavior. So you might find it convenient to "forget" to check back on the progress you've requested. Don't let yourself off the hook.

In your follow-up interview, you made some kind of statement, wanted to know whether you were understood and added a request, specifically related to the follow-through. So first, be sure you've completed each of the previous evaluation exercises in this chapter, which cover those areas. Then answer the following questions:

1. What was the date I was told the action would begin? _____

*2. If that date has passed, what percentage of the agreed upon changes were made?*_____

3. By what date was I told the action would be completed? _____

4. If that date has passed, what percentage of each part has been completed?

---

5. If the actions have not been taken care of as promised, what have I done to see that they will be? _____

6. If I agreed to check back with the boss/co-worker, has the date for that passed? _____

If yes, what am I going to do about it? _____

---

7. If the date for checking back is coming up, have I prepared and practiced what I want to say? _____

8. Do I have a plan for responding to what I'm told about progress? ___

9. What is my plan? _____

_____

10. If I have no plan, what's causing me to stall? _____

_____

11. If this person really can't make the changes without a third party's okay, who can make them? _____

12. How can I discuss the problem with the third party directly?

_____

13. If there are obstacles to speaking to the third party or other obstacles in the way of progress how can I handle them?

_____

_____

14. What is my plan now for handling the next step? _____

_____

15. When? _____   *How?* _____

16. Am I ready to give up trying and withdraw? ___   *Why or why not?*

_____

The Retreat: Graceful or Forced

As you can see, the tactic to pin *yourself* to a commitment resembles the one you use for dealing with the person who may be waffling. You need to get tough with yourself. But that still doesn't mean you have to do anything you don't want to. In answering the question about why you "stall," you might have said the agony outweighs the slim possibility of success or that personal problems or commitments take precedence right now. Those may be good reasons to discontinue your campaign. Just double-check that you haven't used them as excuses to avoid action that you'll later wish you had taken.

Dr. Margaret O'Toole, a junior researcher in molecular biology who blew the whistle on her boss for falsifying scientific data, paid a steep price for speaking out. Her boss fired her, and other scientists created rumors consisting of "everything from reports of incompetence to suggestions that, as a nursing mother, she was not acting rationally." That treatment continued for five years. She says that during that time she was made to "'seem like the worst lunatic that ever walked the face of the earth.'"

In this case O'Toole's withdrawal was forced when her boss fired her and when other scientists tried to push her out of the field. For several years she was unable to find another professional job and it seemed that virtually no one would defend her action. But after four years she did find professional work, and gradually some of her colleagues did come forward.

Withdrawing can create opportunities to explore new approaches to handling your work problem when you've exhausted the possibilities or the price of "winning" seems too high. But think through how you'll retreat from this immediate struggle. Even if you resign without risking a protest while you're on the job, you might file some form of grievance later.

Some women have chosen to present in writing their reasons for leaving a job as they walk out the door. Others arrange for an interview at the time they resign the job or even after they've left. Consider the timing of a resignation and complaint carefully. If you report an abusive person to an authority and then resign with notice, he may choose to make your life hell during the period before you actually leave. Some of the most harrowing abuse we've heard about has occurred under these circumstances. Try to anticipate the worst that can happen in retaliation for your action.

If you decide not to confront the abuse and to continue working on the job, you face a different dilemma. How will you be able to endure the abuse without letting it take a serious toll on how you feel about yourself? You can take action to reduce stress. But you might also choose to quietly organize for later action with a few other colleagues. Or you might approach the problems collectively with a large group, planning for long term, possibly even systemic, change.

SECTION VII

Action with Others

Chapter 17

You Don't Have to Go It Alone

We mobilized in my office. I said to the staff, "Divide the resource list, write letters to the board, the newspaper, the agencies who refer us kids. . . . We have no power ourselves, but we can mobilize outside power." We constantly worked as a team; no one orchestrated. When I was down, someone else would be in a higher place. I'd feel myself energized.

Hattie, youth advocate

If individual action hasn't worked, you'll probably review the possibility of maneuvering around the abuse, resigning or waiting for a transfer—yours or the perpetrator's. But, before you make a final decision, consider a group approach. Joining with others may succeed in stopping abuse where individual efforts failed. Working cooperatively can bolster your courage. It might also prevent your boss or co-worker from targeting you for punishment.

A group might consist of you and just one or two co-workers. One day, three of you get tired of hearing each other's chronic complaints about your supervisor and decide to act or you whisper to your co-worker that you feel intimidated by a threatening co-worker and she says, "Yeah, me too. Let's go tell him to cut it out." Sometimes spontaneous action on a joint decision accomplishes a goal quickly, especially with a small group. But cautiously weighing the pros and cons of group action can also serve you well.

A group is like a chemistry experiment. Each time the temperature changes or the mix is stirred a new substance seems to evolve. Exhaustive guidelines, allowing for all possibilities, would take us beyond the scope of this book. But we do suggest ways to evaluate the potential for cooperation among co-workers and include brief guidelines for planning an action together. We also relate examples of workers who organized collectively to oppose abuse. In general group and individual actions differ in these ways:

GROUPS	INDIVIDUALS
Many ideas and choices; compromise	*Precise focus on individual needs*
Camaraderie	*Loneliness; independence*
Safety in numbers	*Confidentiality assured*
Collective responsibility	*Individual responsibility*
Success affects more people	*Success is yours alone*
Shared responsibility for failure	*Individual responsibility for failure*
Informed support on the job	*Safer support outside of work*
Complex decisions: slow action	*Action quickly follows decisions*

Your personal history of work with other people and as an individual gives you insights about how these differences affect you. Maybe each experience differed dramatically from the other. Recall your interactions in any group you have been part of, whether in church, politics, at work, on a sports team, in a support or therapy group or book club. Then tailor our exercises to fit the practical knowledge you've gained.

Which is best: organizing with others to confront an abusive person, or working alone? Four people competing to diagnose and repair a faulty kitchen sink or computer program can bruise each others' knuckles and egos. But, working together, those same individuals may resolve the problem in one-fourth the time. Similarly, cooperating on the job might give you more satisfaction than going it alone. The following questions help you evaluate risks in group or individual protest against abuse.

EXERCISE 17A: What's Best For You?

1. Which positive aspects of group action are important to me? _____

---

2. Which benefits of working alone are important? _____

_____

3. What advantages of individual action am I willing to give up in favor of
working with a group? _____

4. Which of my goals or my usual work style am I willing to compromise to
keep a working group together? _____

_____

5. What compromises would I not make under any circumstances?

_____

_____

6. What adjustments am I willing to make just for a short-term project?

_____

_____

7. What adjustments am I willing to make on a long-term basis?

_____

_____

Small Groups; Short-Term Action

Spontaneously formed small groups are often appropriately short-lived. The planning stage might take ten minutes. Your group may stay together just long enough to file a complaint with the troublesome person and to congratulate yourselves after the encounter. When action immediately succeeds, the group has no further need to continue, though members sometimes choose to stay together in case other problems arise.

You and a few others might have cooperated on different work projects without considering yourselves a group. When you organize to stop emotional abuse at work, you may have already completed the important initial group task of establishing trust. Earlier group experience in working together may enable you to plan quickly on a new issue. If your goal takes longer than expected you may enjoy each others' company so much you're glad to extend the life of the group. Confronting abuse can even provide you pleasure, rather than a crucible of anxiety, as sometimes happens when people act alone.

Trudy, a bank bookkeeper, became upset about crude sexual gestures and remarks made by Patrick, her immediate supervisor, who apparently considered his actions humorous. She often let off steam about him to her friends and co-workers, Faith and Marsha. These three women, each supervised by Patrick, gained some satisfaction from making fun of him. But when one of his "jokes" embarrassed Trudy in the presence of a customer, she felt he had gone too far. She discussed the situation with her friends during a morning break. The three women decided to make a complaint, went directly to the branch manager and explained what they found objectionable. Their request was casual but definite. "Tom, we've got some problems with Patrick's idea of humor. We object to some other things he does too, and we want you to talk to him about making changes." Tom listened as the women described the problems. The next day the offensive behavior stopped.

In this case several circumstances contributed to immediate action and response. The women knew each other well and shared many values. Since the group consisted of only three people, each could easily get a hearing from the others. They had discussed the issues many times. Their jobs allowed flexibility and the mobility needed to act immediately, in contrast to tellers or others who must remain at their stations. Had it been necessary to postpone action, time to reflect may have changed their decision. Group members often reconsider consequences during any delay in implementing a decision. New perspectives often result in at least some withdrawals from an action plan.

The small size of the bank and informal communication system encouraged a spontaneous knock on the manager's door, with no advance appointment necessary. The manager, respecting the work of each woman, did not use his position to intimidate them. He recognized the potential loss of three skilled employees because of one faulty supervisor. Patrick, who was more ignorant and insecure than cruel, did not retaliate. The similarity of all players' race (white), class background, ages and life-style contributed to ease of communication.

Nevertheless, had Trudy complained on her own, she might not have been taken seriously. The three women gave each other confidence to speak up to authority. Each of those factors contributed to an immediately successful action that was low-key and short. Although a small group can operate over a long period of time, and a large group can take on a single brief act, generally there is some relationship between size and duration.

Larger Group: Long-Term Action

Now we will describe in detail one group action by an agency staff determined to get free of an abusive director. The story illustrates many problems and several approaches. We begin with a description of a pre-group stage, common to many situations. Each employee privately assesses her relationship with the boss, wonders if anyone endures the same treatment and examines her own possible role in the problem. Then she might consider the risks necessary to challenge the boss head on.

Hattie, quoted at the opening of this chapter, worked for six years as a supervisor and youth advocate at an agency that provides a group home and counseling for young women who run away from home or the law. Staff, administration and board worked well together for several years and became a closely knit working group until the board of directors hired a new director, Marva. Her management style combined the characteristics of dictator, crazy person, admiral and manipulator bosses described in Chapter 12. The staff was dismayed as these tendencies emerged during the first couple of weeks of her tenure. But Hattie resolved to give the new boss some slack until she learned her job. Hattie adopted a kind of cheerleader role, persuading staff to give Marva a break, listen to her ideas and help educate her about the agency's methods of operation.

Marva made serious mistakes, for which she frequently blamed staff. Then she hurled loud verbal assaults at the nearest employee. Workers inwardly raged or grieved as they watched their boss dismantle or radically alter one agency program after another. But Hattie still thought that with the help of the staff, she could rescue the agency and Marva as well.

Tina, the program manager, recognized serious problems in Marva's treatment of staff. Sometimes Tina reacted by "steaming" with anger. On other days she felt "shocked and confused." Each time she neared the point of despair, Marva convinced her that she would change. She promised to stop belittling Tina and to listen to her. She asked for staff support and time to adjust to the new position. Then she offered to accommodate Tina in some small way. "I kept thinking," Tina says, "the problem was just Marva's anxiety over the new job." Each time Tina "fell for" these "occasional indulgences" she realized the abuse was similar to the cycle of honeymoon, tension-building and battering familiar to women living with violent partners. Yet she wanted to believe Marva would reform.

When Marva pointedly snubbed her and ridiculed her ideas at a public meeting, Tina thought of walking out and even fantasized disrupting the meeting with a protest. But then something shifted. She thought, "You will not humiliate me again, Marva." Following that meeting she stopped trying to influence Marva's management, and determined to resign. But she wanted to stay on the job just one more month. Meanwhile, new problems with management surfaced daily. She needed an ally.

Hattie and Tina each heard so many individual complaints during staff supervisory sessions they agreed on the advisability of a joint team meeting to compile a list of issues for Marva's review. Tina thought the pressure might force Marva to see that she didn't hold all the power, while Hattie persisted in the hope that Marva could learn from staff feedback. At the team meeting, as advocates pooled information about Marva's treatment, the group's anger heightened. They feared for themselves and for the life of the agency.

The Case Against Marva

Staff collectively realized that the director:

1. Screamed at the bookkeeper, standing over her desk with fist raised.

2. Several times a week shouted orders, immediately retracted them, and blamed staff when they weren't carried out.

3. Asked relatively new staff members to take over projects

of old-timers without discussing changes with experienced staff. In some cases this was an attempt to lay the groundwork for firing without notice.

4. Erased data from computers and then accused staff of stealing it.

5. Met with staff one-on-one, promising each one similar rewards for working with her against others.

6. Changed longstanding program routines without informing program managers.

Turning Points

Marva learned the meeting had taken place even before Tina and Hattie could prepare the list of grievances to present to her. She gathered all staff and shouted at them: "I was hired to command this agency and that is what I will do. If you don't like it you can leave." She demanded that each worker account for every minute of her time, even time in the bathroom. She prohibited all meetings of more than two people. Tina reacted with "shock and confusion." She viewed her public humiliation as one turning point. Now she faced another. She simply wanted Marva out of the agency. Hattie tempered her outrage by repeating to herself, "Embrace, educate, leave no rock unturned to be helpful."

Three days later Marva terminated seven staff members without warning, ordering them out of the building instantly. That night the fired women met with most of the staff still on the job. Not all workers had attended the previous meeting and some had continued to wonder if they were at fault. Believing no one else had seen Marva's "crazy" and insulting behavior, they hadn't trusted their own judgment. Now, hearing their own experiences echoed by others, they believed.

Hattie had been at a conference when the firings took place, but as soon as she learned of Marva's action she rushed to her office and asked, "What's going on?" Marva, apparently referring to her attempts to transfer workers to jobs they weren't trained for, said, "These people just don't want management positions." Marva's termination of the employees and her response to Hattie's question combined to shift Hattie's attitude completely. "We've tried," she thought, "and you've pulled out the rug."

She immediately began to think about organizing staff. "The problem," she said to herself, "is how to take our pain and get the attention of people with power to see that we have a monster here."

From Support to Action

One week after the firings, the staff convened again. They unanimously agreed to present the group's grievances to the board of directors, their first organized group action. Without exactly realizing it, however, the staff had forged the groundwork for operating as a group almost since Marva arrived. Meeting in twos and threes, they had compared notes and supported each other whenever Marva attacked. The planning meeting to compile grievances had taken them a step further. This third gathering melded them into an action group. Weekly sessions followed the initial get-togethers, and as organization progressed, focus shifted to whatever situations evolved. Individual discontent and anger had set the stage for group action, and the precipitous unsupportable firing of staff had rung up the curtain.

Marva's disparaging treatment of workers and their programs escalated rapidly. After just three weeks of her direction, most of the staff agreed that Marva's actions endangered the agency as well as their mental health. Marva might have co-opted some of the workers had her mistreatment been less extreme—if she had, for instance, resisted the urge to fire so many staff in one fell swoop. But agency workers felt the immediacy of the threat at nearly the same time, which enabled them to form a cohesive action group, as we will discuss in detail later in this chapter.

What Would Your Group Look Like?

These glimpses of developing group action may have stimulated your thinking about the potentials for organizing at your own worksite. You may not have the kind of natural group or long-term trusting relationships that were available to the bank bookkeepers or agency workers. But you still might benefit from considering the possibility of group action among your co-workers. Here are some questions to help you decide whether the possibility is worth exploring:

EXERCISE 17A—Can I Form a Group With Co-workers?

1. Who are the people who might join with me in a group action?

_____

2. How much time would I be willing to devote to working with a group?

_____

3. Would group support be enough of a trade-off to forgo some of my individual control over decisions?

_____

_____

4. Might I feel relieved at not having to take all the responsibility for what I do about the abuse?

_____

5. How would I feel about any of the potential group members representing me?

_____

_____

6. If I had reservations about anyone in the group as a spokesperson, could I speak honestly about my doubts?

_____

_____

7. Among possible group members, would anyone be likely to take over decision making without consulting the group? _____ Or insist I take over? _____ Or not do their share? _____

Who? _____

_____

Action Requires Trust

Although the degree of trust necessary varies, organizers must be able to count on each other in some important ways.

Trust issues include confidentiality, carrying out responsibilities and loyalty. Hattie and Tina, as well as other workers at the agency, benefited from well-established relationships. Most of the employees had worked together for years, and similarities in work values enhanced their closeness. They could reasonably well predict how each would operate in a group. Working for a cause larger than themselves fueled the group's passion to "take the agency back." The staff already knew the benefits of teamwork in gaining the confidence of young women wary of almost all social-service agencies. Now they committed themselves to a similar group process to stop Marva's betrayal of that trust.

The staff reached a near consensus about Marva's destructiveness. Only one long-term worker, Bonnie, refused to join the group action against Marva and actively supported her. Most staff viewed Marva's behavior as so outrageous that they had little patience for anyone who remained loyal to her. Feelings of betrayal, sadness and anger made it difficult for some of the advocates to work with Bonnie. Although they tried to respect her, they felt they had to guard against her reports of their activities to Marva, so eventually they severed all but essential communication with her. Had Marva retained many loyalists, the problems of trust and of working together might have taken a much higher toll.

If you and other dissidents don't know each other well, your group may approach decisions more deliberately than this agency staff. You'll require varying periods of time to explore your trust in each other. You will make different decisions on how open to be about your opinions or feelings and which of the group members you'll confide in. Whether to organize only on your own management level or with a group of protesters from different levels of the work hierarchy offers a particular challenge.

Alana, the community college teacher, was asked by her staff what they should do in response to her boss's abuse of the entire department. She said, "I think you have to answer for yourself, because you have your own issues and I intend to think about it for myself." She felt it was "not appropriate to rally them to the cause," though she did discuss her feelings about the abusive process they had all experienced. Zoe, counselor at the agency for people who are hard of hearing and deaf, called a meeting of her staff, encouraged them to take action, and once they organized themselves she withdrew to avoid exercising undue influence.

One person may be trusted to support you emotionally, but not to speak up to the boss. Another may be willing to work with you as long as her job is not on the line. Perhaps she will type a leaflet, but can't be counted on to put her name to it or to keep a secret. Julia, the agency bookkeeper, wanted to support the dissidents without risking loss of her job, so she supplied information. For instance, during a period of frequent firings, she warned Tina she had been instructed to write her severance check. That information enabled Tina to plan her last few days before Marva forced her to leave.

When you think about whom you can trust, consider people as individuals. It won't help to lump all the people of privilege or all of the Others together, as either trustworthy or not. If some of the people on the "other side" of a professional or social status line differ in their values or lifestyle, that doesn't mean they all do. Besides, they might agree with you on certain points even if they differ on others. Think about which individuals might join you regardless of other affiliations. Plan carefully and then make discreet inquiries about people's alignments.

Once you've made preliminary judgments about including particular individuals, you might approach a caucus or other group for joint action or support. How might they help? Do their particular traits or positions present potential hazards to your plans? Who in your organization can act as a bridge to them? The following questions, to be answered by your group, can help you decide whom to include:

EXERCISE 17B: Whom Can We Trust?

1. Which individuals from our level of management/ nonmanagement might join our group to protest abuse? What are the advantages and disadvantages of sticking with people at our own level?

---

2. Which workers on lower or higher levels of the management hierarchy might join us? What are the advantages and disadvantages?

_____

_____

3. If none of us is a supervisor, which supervisors, if any, might we risk recruiting?

_____

4. If the abuse is a form of discrimination against women, people of color, gays or lesbians, older or disabled workers, what are the implications of forming a group consisting only of members of those groups? Which individuals in what groups?

_____

_____

5. How can we decide whether certain workers are really on our side? For instance, what have those in question done in the past to develop our trust?

_____

_____

6. If our actions are open, is it important to rely on others not to discuss the group's discussions? In confidential meetings, who will keep our discussions private and who might not?

_____

_____

7. What might be the benefits and risks of trying to involve other workers in general in our cause?

_____

_____

8. Might workers who aren't asked to join us sabotage our efforts because they feel excluded?

_____

_____

These questions might be answered individually first, then collectively in a group meeting. Each group action may result in members becoming aware of new problems, which will create a potential for shifts in group membership. Keep the questions handy to review as your group's situation changes.

Timing and Support

In Chapter 13 on "shadow organizations," we mentioned police officer Rose Melendez's support group. Melendez also benefited from an officers' group designed to address sexual harassment on the police force. Her story illustrates the importance of timing and administration support.

We developed a professionalism panel—men and women—who had experienced sexual harassment, and now we're providing awareness training. We discuss different types of harassment that occur subtly: the ignoring, the obnoxious comments that aren't meant to be heard by anybody except you. The training is working; it's changing attitudes. It's opened up communication and allowed us to confront the issue. You can say, "Hey, Joe, cool it. I don't like that," and he knows what you mean. Reports of harassment are now heard by the professionalism panel and directed to the chief's attention for disciplinary action, and the number of incidents has slacked off as a result. . . . The administration's behind us, and I think our efforts are improving working conditions for everyone on the force.

Melendez's group had several advantages in reducing harassment. First was support: male officers who were ridiculed by colleagues for affirming women co-workers, refused to be intimidated into abetting the harassment. Instead, they cooperated in the campaign to decrease hostility toward women officers. Second was timing: administrators previously tolerant of sexual harassment had increased their understanding of the problem and made a commitment to stop it. Third was a potential trade-off: the committee benefited from the administration's awareness that reforms furthered its own interests.

Officer Cheryl Gomez-Preston of the Detroit Police Department, endured a markedly different situation. As we mentioned in Chapter 3 on sexual harassment, her appeal to her supervisor to stop gender- and race-based mistreatment by co-workers met with worse treatment. The supervisor stated that he wanted sex with her in exchange for helping to stop the abuse. Officers who had staunchly stood by her at an earlier period now refused to join her in confronting the administration or co-workers. They wouldn't even hear her out. Her best choice, finally, was to resign. An uncooperative administration, hostile colleagues and unfortunate timing all contributed to making group action impossible.

EXERCISE 17C: Is the Timing Right?

Your group might be justified in insisting that a particular person or system immediately stop abuse of workers. If you're organized and geared to act soon, and participants begin to question the timing of the risks you plan to take, you might feel disheartened. As each individual weighs her personal alternatives, the group as a whole can consider these questions:

1. Will working as a group put enough pressure on administration to act on our complaints, even though they didn't respond to us as individuals?

---

2. Will personnel shifts or other planned reorganization give us a better hearing later than the current possibility? If so, what are the expected improvements and how will they help us?

---

3. What are the best and worst results that can happen if we act now?

---

4. What are the best and worst results that can happen if we wait?

Group Assertive Action

Who speaks for the group? Administrators often prefer to negotiate with one leader. Yet one person designated as spokesperson or representative may gradually convince herself that she holds the power. That belief could develop into a self-fulfilling prophecy if others equate "spokesperson" with "leader." When one woman has access to most of the important information, that knowledge gives her the tools to make decisions. The more decisions she makes, the more control she can exercise.

Some groups have found that rotating the representative job among several people encourages a democratic process and group trust. However, that system produces complex problems. Once a particular organizational system has become established, the group may resist switching to a different way of operating. So try to make an early and thoughtful decision about whether to organize along traditional hierarchical lines or with shared leadership.

Practice the same principles for group confrontation that you learned to use in taking individual action. Speak or act straightforwardly, with respect for yourselves and the other person. Plan precisely and rehearse each participant's part in the expected interaction. During your group practice session, pay attention to how each person delivers her message, as well as to its content. Give each other honest and supportive feedback.

Rehearse as a group how to handle all the possibilities you can imagine. Groups lack the flexibility of an individual who can switch her approach on the spot if necessary. Unless you rehearse all probabilities, your spokesperson may not be certain how best to represent the group in unpredictable circumstances. During a confrontation with a powerful person, if each of several representatives reacts individually to his offers of compromise, confusion and embarrassment may quickly follow. You risk erosion of your sense of solidarity and trust. The opposite problem arises if only one of you wants to negotiate and the other two disagree with such a move, but hesitate to expose your differences to someone in power. If the two who dissent from the third don't speak up, they hand over power to the one who wants to make an agreement on the spot. You can minimize these potential problems by choosing one spokesperson.

When you give power to just one representative, agree ahead of time on the limits of her negotiations for the group. You may decide that unless the person you're appealing to accedes to all your demands, your spokesperson will take all proposals back to the whole group for its collective decision. Representatives won't be empowered to make compromises in the name of the group. In addition, if one or two others accompany the person authorized to speak for the group, their presence may remind her of exactly what she's been empowered to say. If she makes a critical error, the others can say, "Excuse me, but I think we'd better take this issue back to the group." This kind of challenge should be built into your practice sessions. When witnesses to the interaction report back to the larger group, three people can present a richer perspective on what happened. Like other guidelines in this book, use these suggestions when they work and substitute your own alternatives when appropriate.

Staff Takes Action

As we saw earlier, individual workers at the agency for young women appealed unsuccessfully to certain board members for relief from Marva's abuse. By their third independent staff meeting, facing the failure of cooperation and confrontation to create change, the staff upped the ante. They agreed to attend the next board of directors meeting to state their case, including a nonnegotiable insistence that the board fire Marva.

The group designated one person to state that demand, backed up with specific facts about Marva's behavior. In addition all staff were encouraged to speak about their own experiences or observations within certain guidelines. Each person was encouraged to "appeal to the hard-core practical, not the emotional." Some workers did exactly that, while others became emotional. At least one woman cried, comparing Marva's treatment with an earlier traumatic experience of having immigration papers "flung in the garbage." Since each spoke only for herself, such variations were acceptable. Board members indicated their impatience with the procedure by periodic suggestions that they move on to other agenda items, an attitude Tina described as saying, in effect, " 'Thank you for sharing. Next item please.' "

When the workers later asked for help from a county coalition of juvenile probation officers and youth groups, they used the same system of each person speaking from her personal perspective.

Tina agreed to speak, in spite of her fear of directly confronting Marva in a public arena. She says:

> *I felt like a woman going into court to face her batterer. Marva wasn't playing by any rules I knew. She was devious, slippery. I could never get my hands on the smoke. I don't know how to live like that. In my mind, only two people would be there: her and me. I wouldn't be able to defend myself.*

To prepare, Tina spent time with a good friend and carefully planned what she would say. In spite of her misgivings, she later felt pleased that she had "mustered up the strength" to speak.

Hattie also had misgivings before the meeting with the coalition. Members of the coalition, reluctant to take an active role in censuring Marva, listened guardedly while Hattie spoke of the isolation, secrecy, lack of group process, canceled management meetings and insults. "Sounds like abuse to me!" someone said. "That just broke it," Hattie says.

The coalition membership decided that Marva's mistreatment constituted "abuse in the workplace" and agreed to consider action, but delayed for a month their decision on exactly what to do. All of the staff messages had come across powerfully in the two situations. Had the group engaged in complicated negotiations with the board or coalition, a less individualized, more controlled approach might have been necessary.

The staff decided to direct its appeal to a new audience. They began a campaign to inform as many social agencies and funders as possible of the problems Marva had created. Each worker spoke to as many people as she could, depending on time available and which people she knew. Staff agreed generally on what message to convey. "We're in crisis. You may have read about it in the paper," they would begin. But they left the style of delivery and details to each worker.

Over time the staff learned that colleagues in other agencies responded most readily to the key words, "fired in secrecy." Funders were galvanized into action when they heard, "We're not in compliance with grant regulations." This plan called for a high degree of initiative and trust, and it worked. It required minimal formal organization and little meeting time to distribute responsibilities. The community responded with letters of inquiry and requests for accountability from the board.

When Trust is a Question

In another organization, where workers don't know each other well, you might assign tasks more formally, with more time to spell out expectations for each participant and to check back often on progress. Grace, a public school teacher, organized leadership at her junior high school to protest the central school administration's racial discrimination against teachers and students. The initial meeting brought enthusiastic cooperation of teachers and other staff. Then before the newly formed protest group had time to think about what steps to take next, eight other schools spontaneously asked to join.

Many teachers in the enlarged group didn't know each other, so they lacked the trust and understanding of workers at the agency for young women. In addition, members of the new group represented a wide variety of cultures, ethnicity and class background, which brought potential mistrust and misunderstanding. So it was important that elected leaders formally divided the tasks of writing position papers, contacting the press and calling parents, with scrupulous attention to equal division of responsibilities. Committees drew up a group statement to present to the school board and another for the superintendent, both subject to approval of the entire group. Spokespeople, authorized by participants as a whole, spoke publicly only about what was agreed upon by the entire group.

A union or professional organization may offer help but restrict what your leadership can publicly state or negotiate. Their organizers could offer to "relieve" your group of the leadership role. At worst, they might show more interest in building their own organization than in your immediate problems. One union representative advocated well for Jessica, the East Indian nurse. But later a hospital administrator insisted that a "union liaison" hired by the hospital take over the role of representing her, in place of the real union man. Knowing the hospital would try to force her to take "administrative leave," Jessica asked the assigned liaison what he thought of such a plan. When he said it was fine, she realized he would not help. Matter-of-factly she said to him, "Then I don't think you will be representing me." That was that. She later was represented by a lawyer.

Be sure your entire group agrees at least on the principles for negotiating (or not negotiating) with the person in power. The group can also decide whether the representatives will conciliate, be tough or take a stance somewhere in between. The designated representative can then rehearse the expected interactions with a few group members. Or two or three people chosen to speak for the group can practice what to do in the event of differences of opinion or unexpected offers from the person confronted. A review of Assertiveness Guidelines and evaluation questions will help them give each other feedback.

Community Action

Confrontation often begins at the local level, when a worker tells an abusive person, "This offends me. I want you to stop it now." The next step is to appeal to someone at a higher level or to speak to the same person again, this time with several co-workers. If these approaches to higher administrators or a board of directors doesn't bring the desired results, you and your colleagues may turn to an outside agency.

If you work in a profit-making business, ask a licensing or monitoring bureau, such as a real estate association to censure the offending party. It may not see its role as doing exactly what you want, but perhaps you can persuade it to make an exception. You don't need a union to publicize your cause to customers, the local press or the public through pickets or even direct mail. In some instances a forceful group threatening to inform pertinent people might cause administration to negotiate.

Filipino workers at a public hospital complained to their union about being denied use of their native language, Tagalog, and the union eventually mounted a county-wide public campaign on their behalf. But intervention by city and county governments, as well as by Asian and Latino organizations and newspapers, ultimately succeeded in winning them a number of their demands.

From Individual to Community Action

The agency Marva directed offers an example of progression from individual workers trying to handle abuse individually, to confronting the director as a group, then broadening their campaign to the board of directors, newspapers, funders and a county organization. They could not predict what would occur at each step. When agency workers asked the county coalition, to help resolve their problems with Marva, coalition members resisted involvement at first, not seeing such a role as their responsibility. However, once they understood the magnitude of the situation, they agreed to expand their previous responsibilities by holding a hearing. Agency staff shifted tactics and goals according to what was needed at each stage of their campaign. Although some activities overlapped with each other, if staff actions and reactions were charted, they would look something like this:

The group:

1. Made individual requests for change; Marva didn't comply.

2. Instituted informal staff program to educate Marva on agency philosophy; she didn't seem to understand.

3. Held staff meeting to plan agenda for appealing, as a group, to Marva; Marva responded with shouts, insults, new restrictions.

4. Began appeal to board of directors with new demand that Marva must go; board didn't listen.

5. Informed funders and referring agencies of agency disarray, funding noncompliance and Marva's abuse; referrals fell off, but funders didn't act.

6. Several employees resigned en masse; no effect.

7. Called press; board and Marva responded defensively to negative newpaper articles.

8. Appealed to a coalition of probation and youth agencies, which agreed to a hearing.

9. When criticism and protests from funders, community agencies and newspapers mounted, the board finally demanded Marva's resignation.

Parallel to these escalating decisions and actions, each worker wrestled with her own personal action plan. Some decided that "if X happens, I'll quit." Others said to themselves, "I'm going to speak up about this, or refuse to do that, and if I'm fired, so be it." During a period of three months several individuals resigned as well as one group of eight people who left en masse after handing the board a written protest.

The board had ignored the staff's individual and group appeals, but ultimately too much pressure descended on them from too many sources. They couldn't ignore bad press notices, falling referrals, questions from funders and the resignations or firings of over three-fourths of the staff. The agency limped along with new, undefined programs, untrained staff, low morale and few rebels to continue the struggle from within. Working more and more outside the agency, staff members had appealed to virtually every source of power available in their community. There was nowhere else to turn.

But the hard work paid off. Under pressure from all sides, Marva reluctantly complied with the board's formal request for her resignation. During the next few months an interim director rehired most of the old staff, who then began the hard job of rebuilding relationships with each other, new employees, young women clients, the board and community agencies. Wounds to the agency and the staff did not heal quickly. Board and staff members and clients continued to suffer the pains and stress brought on by disruption of services and relationships. But all are relieved that the injuries to the agency have not been lethal, and they now have reason to hope for recovery. None of the staff members doubts the necessity and value of her commitment to stop the abuse and save the agency.

When the Group Changes

Your group of protesters against abuse could remain small and informally organized or it could develop into an ongoing support, problem-solving or political action group. If your original interest was only in a short-term commitment to resolve an immediate problem, you might have second thoughts about continuing your involvement. Shifts in the purpose and size of the group might unnerve you. They may not represent what you expected at first. But the new situation could provide even more satisfaction than your original plan.

The expansion of group purposes calls for a review of your

original goals. It may require new decisions about whether to enlarge or compromise those goals, attempt to change the group, or try a new tactic on your own. As you review those choices, you can also consider other options: working with unions, beginning a lawsuit or appealing to human rights agencies.

Chapter 18

Collective Action

Go with your instincts if you think something's wrong. You wouldn't feel funny if it wasn't something. If you don't feel confident by yourself to protest, use a co-worker or a union. You can be part of change, to make a better society, to build your self-esteem, to tell yourself who you are.

Marlene Pedregosa, union organizer

So far this book has focused on how you might confront your boss or co-worker alone or with a group of co-workers. Now, we move to broader arenas—more formal organizing through unions and, in the next chapter, the legal system. Although you may not proceed all the way, some steps included here can be useful in challenging work abuse.

Many women have improved their work conditions by organizing through unions or by using the law. Moreover, the process of striving to change unjust systems changes the activists themselves. They become more self-confident, more certain about their rights and less likely to tolerate abuse of any kind. That's the theme of this chapter: Organizing may bring important practical results and the change in you may be extraordinary.

Labor unions, legislators and judges have not yet put emotional abuse on their agendas. But sexual harassment in the workplace didn't gain a place on anyone's agenda until the late 1970s. Now, several important Supreme Court decisions and state and federal laws uphold women's rights to be free of sexual harassment. We believe emotional abuse at work can become the next frontier of public acknowledgment.

For example, the office workers' union, 9 to 5, has broken new ground by bringing formerly private issues to the level of public debate. Respect and dignity for the woman worker is the first item on the union's Bill of Rights, preceding salary or promotion opportunities. This union has made public issues of the longstanding private complaints of women office workers, complaints such as making the coffee at work, doing personal errands for the boss or being personally humiliated. Regardless of what work you do, if you think someone acts unfairly, whether the action is illegal or not, 9 to 5 leaders want you to "hang on to your outrage." Emotional abuse is on their list of "wrongs," even if not yet illegal.

Making emotional abuse a serious public issue will require much effort by many people. But before you get discouraged about that, let's consider other workplace changes that have come about by public protest and the hard work of many.

In the United States until the mid-1930s, these workers' benefits were non-existent:

- health benefits
- safety regulations
- a minimum hourly wage
- paid sick leaves
- pensions
- paid vacations

A ten- or eleven-hour workday was standard, as was a six-day week. And that's only a partial list. Changes occurred because people struggled for them collectively, often in labor unions. Now we take these benefits for granted.

What You Gain in Organizing

Whether you choose small or large groups, unions or professional organizations, there are some clear advantages to joining with others when you have grievances.

Multiplying Your Clout

A group of legal secretaries, each with at least eight years of seniority, learned that newly hired secretaries earned nearly as much as they. They held a number of meetings, gathered information about salary levels at other firms, and together, presented their findings and their complaint to the senior law partners. The partners agreed to pay them fairly and to change the method of determining salaries. One of the women later said: "If we'd gone in individually, we'd have gotten nowhere."

A manager can easily dismiss your complaint when you're the only person confronting him. You may have filed individual grievances for weeks or months with no success. But a group of workers with documented complaints can't be so easily ignored.

You and other women, working together, can articulate your complaints and make an impact. In addition, you learn how to strategize, run meetings and take action to deal with abuse.

If you leaf through the yellow pages of a telephone directory, under the heading "Associations," you'll find page after page of organizations formed by groups protecting their own interests. People in all fields use these formal associations for their own benefit. Many of them wield tremendous political power.

Your boss may belong to the Chamber of Commerce or the National Association of Manufacturers or a number of other associations. He uses those organizations to protect the interests of the company and his status in it. Large organizations have lobbyists in state legislatures and Congress, solely to advance their own interests.

Why shouldn't women workers do the same? In fact, if your boss or supervisor is annoyed that you formed or joined some kind of organization instead of addressing the issue of abuse on a personal level with him, you might keep in mind (or even tell him) that you assume he also uses organizations because of their effectiveness.

You may get to know and appreciate people at work better as you deal with common problems. You find that you and other women at work can articulate your own complaints and strategies, and make an impact. You develop skills you never thought you possessed.

But Organizing Is Not For Me

Like other women, you may have reservations about organizing to protest mistreatment at work. Do some of the following sound familiar to you?

- I'm afraid I'll be fired if I do this.
- This just doesn't fit with my self-image. I don't have the self-confidence to speak out, especially for myself.
- Personal relationships at work are more important to me than the work I do. I don't want to take the chance that those relationships will change.
- I don't want to offend anyone. Women are supposed to behave like ladies.
- My husband (or partner or family) won't like this idea at all. They certainly won't like it if I attend meetings after work.
- If I get involved in anything like this, it will upset the precarious balance I'm managing now between my family and my work.
- I only work part-time so I'm not a regular part of the company.
- I think my boss really has my best interests at heart.
- I know women get put down generally. That's life. I never thought of this as a reason to protest.

Despite such misgivings, many women have decided to organize with others. They generally find that the reasons for their initial reluctance fade in importance, though they may still be of concern from time to time. In the long run, the benefits of collective action become clear, especially in increased awareness of your right to respect at work.

You may believe that unions are mainly for factory workers, office staff or women in the trades. But the successes of teachers, nurses and other recently organized professionals may change your ideas about the appropriateness of unions for you.

Before a nurses' union in Washington state called a strike in 1989, many of the nurses had been apprehensive about taking such a stand. They were worried about losing their jobs. Then they checked and found that other jobs did exist for them. They also worried about the anger of doctors, but they overcame that fear. Although they had been trained to be compliant with doctors, they believed they had a right to protest their valid grievances. And they did so successfully. Later, many of the nurses said that working collectively for change was the most significant action they had ever undertaken.

Perhaps you've joined groups at other times in your life—a tenants' organization or a group protesting a school-board action, for instance. That may have seemed acceptable because it would benefit your children or the whole family, rather than yourself primarily. Maybe now is the time to consider what you need at work.

Getting Started

When you and your colleagues have identified a common problem of mistreatment and think beyond your particular situation, you see that the organization or the broader system constitutes the problem. Now you are ready to consider formal collective action.

The small groups we described in Chapter 17 may prove useful as you choose among a number of alternatives for more formal action.

A "New Girls" Network

You can organize a women's network, drawing from all levels of your workplace, including management and front-line employees. Since abuse strikes women at all levels and in all jobs, a coalition of women across levels can be an advantage. Women with more power in the organization can use their additional leverage to bring an issue to the attention of higher management as a company-wide concern.

If you're not in management yourself, you also need to be alert to any drawbacks of including management women in your network. Some of those women managers may themselves be perpetrators of abuse and of course, you'd be wary of them. Also, women managers may have dual loyalties. They may feel caught between loyalty and obligations to their bosses and concern about women at all levels in the company. They may fear that siding with other women will interfere with their climb up the organizational ladder. This conflict could prevent them from acting on the network's agenda. If you are a manager yourself, you need to consider how you will manage this dilemma. Thinking this through beforehand can help you to act with integrity.

Many women have organized networks with others in the same type of work. For example, the American Society of Women Accountants, headquartered in Memphis, Tennessee and with local chapters nationwide, provides both formal and informal ways for women accountants to share expertise as well as workplace problems. You may be able to tie into a similar network in your line of work.

You can call in other outside resources to aid you in your efforts. For example, 9 to 5, the women's clerical union, will plan workshops for your group to provide information about useful strategies for improving personnel policies. (The union's hotline number is 1-800-522-0925). You don't have to be a member of 9 to 5 or even a clerical worker to request that service.

When the Network Becomes Official

Many women have found they can be effective as a formal group, short of union organizing. Some of these women had never taken part in organizing efforts. Joan Sharpe had been employed at the Schlage Lock Company in North Carolina for many years. Eighty percent of the workers at the plant were African-American women like herself. When the company moved its operations to Mexico in 1987, Sharpe joined a group of fired workers to protest the lack of severance pay and other benefits extended to management but not to workers. The group made their case to various governmental agencies. As a result, the company acceded to several important demands, including severance pay. Joan Sharpe said of the experience:

> *Most of us came right out of high school to work for Schlage. This was our first experience at educating ourselves about worker rights. BWFJ [Black Workers for Justice] showed me that in a nonunion workplace people can fight.*

Perhaps you will meet with women in your department or on your shift at lunch in the company cafeteria or after work at someone's home. At the start, these meetings may occur spontaneously as problems arise. Later, they may become regularly scheduled. You carefully document instances of emotional abuse experienced by women, keeping written records. Later, your group may make formal complaints to management. The group keeps going to deal with other issues as they come up. Management begins to take your group seriously. Sometimes such groups become "employee advisory councils" with a semi-official standing.

Unionizing as a Strategy

Fifteen percent of women workers as a whole and forty-three percent of both women and men who work in government agencies are union members now. Unions are the strongest form of worker organization because, once they are recognized, the employer must negotiate with union representatives.

You and your co-workers may even start a union. That may seem like an outragous idea to you now, but someone started the unions that we accept as established today. You could be that someone tomorrow.

Ellen Cassedy and Karen Nussbaum, two clerk-typists, founded 9 to 5, the office workers' union. They tell their story:

For us, it began when we were twenty years old and clerk-typists at Harvard University. One day Karen was staggering down the hall carrying a load of doctoral dissertations. "Why aren't you smiling, dear?" asked a passing professor with a wink. Another day, Ellen's boss ceremoniously placed a note on her desk before disappearing back into his office. "Please remove calendar from my wall," it said. Ellen went to his office, unstuck two pieces of masking tape from the calendar, and put it on his desk. Why had he wasted time ordering her to do something that he could have done himself in ten seconds? Then, one afternoon a young male student came into our office. Standing in front of Karen and looking directly at her, he asked, "Isn't anyone here?" At that moment, we realized what it was that our working lives lacked. It was respect.

This happened in 1972. Next, Nussbaum and Cassedy attended a workshop for women office workers where women listed their grievances. Many of those complaints dealt with lack of respect. Ten women from that workshop produced a newsletter, which they distributed to women office workers in the Boston area. When a memo about the group appeared in a business journal, the women received 3,000 calls and letters from secretaries throughout the country. In a few months, they had founded what has since become a national association, affiliated with Service Employees International Union (SEIU).

Now titled SEIU District 925, the association maintains a clear orientation to women's concerns, resisting the male leadership approach of many mainstream unions. And it all started with two women fed up by the lack of respect shown them as office workers.

When Management Gets in the Way

If you take organized action with others at work, you will probably face management objections. Managers or heads of companies clearly prefer to deal with workers one at a time in order to "divide and conquer." Managers maximize their control to discourage organized activity using tactics ranging from personal persuasion to illegal and threatening intimidation. For example, Darlene, a hospital licensed practical nurse and union representative, was threatened with firing if she brought union materials to work.

In some situations, rigid control of worker activities inhibits organizing efforts. Supervisors in an electronics factory in Massachusetts monitored the women much more closely than the men, which made it very hard for the women to get together and discuss their grievances.

In another instance, initial organizing by women workers was seen as a threat to an insurance company in Wisconsin. Managers staggered workers' coffee breaks and lunch hours and monitored phone calls. They even followed women workers into the bathrooms. In any way they could, they tried to prevent the women from planning any protest activities. Despite these obstacles, the women successfully formed their union.

Sometimes management tries to foster friendly relations between supervisors and workers by making the workplace appear democratic. Supervisors are encouraged to consult with employees and include them in decision-making. You might think such an arrangement gives you more autonomy and improves your work situation. But a problem arises if this "friendly" supervisor mistreats employees. Challenging abuse in that situation becomes more difficult since you might believe even a legitimate complaint could disturb the "democratic" arrangements.

Sometimes nonprofit organizations, specifically designed to do public good, treat their own women employees with disrespect, including intimidations and insults. But the employees may feel in a bind because they view those who run the organization as "nice, dedicated people," often underpaid and overworked themselves. It seems harder to object to mistreatment when it comes from someone who otherwise appears concerned about people in the community.

Changing the "Old Boys'" Unions

By listing unions as an avenue for action, we don't want to give the false impression that appropriate unions are always available to workers, or that all unions welcome the active participation of women. Unions, by and large, have not paid attention to the special concerns of women. For example, child care, family leave policies and flexible work schedules have not been high on most unions' agendas. Also, few women achieve visible leadership positions in unions. Although more women fill union roles than ever before, many women remain skeptical about the possibility of unions serving their interest.

A beautician recalls her encounter with the "beauticians' union":

> *The only union representing beauticians in the area . . . is officially called the Journeymen Barbers, Hairdressers, Cosmetologists and Proprietor's International Union of America. Note the barbers come first. And note proprietors. I am genuinely taken aback.*

When the beautician talked with the head of the union, a proprietor of a barber shop, he told her he saw nothing wrong with owners and workers being part of the same union. He acknowledged that barbers make up ninety-seven percent of the union, and that most are barber-shop owners. He also admitted that barbers earn about thirty percent more than beauticians. Still he didn't see anything wrong with that:

> *We don't try to justify it, but we do have different contracts for barbers and beauticians, and the barbers, yes, are guaranteed more. But they are men after all, they have families to support.*

Although this beautician saw little advantage in joining that union, union attitudes may change because the composition of the work force is changing rapidly as more women enter jobs. Women constitute the greatest number of new workers each year and continue to join unions in increasing numbers. In 1968, nineteen percent of union members (or people represented by unions) were women. By 1989, that proportion had risen to forty-seven percent. Currently, unions feel pressed to attend to women's needs; more national unions have established departments of women's affairs.

Women's Unions Aren't New

Women have secured an important place in the history of labor-union activism. Though not all their efforts succeeded, knowing what women have achieved shows us their capability and courage in the face of difficult circumstances. Working with others, you might add to this impressive history.

• In the 1830s, young women—the "Mill Girls"—went on strike in the New England textile mills to protest the twelve-hour, six-day week.

• In the 1920s, 26,000 textile workers, eighty percent of them women, waged a successful strike.

• In the 1930s, African-American and white women formed the United Laundry Workers Union and joined men workers in the Food and Tobacco Workers Union. They gained pay increases that doubled their wages.

• In 1936, African-American women formed a domestic workers union. They demanded and received a triple increase in wages and more respectful treatment from their employers.

• In 1938, Chinese women in the garment industry organized their own chapter of the International Ladies Garment Workers Union and gained higher salaries and better working conditions.

• In 1974, 3,000 women union members founded the Coalition of Labor Union Women (CLUW) to advance the interests of women workers. By 1992, CLUW membership had increased tenfold.

• In 1992, women's labor unions and other women's groups joined a coalition of other community organizations and succeeded in getting a bill passed in the Georgia legislature on family and medical leaves for state employees.

This is just a partial list of women's union activities and successes. In a number of instances, white women and women of color struggled in the same battle. They forged alliances that broke through long-held prejudices about each other.

Organizing Brings Strength

Organized, public activity can benefit women by providing an increased sense of personal power. A clerical worker in a Wisconsin insurance company described her experience when she went on strike with other workers:

Before the strike, I would have done whatever I was told, not thinking I had the right to say otherwise.... Now I realize that ... if you are not getting treated equally and fairly, you do have the right to say otherwise.... I learned not to be afraid.... [Before] I felt like I was stepping on pins and needles all the time.... I learned I didn't have to take that anymore.

Dian Murphy, an African-American flight attendant who had been raped found herself threatened with a job dismissal when she couldn't meet her usual flight schedule the morning following the rape. She later addressed 12,000 union members, civil rights activists, senior citizens and others at a Jobs for Justice rally in Miami and said:

It's very difficult to stand here and talk to you about what's happened to me.... I have lost so very much and to have Eastern Airlines further humiliate me and try to take away my dignity is appalling. I was victimized twice: once by a rapist and once by my employer.... And I refuse to continue to be a victim.

In Wilmar, Minnesota, eight women bank tellers challenged sex discrimination at their bank from 1977 to 1979. They objected to low pay and grew tired of training men to become their supervisors. These women never thought of themselves as union members. After they made initial complaints, the bank's management subjected them to serious harassment. Angry at such abuse, the women formed a small union and went on strike.

Some family members objected strenuously to their activities. But these women, joined by many others in the community, formed strong bonds and bolstered their resolve. They walked a picket line in front of the bank for years, even during long winters in temperatures of sixty-degrees below freezing. Many people in the community withdrew their bank deposits in sympathy.

Although their strike gained national publicity and some support from government agencies, the women lost the strike and their jobs. Only one was later reinstated. The image of these ordinary/extraordinary women struggling for their rights in the freezing weather remained in the minds of other women years after their campaign was over. The women themselves speak of the personal benefits of the experience:

> *When asked whether the strike was a mistake, one of the women, probably speaking for all of them, replied: "No, I'd do it all over again. I really grew up and learned the meaning of responsibility. I have a new perspective on life."*

Analyzing the Willmar experience, Joseph Amato, an historian, added:

> *Women whose work was valued only slightly above the minimum wage discovered they could lecture in college classrooms and address rallies; they could negotiate with bankers, politicians, and union chiefs. . . . [T]hey could organize a union, run a publicity campaign and conduct a strike by themselves. . . . They have acquired a dignity denied them at work.*

These women dramatically changed their attitudes about what they were willing to tolerate. They became strengthened by association with others who understood indignities or injustices in the workplace. They moved from passivity to a more self-respecting attitude.

Going Beyond the Obstacles

Women at an electronics plant responded to a union call to attend union meetings and made three discoveries: 1) their own particular mistreatment—including low pay—was related to their status as women, 2) some of their problems were the same as those of the male workers, and 3) the plant had no formal procedures for dealing with grievances.

Some of the women's husbands tried to stop them from organizing. One woman's boyfriend would not allow her to appear in public without him and he refused to accompany her to union meetings. The husband of another woman threatened her with abuse if she participated in organizing activities at work. These two women learned to handle abuse at both home and work in creative ways. Though they did not attend formal meetings, they each assumed leadership roles inside the plant during working hours.

Their activities and those of other women paid off. When an election was held, the majority of workers voted to be represented by the union. Furthermore, women joined the union in equal proportions to men.

A group of unionized women workers in an insurance office in Wisconsin devised creative ways to share information and discuss their plans for a possible strike despite management opposition. The company had placed the women in separate carrels to deter their efforts. Out of sight of the supervisors, the women used the phones to develop strike plans with their co-workers. As part of the same effort, the women responsible for mail delivery carried news of the latest organizing efforts between departments. These strategies helped the women develop and maintain a consensus about their activities.

When some of their husbands objected to the women's attendance at meetings, the women used carpool time and night-time phone calls to attend to the organizing efforts. They held some of their meetings at lunchtime or coffee breaks. On the afternoon before the strike vote, these office workers learned that two male negotiators for the parent union had accepted a management proposal without the needed approval of the women's bargaining unit. The union women voted unanimously to proceed with the strike.

During the strike, the fifty-three union women developed strong ties with their co-workers. "As the strike progressed," one woman recalled, "the issue became not only gaining a good contract but also protecting my friends."

The women felt they needed to challenge management's attitude that "we were just a bunch of dumb little women who didn't know what we were doing." Their challenge succeeded. As a consequence of the strike, the new contract included improved grievance procedure language and strong union input into work rules.

In each of these situations, women used creative strategies to improve their working conditions and gained a greater sense of personal power.

The film, *Salt of the Earth,* based on a 1951 strike at a silver mine, highlights the women's important roles in the strike efforts. But many husbands and boyfriends resented the women's activities and assertiveness. In the film, one woman says to her husband:

> *Have you learned nothing from this strike? Why are you afraid to have me at your side? Do you still think you can have dignity if I have none? . . . Why must you say to me, "Stay in your place." Do you feel better having someone lower than you? . . . I want to rise. And push everything up with me as I go.*

Changing Yourself and *the Workplace*

Women have acted collectively to change their work conditions and themselves in another arena. In Washington state, women involved in the fight for comparable worth helped secure more money for many women state employees. And these women also became more self-confident, more certain their work was valuable. They developed a strong sense of their own power to change systems. Here's a brief background of their activities.

The well-known slogan, Equal Pay for Equal Work, means that two people doing the same job should earn a similar salary. Proponents of "comparable worth" maintain that very different jobs can also be equated by using such criteria as the amount of training needed and the extent of the employee's responsibilities. Thus, people doing very different jobs would earn similar pay. Take two employees at a hospital: a male ambulance driver and a female nurse's aide. Although their jobs appear quite different, evaluations show these two employees have the same degree of responsibility and training. The two jobs would then receive the same basic pay rate. Women would benefit: since drivers traditionally have earned more than nurses' aides, the aide's salary would probably increase.

Many people believe that such comparisons aren't really possible, but private companies have been making these comparisons for years. They develop their own salary structure that way.

Although comparable worth has been implemented in several states and in many cities and municipalities, it still remains controversial. However, it represents another example of how laws can change women's work situation. Being paid a low salary for "women's work" is not inevitable.

An office workers' union, representing many of the clerical employees at a university in Washington state, increased its membership dramatically when it entered the comparable worth effort in the 1970s and 1980s. Because of the union's involvement in that issue, many women joined who had never belonged to unions. Organizers found that the comparable worth issue seemed "to touch a chord in every woman and many women responded with a 'gut level' sense to the unfairness of their salaries."

Many of these women did things they never thought they could do.

- One woman lobbied legislators. She had never done anything like that and felt intimidated the first time. But the next time and the time after that, she spoke her mind clearly.
- Women created slogans to describe their feelings about their work. The buttons said, "We're Worth It" and "I'm an Office Worker and Proud of It."
- Women reported the excitement that came from within when they knew they had become instrumental in achieving an important change for women. They knew they were part of the political effort that increased salaries for underpaid state employees.
- With the success of comparable worth, union members felt emboldened to take on other issues. Women were galvanized to fight for equitable treatment as well as for pay and promotion. As a result, the preamble to the union's current contract with the university contains a declaration of the

right to dignity and respect.

• Since the successful fight, a union leader commented, "You never hear women say: 'I'm just a secretary' anymore."

In the process of developing political skills, women became less tolerant of abuse on the job.

Maybe Organizing is For Me

Here's another list to think about—this time a list of reasons *for* considering organized action.

• If I decided to join a union, I might earn as much as thirty-three percent more than I do now. (That's the average wage difference between union and non-union women workers.)

• Our group might receive official status as a union and maybe get our grievances heard.

• I might develop skills I never imagined I had.

• Other people in my family and at work have benefited from unions.

• A union or any other formal group might give me the added impetus to fight abuse at work. Then I'd be under less stress.

If you consider becoming involved in collective action at work, you may believe that you and other women don't know enough about how to organize. When you look at most workplaces, and notice who's on top, it's easy to overvalue men's organizational skills.

Yet the nature of women's lives can prove useful as they organize with others. When women use their caregiving traits in organizing groups, they can become very effective leaders. Listening to the concerns of others, they often compromise creatively and retain unwavering commitments to the issues at hand and to others in the group. Women often need to meet many demands in their daily lives. These same experiences tend to develop sensitivity to many kinds of people. This can be a clear advantage when you're working in groups.

In conjunction with collective action or instead of that route, you may decide to take your complaint about emotional abuse to an outside agency or to the courts. The next chapter focuses on those alternatives.

Chapter 19

Using the Law and Government Agencies

I would do the trial again if I had to. I'm a stronger person. And I now stand up for myself. And there are now signs all over the campus about sexual harassment. They are taking it seriously because they got socked with a lawsuit.

Kimberley Abbott, cosmetologist

Sometimes the alternatives for confronting abuse that you've considered so far just don't work well enough. You may have talked with your friends or co-workers about your frustration. Maybe some of them have said: "Sue the creep!" or "Take him to the Human Rights Commission," or "Get the EEOC after her." Others might be cynical about any public agency following through on your claim; some may caution you about going to court.

How do you decide? Some lawsuits have brought rewarding results. Both through private attorneys and public agencies, women have won considerable financial settlements for the abuse they've endured. But seeking justice through government agencies or the courts is no easy task. It may mean months or even years of waiting while the process unfolds. Sometimes the results can be disappointing. Like accepting the need for surgery, you know it will be a painful experience. But often a cure for the illness awaits you at the end.

This chapter doesn't provide a step-by-step description of how you make a claim through an outside agency or through the courts. Instead we describe the major aspects of that process, how you can get more information and how you can prepare yourself for the procedures. Knowing more about making a formal complaint to official agencies, including the time and effort it takes, gives you the tools to decide whether you want to start the process.

We discuss public agencies, such as the U.S. Equal Employment Opportunity Commission and state human rights commissions. Also, we explore the process of going to court and give examples of women who have used both these strategies successfully.

You can use public agencies or the courts because laws have been passed by the U.S. Congress and state legislatures to protect the rights of workers. The right to work without being subjected to sexual harassment is an example of a newly won right. Although the term, "sexual harassment," was coined only in 1976, lawmakers and the courts now view sexual harassment as illegal sex discrimination. Emotional abuse is more difficult to prove in and out of courts, but women have won such claims.

As a woman, you can make a formal complaint about either of two kinds of personal abuse:

1. Sexual harassment
2. Sex-based harassment

Sexual harassment refers to the kinds of sexual behavior discussed in Chapter 3. If men at work tease you sexually, persistently ask you for dates, tell sexy jokes or physically touch you, that's illegal sexual harassment.

"Sex-based" harassment refers to mistreatment that does not have a sexual context but that targets you because of your female status. These sex-based abuses have also been outlawed. In sex-based harassment, you have to prove that someone emotionally abused you because of your gender. So if your boss or co-workers, whether they are women or men, threaten and demean male employees as well as you, they have not broken the law. But if they emotionally abuse you but not male employees, they have violated the law. The same holds true if someone mistreats you because of your race, age or disability.

The First Steps

Preparations for reporting to outside agencies are similar to those for confronting your boss or co-worker:

1. Talk to your potential support group. Explain what you are thinking of doing. Get specific commitments from as many people as possible. These people may not be the same ones you recruited to help you confront the boss. If you plan a lawsuit, some people may be afraid of being subpoenaed and reluctant to testify in court for you. Others will be pleased that you intend to take more official action.

Certain people will believe you need only a union or professional organization working for you. Maybe friends and co-workers offered to support you before, but now they suffer "burnout" or think you are going to extremes on the issue. On the other hand, some people may come through for you because you've persevered. They admire your courage and now believe something may come of your complaint. People who have survived similar procedures can provide invaluable support.

Rana, the African-American insurance office manager we mentioned in previous chapters, describes her decision to sue her employer and the reactions of others to that decision. Rana is a woman of fifty with an almost regal manner that reflects her self-confidence and her pride in her work. She had been an office manager for fourteen years when her newly appointed boss, a white man in his early thirties, began a campaign to force her out of her job.

The boss refused to provide necessary equipment for her staff and made humiliating demands of her. It would take a month or more just to get office supplies. Instead of providing computer equipment as he had with the other managers, he gave her an old typewriter. He took months to fill an empty position in her department. She became concerned that her staff felt she wasn't getting her job done. At the beginning of his harassment she says:

> *He seemed to be only posturing. I'm not thin-skinned so I let that go. Then he asked me to step down from my position. He simply said he wanted someone else for my job. I started a grievance process within the company and after that, he made my life very difficult.*

I thought: would I go meekly? It was not in my genes to lay down and die. I had my dignity to uphold. I also had a very fine support system—family and especially friends who urged me on. A co-worker said to me: "If you tell anyone I said this, I'll deny it: But go get him!" Many people gave me information—just put it in my box. Someone gave me a packet of information about her own problem.

2. Gather as much information as possible from official agencies and reference books. Talk to people who have used complaint procedures or the courts in the past. Try to talk with women who have been successful this way as well as those for whom the process didn't work. Get an idea of the range of options before you make irrevocable decisions.

3. Agencies, such as the Equal Employment Opportunity Commission (EEOC) and state human rights commissions are established to help you. But staff see their jobs in a variety of ways. Some may serve you with warmth and efficiency; others with cool, authoritarian attitudes. Prepare yourself for all reactions.

4. When you start the complaint procedure at an agency or seek information from a lawyer, ask a friend to accompany you and take notes. She can help you sort out your reactions to the interview after you leave.

It sometimes seems that lawyers have designed the language of their profession to bewilder and intimidate ordinary people. You might feel inadequate or confused by a barrage of "legalese" and "tune out" from time to time. Ask for statements to be repeated as often as necessary. Bring notes with you on what you want to say or ask, and record advice and information as you receive it.

5. In consulting an agency, get specific information about the following:

    a. The agency's step-by-step procedures.

    b. The time line for each step. How long will it take? Does the agency need to complete each step within specific time limits? What is the first step? What are the limits for the second step?

You don't have to ask all these questions if a handbook spells them out. But the agent may claim there is a shortage of handbooks "at the moment" or give another excuse for not providing the information you need. You might have to ask for a copy of the pertinent pages while you wait.

    6. Get specific information about the following:
        a. Your role in the agency's procedures.
        b. Things you can do to speed up the process.
        c. Policies on confidentiality. How will the agency conduct the investigation while maintaining your confidentiality? At what point will that change? Will you get a warning before the boss or co-worker is informed of your charge? Is there any way a future employer can gain access to this information? If you live in a small community, you may want to ask even more detailed questions about confidentiality.
        d. Procedures for withdrawing your complaint.
        e. Procedures for filing a lawsuit. Will these agency procedures affect a potential lawsuit in any way, in case you want to follow that route?

    7. Be prepared to re-evaluate your action at each step. Many aspects of your living situation, your feelings and your job may shift during the period you take the steps required by the system.

What Are the Practical Tasks?

To make a claim of harassment to someone or some place outside your place of work:

    • Use the informal or formal grievance procedures available at your workplace, as well as individual efforts to stop the behavior directly. In addition, explore the possibility of formally complaining to the personnel department, board of directors or a grievance committee at work. If you make an appeal to agencies such as EEOC, they will want to know if you have attempted such solutions.

    • Keep a special notebook to record each event that has anything to do with the mistreatment. Write down such specific behavior as who did what to whom, what day, what time, how often, who witnessed it, etc. Ask a friend or co-worker to review the letter and give you her reactions and suggestions. Send a copy, with all the specifics, to someone who has the power to take effective action on your behalf. If you later bring a lawsuit, your notebook or records may become public in court. However, your ability to establish a clear, specific pattern of behavior through written records increases your credibility.

• Record your reactions to the abuse, including your feelings.

• Keep a record of all the people you spoke to about the mistreatment at the time. If there were no witnesses, your complaint may sound more believable if a co-worker testifies that you told her about the behavior at the time, and how you reacted.

For two years, Kimberley Abbott tried every tactic she could think of to stop the sexual harassment on her job as a college custodian. Only then did she begin to take notes. Nine years later, she sits comfortably in her pleasant apartment, self-assured and optimistic about her current life as a trained cosmetologist. But when she talks of those earlier, difficult years, she's visibly upset. Her anger and frustration about enduring harassment seem like open wounds.

> *My boss started in on me the very first day. At first, he seemed like a nice older gentleman. He was about fifty and I was in my early twenties. He would come up to me very closely, pat me on the buttocks and stroke me. This was always out of sight of others. He would hang on to me like he was playing with a cat. No one else had this kind of experience with this boss. They were all older people—married—I was the youngest.*

Kimberley told the boss she didn't like his behavior and that she was just there to do her work. But when she complained to him, he threatened to force her out of her job.

> *He'd write memos saying I wasn't doing my job. He'd write that my work area wasn't clean, which it was. He'd state I was out of my work area, which I wasn't. He would say I didn't call in sick, which I did. He was calling me at home, after hours. I finally faced him. I said I'm here to do my job and just want to be friendly with everyone. Then the next day, the "paper chase" would begin again.*

Once Kimberley started to take notes, her boss's memos became part of *her* records.

Kimberley often had nightmares about her boss and sought counseling to deal with her anxieties. She called the rape relief center for help in thinking clearly about the problem. To try to stop the harassment, she appealed to the personnel department, the affirmative action office and the police department on the campus, but was not satisfied that they would be advocates for her. She says:

> *Even now when I talk about it, I still have a lot of anger. That someone had power over me and there wasn't a damn thing I could do about it. People say why didn't I quit? I was financially strapped. I couldn't quit.*
>
> *The harassment went on for four years and I was in tears a lot of the time. The harassment just continued and the college wouldn't transfer me out of my boss's area. I went to my family doctor because I felt I was cracking up. He said what was happening to me was against the law and that I should take it to court.*
>
> *After two years, I started to note down details of every incident. Who was there. Who said what. I kept a calendar of all the events. I did that for the next two years. That helped a lot when I started a lawsuit. Otherwise, I would have forgotten a lot of what happened.*

Putting Together Your Initial Complaint

Let's suppose you're ready to be interviewed by an EEOC staffer or an attorney about your abusive boss. When you appeal to an agency for help, you place your job, some of your peace of mind and possibly a big chunk of your future in the hands of strangers, those who will advocate for you.

Initially, you may feel anxious about the whole process—so anxious that it becomes easy to misunderstand instructions or information about what to expect. Therefore, even if a friend accompanying you takes notes, don't hesitate to ask the agent for explanations and for repeated answers to your questions. You are the customer here. The other person in a very real sense works for you, and wouldn't have a job if people like you didn't make complaints.

If you don't understand the jargon of the agency or system, ask the agent to speak in ordinary English. If you don't speak English, or if English is your second language, ask for a translator or bring your own. If your hearing is impaired or you are deaf, you may want to speak through an interpreter. But if the agency or attorney hires someone to assist in the interview, you may have to pay for this. If you possibly can, provide your own interpreter or translator. She should work for you, and not try to please the agent or attorney who employs her.

At this point it might be a relief to let some outside agent take over full responsibility for resolving your problem. If that means you simply follow their instructions without question, think twice about it. Once you've given up control, you will have a hard time getting it back.

Ask whether the agency will maintain confidentiality about your complaint and the investigation. Sometimes the agency will permit you to make a complaint without giving your name. Under what circumstances will they do that? When the person who mistreats you is informed of your complaint, what will they tell him? If your workplace has few employees or if you are the only one being mistreated, the other person may easily figure out that you have made the complaint even without your name.

If the agency you've appealed to makes the process difficult for you, put into operation the same actions you used in dealing with the abusive person:

1. Before an interview with an agency representative, explore with a friend the positive and negative aspects of the entire procedure. Then discuss the best and worst response you might expect from the particular interchange coming up.

2. Rehearse with your friend what you want to say.

3. At your meeting with the agent ask for specific commitments, including how the agency will follow through on promises. Use the guidelines discussed in Chapter 16, "Evaluation and Follow-Through," for making a request and getting an answer.

4. Monitor yourself for faulty automatic thoughts, especially negative predictions.

5. Use other methods for staying in top condition for an ar-

duous task: eat nutritious enjoyable food, sleep as regularly as possible, exercise, take time to have fun.

A complaint process or lawsuit may take months or possibly years. Long, unexplained and seemingly unreasonable delays may frustrate you, and agents may stall in providing explanations for why they occur.

You need to find out when the agent plans to inform the abusive person of your accusations, so you can prepare for the reaction, which may be explosive. At least, you can psychologically prepare for it. You might decide to stay away from work that day. Give the accused person time to cool off a bit before you see him. He may punish you with escalated acts of intimidation or threats of insults. But if he realizes he now faces a serious threat, he may simmer down a little. If he fears losing his job or getting into trouble with his boss, he could start handling you cautiously. Prepare yourself for all possible reactions.

Rana continued to work at her insurance job for nine months after she filed a formal complaint. Her boss tried to ruin her reputation among her peers, a common method of intimidation and control. He gave her a low evaluation even though she and her staff had records that confirmed their excellent performances. Rana had grown up in an extended African-American family in which each of the adults stressed the dignity of all individual family members. As Rana recalls the impact of her boss's actions on her sense of self, her voice reflects the anguish she felt:

> *Those nine months were terrible for me. The agony was excruciating. He tried to break my spirit and I had to find a way to hold on to my dignity. Some people just didn't want to be seen with me. I kept my door closed. I dreaded any telephone call and feared further harassment.*

Fearing punitive reactions to complaints, some women decide to file grievances only after they have resigned and found other jobs. At that point, follow-through might still be important in order to get reparations of some sort. A woman may want to be instrumental in creating a better environment for other employees, or just want the offensive person to know action was taken against him. All those might be important reasons to continue the process. When the stess of enduring abuse every day has ended, the grievance process becomes more manageable.

The Equal Employment Opportunity Commission

The federal EEOC can investigate a complaint if you're a member of a "protected class," that is, a woman, a person of color, or one who is old or disabled. They also handle cases of wage discrimination and other workplace complaints, such as unfair hiring practices.

The EEOC has established offices in every state. (If you want to know the location of the office near you or if you have any questions about their procedures, call 1-800-USA-EEOC.) You can walk into an EEOC office at any time and pick up written material explaining your rights and the agency's procedures. If you decide to set up an appointment to make a complaint, this is what will happen:

1. The agent will take information from you about your complaint and will tell you whether the agency can handle it. EEOC *can consider your case only if your worksite has fifteen or more employees.* Violations must have occurred within the preceding six months. The abuse may have occurred before then, but if you can show that the same kind of mistreatment continues, you can still make a complaint. (If you're thinking of a lawsuit, check out the procedure in your state. In some states, you can bring a legal claim no matter how long ago the abuse occurred.)

If EEOC accepts your case, the agency will explain its procedures to you. If it files charges on your behalf, it will notify your employer about the complaint and assign an investigator to your case. As we mentioned before, you will want to find out exactly when the agency will do this.

2. Usually you need to give your name. But you can sometimes have a third party, such as a union, file the complaint for you without identifying yourself.

3. It often takes several months for an EEOC officer to start to work on your complaint and from two to four months to investigate it. EEOC offices attempt to get through the whole process in six months, but generally it takes longer.

4. If their investigation shows reasonable cause to believe you've been the victim of discrimination, EEOC staff will initiate a conciliation process. That means they will seek an agreement with your employer to stop the abuse. Most of the cases where

reasonable cause has been determined end with some kind of conciliation settlement.

A settlement can look very good after months of waiting and worrying. Some conciliation agreements include the employer's agreement to provide training for employees on how to recognize abuse and how to stop it. If you had to leave your job because of the abuse, you could get back pay and be reinstated at work.

5. If conciliation fails and the national office in D.C. agrees with the local office that your case has merit, EEOC can file a lawsuit. "Merit" means EEOC has decided that you have experienced gender discrimination; your evidence sufficiently supports your complaint and you are considered a credible person. Supporting evidence from other people and similar complaints against the allegedly abusive person also contribute to the merit of your case.

Because EEOC judges that some cases don't have merit and because many out-of-court settlements are arranged, only about five percent of complaints filed with the EEOC go on to litigation. The agency chooses to litigate some cases because it expects the outcome to affect many people.

If there is any possibility you might hire your own lawyer in the future, you will want to consider EEOC's limitations at the outset. If EEOC accepts your complaint, conciliation fails and the agency decides not to proceed with a lawsuit, you cannot take the case to court privately without its permission. You need to request a right-to-sue notice from the EEOC allowing you to go to court. If you file a lawsuit in federal court, you must first use the federal EEOC agency. States differ about whether you need to make a complaint to EEOC before going to a state court as well. You'll want to check this out with an attorney in your own state.

If the litigation by EEOC brings results in your favor and you have resigned from your job because of the abuse, you can receive back pay, back benefits such as pension payments, and reimbursement of out-of-pocket medical expenses. The Civil Rights Act passed by Congress in 1991 now makes it possible to collect compensatory damages for effects such as mental anguish or for expenses such as therapy costs.

The EEOC successfully brought suit on behalf of Margaret Johnson, an African-American woman who worked in the housekeeping department of a Holiday Inn hotel. She endured both sexual harassment and race discrimination. The manager had placed pictures of nude and partially nude women on the walls of his office and commented about them to female employees. He harassed female employees by touching them, kissing them and making suggestive comments about their clothing. The female assistant manager told ethnic jokes at work and referred to African-Americans as "niggers." She laughingly displayed a picture of a nude black woman to employees in the lunch room, glancing first at the picture and then at Margaret Johnson. Johnson quit her job because of this harassment.

As a result of EEOC litigation, Margaret Johnson received $8,500 in back pay from the hotel. The court ordered the hotel to post notices explaining the illegality of sexual harassment, to train supervisory personnel in preventing harassment and to establish grievance procedures. EEOC monitored compliance with these orders. The process of winning these victories did take a toll. Although she originally filed the complaint in 1988, she had to wait until 1991 for a settlement.

Because most complaints to EEOC end with agreements that forbid publicity on the outcome, the public cannot learn of these victories. This limitation makes the lawsuits that do take place especially important in educating the public and as a warning to other offenders.

EEOC has not placed high on its agenda the kinds of emotional abuse we have stressed in this book, possibly because they are harder to prove than sexual harassment. But you can bring a complaint about gender-based harassment, which the EEOC calls sex-based harassment. Some women have won cases against people who mistreated them solely because of their gender.

Susan Bassett started work as a part-time secretary in 1980 in the security department of Safeway Stores in Washington state. By 1983, she had worked her way up to the position of security investigator. In 1987, she filed a complaint with the EEOC. Her supervisors frequently made belittling remarks about her as a woman. They yelled at her and called her "bitch." They fraternized with male employees at work but never with her. A supervisor made it very clear that a woman could not hold the job of an investigator. Bassett heard the following kinds of comments: "If you can't pee in a bottle, you can't be an investigator" and "That's what happens when you send a woman to do a man's job." She finally quit.

The EEOC established that Susan Bassett's experience constituted sex-based harassment. As a result of the litigation in 1990, she received compensation of $34,000, including $18,000 in back pay. Similar to the case of the hotel chain mentioned earlier, Safeway Stores was required by the court to set up procedures to prevent harassment and to hear grievances.

Of course, bringing a complaint to an EEOC office doesn't guarantee you such successful results. Many cases that proceed to litigation are not decided in the woman's favor. But we cited these examples to show that the system can work for you and may be worth your efforts.

Another court case in 1991, which was not handled by EEOC, shows that other cases based on sex-based harassment can be won. A supervisor's badgering and harassing conduct toward female employees in an auto leasing company, while not sexual in nature, was determined to be discrimination on the basis of sex. Cost to the company's management: $50,000. The court reached that figure in an interesting way. The management had tolerated the supervisor's abusive conduct because he was very productive. They estimated that he had saved the company $500,000. So the court awarded the women ten percent of that amount, or $50,000.

If you bring a complaint to the EEOC or to any outside agent, the law bars the person being investigated from retaliating. If someone does punish you for filing a complaint, you can sue him or her. Some women have not won awards for their original charges of sexual or sex-based harassment, but they did collect damages on the basis of the retaliation they suffered.

Three advantages of filing a complaint with EEOC stand out:

1. EEOC provides services free of charge.
2. Even if the agency doesn't sue on your behalf, the free in-

vestigations and written records can be useful if you pursue your own lawsuit at a later time.

3. EEOC's investigation can frighten someone into treating you better even if the case goes no farther.

Human Rights Commissions

Most states have an agency that protects the rights of people at work. It might be called the Human Rights Commission (HRC) or the Fair Employment Practices Commission. These offices take complaints about discrimination in employment, housing, insurance and other areas. Getting information about both the EEOC and the state commission can help you decide where to start. The office that originally takes your complaint will do the investigation but will notify the other office about this.

State rights offices accept complaints only from workers at companies with a certain minimum number of employees. Since the number differs from state to state, you need to find out first if you can file a charge in your state office.

The state process resembles that of EEOC. If the agency decides your situation qualifies as a case of discrimination, your employer is notified and the agency has a "fact-finding conference" involving you and the employer. This conference may result in a settlement about your claim. If this conciliation is not successful, there can be a review by an administrative judge who makes a judgment about the case and settlement terms. This whole process can take many months. As with an EEOC complaint, you can go on to use the court system if you are not satisfied with the outcome. In some states you may need the state agency's permission to file a private lawsuit.

When Rana's boss tried to push her out of her manager's job at the insurance company, he did not provide her with either oral or written notice or explanation. She filed a complaint with the state Human Rights Commission. Recalling those events, she says: "I feel anxious every time I talk about this." About five months after filing her complaint, she attended a hearing which included three high-level managers from her company. Rana recalls:

The hearing officer tried to be as objective as possible, but told me that I should not have come down there by myself. But no one had told me I had a right to bring someone. I didn't know at the time I had that option. I guess I had an assumption of trust.

If you can afford it, make use of legal counsel to accompany or advise you as you negotiate your way through the maze of government agency processes. Even without filing a lawsuit, your attorney can be an observer throughout the process and can protect your interests. The attorney can also advise you of your legal rights at each step.

The Legal System

Here's a list of some of the federal legislation that protects the rights of women at work:

• 1963: The Equal Pay Act. Women must be paid the same salary as men doing substantially the same work.

• 1964: Title VII of the Civil Rights Act. Discrimination is prohibited on the basis of sex, race, color, religion and national origin. This law gives the EEOC the mandate for its activities and serves as the basis for claims about sexual harassment and sex-based harassment. It is the basis for private lawsuits as well. The law has also been extended to apply to persons with disabilities.

• 1967: The Age Discrimination Act. Employers may not discriminate against anyone in the workplace on the basis of age.

• 1978: The Pregnancy Discrimination Act. Pregnant women must have the same rights as other workers on the job. In 1991, the U.S. Supreme Court affirmed that right by prohibiting employers from protecting women from hazardous conditions. The court said women themselves have the right to make decisions about risks they will take.

On the basis of these laws and others, women have filed thousands of agency complaints and lawsuits charging discrimination at work, including sexual harassment and sex-based harassment. In some of these cases, women were awarded large financial settlements. In 1991 the Oceanside, California school district made an out-of-court settlement of $200,000 to a woman high-school teacher who charged that her principal had sexually harassed her. The woman has returned to her job in the school system and the man who abused her has left the system.

Kimberley Abbott tells of her experience with the legal system. She left the college custodian job, was determined to better her work situation and went into training to be a cosmetologist. She found a lawyer she could trust and the lawsuit was prepared while she was at cosmetology school. The strain of both weighed heavily on her. Determined to get the training she wanted, she held firm to her decision to proceed with the lawsuit. She says:

> *At first, preparing for the lawsuit didn't seem like a big deal. Then the depositions [sworn statements from people involved] started to be taken. I had to sit around the table while others were giving depositions and challenged my allegations about the harassment. They were lying, but I couldn't ask them questions, just had to sit there. The most difficult was when my boss gave his deposition. Many times I wanted to pull out. But my attorney believed in me. That's what kept me going.*

The jury determined that sexual harassment had occurred and awarded her damages of $75,000. But Kimberley's satisfaction was short-lived. The judge slashed her award to $25,000, alleging she "didn't have that much pain." Kimberley bravely insisted on an appeal process to reinstate the jury's verdict.

> *I told the magistrate during that appeal he had no idea what I'd gone through. No one had listened to me before, but now I want what I want. I decided to stick it out. I was the one who suffered.*

Kimberley finally received $50,000 as well as public recognition of her struggle. In addition, the college had to pay all of her attorney's fees and costs. And she's contented with her present work situation.

> *I'm in a totally different work atmosphere now. I work at a salon. I have my own clients. I don't have to answer to anyone. I stand up for myself more. The managers of the salon say that I've come a long way.*

Even though considerable progress has occurred in sexual

harassment cases, some legal rulings still reflect long-held beliefs about women and men in the workplace. Legal decisions do not consistently uphold women's rights. Here are a few examples:

In 1986, a woman brought a suit of sexual harassment because her co-workers displayed "pictures of nude or scantily clad women in their work areas." The court denied her claim and ruled that in our society "pornographic displays and vulgar comments" are everyday occurrences and therefore natural and acceptable. In a court case in 1988, a harassed woman was "termed the target of his [the alleged perpetrator] affections," not the target of unwelcome sexual advances. And in 1990, when a woman complained her boss made a series of sexually tinged comments to her over a period of time, the court decided the boss' comments had "little or nothing to do with the plaintiff's gender."

But good news prevails as well. In 1986, the Supreme Court validated the idea that sexual harassment can create a "hostile work environment" for women and is illegal.

In 1991, two federal courts decided that women's claims of sexual harassment on the job should be judged by a new test: whether the alleged acts would offend a "reasonable woman." This would substitute for the "reasonable man" standard that had previously governed all kinds of legal decisions. The "reasonable woman" standard recognizes that women and men view sexual overtures and innuendos very differently.

In 1991, a federal judge ruled that a group of female iron workers could sue collectively on the basis of sexual harassment. Normally each woman would have had to file individually. The attorney for the women said that "this represents a major breakthrough that will give all women faced with sexual harassment a powerful new tool in future cases."

The courts have held that the employer is responsible for providing a harassment-free workplace. Many court decisions and out-of-court settlements have required employers to provide training programs on sexual harassment policies and to publicize grievance procedures if harassment occurs. As of 1991, "jury awards to victims of sexual harassment have been climbing past the $1-million mark." Because of this financial vulnerability, many attorneys have advised their corporate clients to enforce anti-harassment policies diligently.

The Pain and the Payoff

Perhaps you've struggled with the decision to initiate a lawsuit. In the progress of the case, you may face another decision on whether to settle out of court. As with other kinds of civil cases, most women who bring lawsuits about harassment at work settle with their employers without an actual trial. Often the employer wants to avoid publicity and court expenses; women may not want their personal histories dragged into a courtroom. Moreover, your lawyer may advise you that even if you go to trial, your cash award probably won't be higher than the amount in the settlement. As part of the settlement, you may want to insist on changes in how your employer trains employees to prevent sexual harassment and in how grievances are handled. You may not agree to settle out of court unless you get these concessions.

Settling out of court means that the public (including other women subjected to abuse) will not know about the case or the reaction of a judge or jury. The public also will not know the specific terms of the settlement. Still, the cases generate publicity for women's rights, albeit indirectly. When monetary awards are asssumed to be significant and other settlement factors are assumed to be favorable to women, the cases encourage other women workers to object to discriminatory treatment and harassment. These settlements announce to other employers that they continue abuse at the risk of some of their assets.

The preparation of Rana's lawsuit took a year and was emotionally draining for her. Finally, she and her lawyer decided to participate in a settlement process. She recounts:

> *The hearing officer met separately with us and then with the other attorneys—kind of like "shuttle diplomacy." And at the end of that long day, they offered a settlement. I may have asked for some other things, but I was satisfied with the settlement. Would I have done it again? Absolutely. I wouldn't have given up the chance to tell my story. It was agony to have to tell the story so many times. And the expenses and the time! But even if I had lost, I would have done it again.*

Of course, you need to make a personal decision about accepting a settlement if you start court proceedings. It takes a great deal of persistence and patience to follow through with a court case. But if you decide you can stick it out, the decision in your case will be a public one, increasing the chances that both employers and women targeted for mistreatment will know about all of the aspects of the case and the decision. This can increase the likelihood of more woman-sensitive decisions in the future.

Emotional abuse sometimes presents subtle and complex dilemmas. Legal recourse will certainly not provide the entire solution. But you take the first step when you become aware that mistreatment exists and know you can take action against it. Whether you act solely for yourself or with the fate of other women in mind, each of your actions affects other women. Your personal actions against workplace abuse combine with other women's individual protests to form a movement promoting dignity for all women at work.

SECTION VIII

Conclusion

Chapter 20

Where Do We Go From Here?

If the personal is political, then so is the economic . . . The whole system must be changed if women in general, not just a hardy, pioneering few, are to gain economic power. . . . Each woman has to feel that she herself can do it, and then she needs the coaching, the education, the opportunity, the support, the time, and the tools to do it.

Rosabeth Moss Kanter, business administration professor

Kanter's comments reflect the balance we've aimed for in writing *You Don't Have to Take It!* We've focused on individual direct action, while recognizing the need to transform each part of the social/economic system. We've emphasized the importance of how you interpret events and talk to yourself about them, and the impact those actions make on your feelings. We've described how those individual, personal reactions sometimes dovetail with social and political discrimination against women. Now we want to take an even broader look at how each of these personal and political manifestations might develop on the largest imaginable scale.

Other Movements Against Abuse of Women

The movements against violence against women offer useful models for action against emotional abuse on the job. Already we find it hard to remember that only two decades ago women rarely protested—or even admitted to—abuse by family members and intimate partners. Rape, battering and incest lay hidden in the shadow of victims' socially imposed, silent self-blame.

Beginning in the mid-1970s, each time women brought a new form of abuse to public attention, a similar path of progress followed. One woman tentatively confided her secret to another during a coffee break at work, at a laundromat or in a hospital ward. Those two women spoke to others. Groups formed and crisis lines followed. They gave birth to a movement.

Whether rape, incest, woman battering or sexual harassment, the first response to public mention of each type of violation took a similar form: "It doesn't happen." When tediously gathered statistics disproved that claim, the response shifted: "Okay, it happens, but not much. And certainly not to people like me/ you/ us." Next came: "She must have asked for it/ liked it/ deserved it." But more and more individual women shared "confessions" of what had been done to them and grassroots women started support groups and opened shelters. They learned that personal violence and the fear of it permeate the lives of all kinds of women, not just those considered Other. Finally police and social agencies began to take the problem seriously.

For the past two decades legal reform, shelters, educational programs, sociological and psychological research have contributed to public understanding that women do not want, ask for or deserve to be violated. That statement, so obvious today, represented the radical edge of political thought just twenty years ago. Finally the public begins to understand that women remained silent because they feared reporting. They were afraid no one would believe them, afraid everyone would blame them.

At first glance, emotional abuse at work seems significantly different from violations at the hands of intimate partners. One is public and economic; the other personal and domestic. But women *experience* abuse at work and at home in similar ways. Women battered by husbands cite compelling reasons for staying with the partner: emotional, social and financial, among others. Many women harassed and threatened at work drew parallels between their situations and those of women battered by spouses. Muriel, the government accountant, puts it this way:

Why do I stay? For the same reason that so many women stay in abusive relationships—financial. I am 51 years of age, my current lifestyle and retirement benefits depend on job stability. In this recession period, not only are jobs scarce, but it is certainly not the time to make a living in private practice.

Debbie Dritz, the air conditioning repair apprentice, quoted at the opening of this book, describes the striking similarity between a woman battered by an intimate partner and her own experience with the man who trained her to do her job:

> *With all this constant badgering I just tried to go about my work, doing my best and making sure I stayed on Tom's good side. This meant always being cheerful and constantly trying to please him. I felt as if I were doing a complex dance, dancing around Tom's moods and prejudices. I was learning to monitor his moods. I was becoming totally dependent on him. He gave me work. He gave me training. He gave me answers. If I got on his bad side and he withdrew from me, I'd be out there all alone. . . . Tom's tactics were affecting me physically. . . . My emotions were going haywire . . . I started seeing a therapist . . . Finally a frightening realization surfaced. Tom and I were involved in a battered wife syndrome, only in this case it was a battered apprentice syndrome.* He could treat me however he wanted because, to me, staying on his good side seemed to be my only ticket to survival. . . . *I joked to friends that I needed a divorce, but it really wasn't a joke. It was time for a change.*

Looking to the Possible Future

No one yet knows exactly what steps will lead to a successful struggle against emotional abuse at work. We don't even know precisely what circumstances enable women to leave violent partners or fight back against rape or sexual harassment. Almost nothing has been learned about how some girls put a stop to incest and other forms of molestation. Studies produce mixed results, but sociologist Lee Bowker theorizes that safety for women who have been battered requires two types of change. The women need assistance from outside agents, usually police, prosecutors, family or religious leaders *and* they must undergo internal shifts in their thinking.

The same principles discovered by Bowker may apply to women mistreated at work. As we wrote *You Don't Have to Take It!*

that awareness pushed us to promote two major methods of coping with emotional abuse at work: those that spring from internal emotional and mental shifts and those that result from organized public campaigns. Each plays a major role in gaining freedom from the abuse of others.

As a woman's internal perspective evolves, it often includes imagining a different way of life. When she puts that image into action, it may appear shockingly sudden to observers. They don't realize that the woman's vision has been germinating over time. The woman may not have consciously recognized the new image herself until long after she modified her way of life. Yet it profoundly affected her emergence from an intolerable present to activate her vision of a possible future.

That process of moving toward freedom from abuse requires the ability to counteract the consequences of brainwashing, which we discussed in Chapter 2. To the extent brainwashing succeeds, the victim loses hope of ever encountering respectful treatment. At worst she no longer imagines she can be any other way than the way she is—an "abused woman." At that point the word, "abused" no longer describes something that another person did to her. It has, together with "woman," become almost one word: *"abused-woman."* Women abused at work experience similar reactions. They told us: "I lost sight of who I was." "I began to think I was hopelessly incompetent." "I thought it was all my fault." To reverse those thoughts they had to recognize the treatment they endured as something *done to them,* not a description of who they *were.*

We hope reading *You Don't Have to Take It!* and learning about other women's experiences has helped you connect your individual situation with that of women in all kinds of jobs. We hope each woman who endures abuse at work will confide in another women at a union meeting, professional caucus, women's group, a company cafeteria—wherever she feels safe in speaking. As women trade individual stories, awareness of the political implications of abuse at work can evolve into the formation of women workers' groups that act organizationally and with purpose to change systems.

As women workers compare experiences they can encourage each other to name the perpetrators, whether men or women.

Because women understand each other's particular problems in resisting abuse at work, they often benefit from organizing exclusively female action groups. At other times it is to their advantage to join men in protesting abuse of all workers, male and female.

When Organizations Foster Destructive Thought Patterns

The principles and practices we've applied to individual action also generally fit collective political organizations. Women's awareness of our victimization, developed in the past two decades, stirred up righteous anger, followed by effective struggles against injustice that benefited all women. But heightened political consciousness sometimes brings with it despair that undermines the very changes the consciousness makes possible. A movement too narrowly focused on abuse risks demoralizing its membership. It obscures a vision of the possible future. Like individuals, political organizations and movements become enmeshed in destructive thought patterns, reinforced by either/or political rhetoric.

The media frequently contributes to both individual and collective negative thinking by providing ready-made either/or and global thoughts. Media reports claim the women's movement failed because women really don't want the hard, dirty work of mining and ditch digging, nor to leave their children while they work eighty-hour weeks at professional jobs. When we remind ourselves too often of our victimized movement status, we easily incorporate these public messages of "failure." Other reports tell us that women on career paths regret they passed up opportunities for early marriage and childbirth and now they find it's too late; that children suffer too much loss over parents' divorces and mothers' unavailability; that women really want a "mommy track," not a serious career.

Those of us who long for both intimate relationships and satisfying work pore over those sensationalized reports and wonder if we blew it. We ask ourselves anxiously, "Do we really want to just stay home and mind the children after all?" We lose sight of the fact that many *men* would prefer to continue the stimulation of their work and still have more time for personal lives. Other men crave relief from back-breaking or mind-numbing labor, but have few choices. We also forget that many women want *more* help at home, rather than *less* work in the commercial world. They want better wages and better treatment, not a life of lounging on a velvet pillow. To the extent we buy into media messages showing us "what women want," we distort our picture of the possible future. Some of us succumb to the idea that perhaps we never wanted to succeed in the world of work at all. Others develop an image of Wonder Woman, who must do everything much better than men. We will not only "have it all," we will "do it all" too. We will accomplish all the "women's work" as well as all the "men's work."

Popular interpretations of particular studies do women and men a disservice by obscuring complexities. At best they oversimplify the truth about current challenges for women and men in the eye of our end-of-the-century cultural hurricane. News reports frequently rely on studies that support the severely limiting biases of researchers. Then a headline style of writing distorts their actual findings. When corrections or responsible discussions appear they often show up on page 33, whereas the startling news that the women's movement has failed was headlined on the first page.

The grain of truth in some of these studies strikes at women's socially engendered fears that they aren't good enough mothers, wives or workers, maybe not even "real women." "They," whether perceived as the media or the "expert" researchers, told us we could have it all. Currently "they" claim we demanded too much, and that now we don't even want it. It is closer to the truth to say that as a young movement we demanded too little. As a result of women's protests, opportunities to pursue exciting careers have opened up for a few women, but those very successes helped us realize we desire much more:

1. Equal pay, equal access to training, equal opportunities to learn and advance for women and men, people of color and whites, lesbians, gays and heterosexuals, disabled people and those of all ages and lifestyles.

2. Careers for all women who want them.

3. Jobs that pay a living wage *and* offer safety and dignity for both women and men.

4. Equal sharing of household and child-raising responsibilities by men and women.

5. Reasonable hours of work for men and women who want to live balanced lives.

6. Child care and parental leave for male and female parents in the work force.

And more.

The media erred when they claimed women don't want equality. Equal access to all kinds of work remains essential. But we do not share equal access, as long as executives, police officers, engineering professors, head nurses and tradesmen humiliate and threaten women colleagues and employees; as long as soldiers rape female members of their squadrons. "Liberated working women" do not exist as long as women also perform most of the work at home, and in growing numbers support families without the assistance of partners.

Each woman conducts her individual struggle for adequate wages, equal access to rewarding opportunities and respectful treatment at work. Along with the organized struggles for safety at home and on the streets, these personal efforts bring women together to work out a common, yet flexible, vision of justice.

The Possible Future: More Radical Than We Know

Backlash, the vicious, sometimes life-threatening retaliation against the feminist movement shows itself as an increase in rape and other forms of violence against women. In fiction, popular songs and pornography, it takes the form of glamorized or justified abuse of woman. In addition direct attacks on women's centers, bookstores and clinics have increased. Backlash truly does menace individual women as well as the feminist movement. Our fears are sound and reasonable. But we get into trouble when we move from realistic assessments of danger to despairing statements such as, "We haven't accomplished anything in the last thirty years," "Men will never share power," "Men will never stop being violent to women."

If we pay attention only to events that threaten us, without appreciating our accomplishments, our collective thinking becomes global and negative. Dire predictions may flow from such group "automatic thoughts," acting as a kind of sabotage to movement goals. These thoughts can be as destructive to a movement as they are to you, if you predict you will never get a better job or be treated as you deserve.

Backlash does threaten women struggling for their rights and it can imperil our safety. It also signals that those who oppose feminist goals thoroughly understand the enormous social implications. We aim to overturn relationships that have prevailed for thousands of years. Naturally, many men and some women fear this agenda. The irony is that those who oppose equality between women and men may comprehend the significance of our goals better than we do. They understand that our successes will ultimately shake up all institutions and relationships in ways we can't yet even imagine.

Perhaps that comprehension explains in part why the U.S. government has not sanctioned the Equal Rights Amendment, which baldly states the revolutionary vision: *men and women are equal.* Maybe international understanding of the political power of a feminist vision explains why the United States and some other governments failed to ratify the United Nations Convention on the Elimination of All Forms of Discrimination Against Women. Powerful world and national leaders lash out against the feminist movement because they fear its progress. National and international resistance to equality mirrors the extreme reactions of some individual husbands, bosses and co-workers to women's insistence on a fair share of both labor and rewards.

Let's return to media's contribution for a moment. In discussing feminism, the media combine both global and either/or thinking. Media reports alternate the message that feminism has completely failed with the opposite: we have already achieved our goals and should stop organizing. "Women can do and have anything they want." To deny that women are abused and discriminated against, to pretend we have achieved equity, is to threaten our social movement. Such a burial of truth creates destructive results similar to those that occur when an individual woman disavows that she suffers abuse, claiming everything is fine, or that the problem lies within her. Yet the idea keeps popping up: "If you women can't make it, there must be something wrong with *you,* because all the opportunities are open to you now."

But we've seen in our discussions of sexual harassment, illegitimate control and intimidation, that some men use whatever tactics are at hand to drive out female competition. When they cannot *legally* prevent women from taking jobs that pay well enough to raise a family, they find other means. As a movement we need constant reminders of both our successes in achieving expanded freedom and opportunities *and* of that long road stretching ahead before we reach equality.

Complexities of Male Power and Privilege

Still another form of global thinking has given us a two-edged mental set. On the one side, the early identification of men as the main threat to women's safety and freedom has enhanced feminist political focus. On the other hand, that very focus has obscured the complexities of our problems.

Clear identification of men as a *class* of people who hold relatively more power than women has been hugely important. Women's intimate relationships with men often make us reluctant to recognize that love and power each play significant roles in our male-female interactions. We forget that love is powerful *and* that power can be used lovingly as well as destructively. We become impatient with men who don't recognize their privilege, and then scold ourselves for acting as if it's their fault they have privilege, when, after all, it comes with the genes. They cannot throw it off even if they want to. Shifting between these two positions, we miss a more complex idea: men are not responsible for the fact that they *have* privilege, but they are responsible for how they *use* it. Failure to recognize that they enjoy privilege constitutes an abuse of privilege. To achieve the equal position we want, women must keep in mind that most men do exercise more power over others—especially women and children—than do most women.

Our challenge is to remember the position of men as a class, while also recognizing other forms of power and privilege. As the women's movement progressed, more and more white feminists realized that power manifests itself not just as maleness but often as an offshoot of white, able-bodied, heterosexual, Christian privilege. Women experience discrimination and abuse in complex ways, at the hands of many kinds of people, depending on our class, race and other aspects of our status. Some of us found it more difficult to accept that women also have opportunities to abuse others, in accordance with our relative positions of privilege. Many white and middle-class women are as reluctant to admit to privileged status as are men of all colors and classes.

Women need to maintain awareness of factors that may seem contradictory: women are often abused at work and elsewhere, and some women also mistreat others. The more privilege and power women have, the more opportunities there are to behave irresponsibly. Women we interviewed continually surprised us by recounting their mistreatment by other women. Abuse by women bosses underlines the need for women to remind each other of a more humane vision for the future, one that embraces responsible use of privilege and managerial control. These reminders focus on the possible future, in which women help each other guard against repeating the mistakes of other powerful people.

Fortunately the overgeneralized faulty thinking of most political movements gives way, gradually, to understanding the complexities of misusing power. Activists are learning that to greater or lesser degrees each of us abuses our privilege at times and also suffers from mistreatment by those who misuse their privilege. There are no innocents. In different degrees each person shares responsibility for the inequalities that governments create and exacerbate.

In recent years political organizations have begun to see the limitations of each group's narrow focus on achieving its own goals, and have grown into the belief that each group must recognize and abolish its own oppression of others. For example, the "careers" of many working-class women consist of caring for the children, cleaning the toilets or packaging the take-out dinners of successful, advantaged women. Some organizations of privileged white feminists have begun to realize that the careers the feminist movement helped them achieve depend on the low-wage dead-end labor of those Other women.

Some environmentalist groups see that their successful struggles to preserve an endangered species may also endanger the livelihoods of lumberjacks or of Native Americans who fish for a living. Working-class people and workers of color face protest closures of weapons plants in efforts to protect the jobs they depend on, but also face the fact that those weapons may ultimately be aimed at their opposite numbers in countries the United States chooses to fight. Gay men pressure government to spend the money necessary for research on AIDS. Slowly they realize government agencies spend even less money to find a cure for breast cancer, a disease far more widespread than AIDS and one that kills even more individuals. Naming the complexities of problems facilitates the search for common solutions.

Coalitions For A Possible Future

All movements have fostered their own social visions of a possible future, which until recent years have been largely separate from each other. But as we worked on *You Don't Have to Take It!* we envisioned both individual women and organizations of women workers joining with numerous other groups of women and men to further social justice in employment for all people, regardless of their social status or position of power.

Political activists express discouragement about the erosion of hard-won rights, such as reproductive choice and affirmative action, and the lack of government concern for enviromental issues. Focusing on their particular campaigns, they often overlook the potential for developing broad, political power bases through coalitions. But glimmers of hope show through the shifting picture as some of those same losses alert movement workers to the potential of increasing power through new alliances.

Some unions that ignored women's issues in past years and wouldn't even organize within women's traditional work arenas, now eagerly recruit women union members. Regardless of organizers' motives, this trend can benefit women. Voices from health-conscious movements support women and men who struggle for environmentally safe worksites. They campaign against highly mechanized job routines that damage workers' health and chemicals that harm male reproductive organs as well as those of women. Civil libertarians conduct legal battles against the use of lie detectors and psychological tests for hiring, as well as other invasions of workers' privacy. Disabled and old people, gays, lesbians and people of color continue to struggle for equal rights in the workplace. Environmentalists strive to become nonsexist or even feminist. Feminist organizations attempt to root out their own racism. The coming together of these separate movements and attempts to incorporate each others' principles provide the most encouraging signs of a social revolution.

International Coalitions

As awareness of each political movement's interdependence on others slowly grows, we acknowledge that the "pie" has not become infinitely divisible after all, particularly the worldwide pie. This means we need to work together internationally. International relations remain lofty and distant in many of our minds. What in the world do *they* have to do with being called a "bitch" by a co-worker, disdained and intimidated by a boss? Although those two arenas seem unrelated, the concept of "one world" no longer represents a dream—or a nightmare.

Everything we do as individuals has social repercussions. When you defy your boss or comply with the orders of an abusive co-worker, your action, in conjunction with thousands of other women making similar and different decisions, makes an impact on your workplace, your community and society. What women and men do in the United States, individually and collectively, affects the rest of the world. This fact perhaps takes on special importance in the arena of work.

Interconnections among nations create both obstacles and opportunities for political movements in all countries. Defying emotional abuse at work presents us with particular challenges in the 1990s, both as individuals seeking the courage to resist abuse and in organizational political struggles. U.S. industry shrinks the availablity of jobs for U.S. residents in favor of exploiting workers in less industrialized countries, especially poor women who have few choices. This situation and workers' fear of losing the jobs they do hold can propel them toward the most conservative positions of inaction. Or it can push workers to expand coalitions beyond national borders and to cooperate with women (and men) in other nations.

Increasingly women throughout the world speak the same language, whether called feminist, "womanist" or something entirely different, about violence in their lives. In countries as disparate as China, Israel, Germany, Belize and Fiji, women protest against battering, rape and incest. Sexual harassment and other forms of mistreatment of women at work have become global women's issues. Here are some examples of women's activism around the globe:

- The European Association Against Violence Toward Women at Work campaigns against sexual harassment at work. But its mission also includes these goals: "to denounce, in order to prevent, abuses of power, blackmail, and other forms of pressure used to control, exclude, dominate or deny the integrity of women." It also states that, "situations of power, based either on organizational hierarchy or directly on sexist criteria, are what makes violence against women possible."

- Although the threat of dismissal from jobs and psychological and physical aggression necessitate the wearing of hoods to hide their identities, Costa Rican women publicly denounce the "violation of fundamental political rights of workers, the deterioration of working conditions and the repeated sexual harassment to which female workers are subjected in over 26 companies."

- India's most powerful women's trade union, The Self-Employed Women's Association (SEWA), organizes the poorest paid women and has succeeded in gaining higher wages as a result of at least one women's strike. But rampant discrimination against women working for companies run by men has caused the organization to change its emphasis. It now concentrates on making loans to women who want to start their own businesses or form cooperatives.

- Women in Korean, Indian and Mexican cities have won the right to special women's busses and train cars to protect them from male harassment on the way to work.

These protests may soon be followed by individual and collective confrontation of other forms of mistreatment at work. It sounds visionary to anticipate industrial alliances with women throughout the world, and to expect male power to listen to us. It *is* visionary. We *need* visionaries. Images of a possible future grow into specific goals, becoming programs for individuals, nations or international groups. Women took major individual steps when we spoke out, first in consciousness-raising groups, then to national governments and finally internationally. The United Nations conference inaugurating the Decade for Women brought women from all over the world to Mexico City in 1975. Dialogue continued in Stockholm in 1980 and at the Nairobi meeting in 1985, intended to mark the end of The Decade. But women determined that The Decade would not end.

Another opportunity to organize internationally under the auspices of the United Nations is planned for China in 1995. Strategy discussions during that meeting promise to profit from the massive amount of cross-cultural communication of the past two decades. Through newsletters, friendships and organizational cooperation women have built understanding and the formulation of common goals. We can build now toward speaking out collectively against demeaning treatment of women at work as well as in homes and on the street.

Women no longer need to voice protests as isolated solos. Nor can we afford the illusion that we constitute a chorus. We more resemble an orchestra, sometimes dissonant, but often blending different sounds into a resonant message that travels around the world. Across national and continental boundaries, women struggle to end interpersonal violence against women, and also to gain better economic conditions. These two movements come naturally together in confronting emotional abuse of women at work.

A petition currently makes its way to countries on every continent by way of women's organizations, its final destination the United Nations. It promotes the "radical" idea that "Violence Against Women Violates Human Rights." It lays the groundwork for working internationally against the many forms of violence and commercial exploitation of women. The widespread abuse of women includes prostitution and imprisonment of women for the pleasure of male "sex tourists" in Thailand and other countries, as well as rape and the stripping of rights of Filipina women imported as maids to work in Kuwait. Abuse also affects women workers in maquiladoras, factories run by U.S. corportations, that create slum industrial towns in the border cities of Mexico. In these shack towns, women are especially prone to suffer chemical poisons at work and they and their children endure polluted water and air. U.S. women's organizations can join those of men who work internationally for workers' rights, but who often neglect the plight of women.

Is it possible to create a worldwide movement working for the respect and rights of all women, including economic and personal rights? This is a wild idea. But no more so than the "new idea" of only twenty years ago that rape, battering and incest present widespread and dangerous hazards to the well-being of women and must be stopped. No more so than the reality that women in numerous countries oppressed by traditional governments take the risks of protesting that treatment. We do not yet have a global movement, but the seeds have been planted.

The vision that informed the writing of this book pictures a world in which every woman enjoys confidence in her safety as she walks, drives or takes a bus or trolley to her workplace in a skyscraper, village market, agency or field. It is a world in which every woman performs her tasks at home or in an office, factory or farm with dignity and safety. Each woman brings home enough food or wages to fulfill her needs and those of her family. No woman feels she must either apologize for her gender or resent other women or the men in her life for their privilege. These ideas seem to us to be "just ordinary fairness." But they are not "just ordinary." Equality and respect for working women of all classes constitute the most radical of goals.

Women become discouraged in struggling for respectful treatment, but find strength in connections with women in the same office, union, nation and throughout the world struggling for the same fundamental goals. Alana, the community-college teacher discussed in earlier chapters, boosted her morale with thoughts like these:

> *I had to reframe it as a larger issue. At this point it becomes a systems issue. The system is abusive. Maybe my job is to work in a system that helps to clean this up.*

We recognize a series of systems within systems, the global industrial complex representing the largest. To affect our own lives we must think and act locally, but everything each of us does may make a significant impact on the global community.

Therefore we must at the very least "think globally, act locally." We choose to organize for adequate wages and respect, but not if our gains come at the expense of men, or on the backs of the poorest of women or of women in impoverished countries. All women and men must think and act both globally and locally.

Whether you listen to your own voice speaking the truth, confront your boss about abuse, learn about working conditions of women internationally, start a union, file a lawsuit or tell your co-worker you won't permit his manipulation—whether you circulate a petition to the United Nations or begin the struggle to name your problem—whichever actions you choose, you become part of a global movement to gain equal rights for women workers.

Our vision pictures worldwide opportunity for all peoples. Starting here. Starting now. Each of us must help the other by sharing "the coaching, the education, the opportunity, the support, the time, and the tools to do it," as our quote at the beginning of this chapter suggests. It begins with each individual woman. It begins with you.

NOTES

Chapter 1: What is Abuse at Work, Anyway?

(1) p. 3. I had a boss...: Anonymous, "The Air-Conditioned Nightmare," *Tradeswomen Magazine* 7,1 (Spring 1988), p. 11. Slight variations of this comment show up in many women's stories. When Debbie Dritz wrote this article, she preferred to remain anonymous.

(2) p. 3. An hour later...: Louise Kapp Howe, *Pink Collar Workers* (New York: G.P. Putnam's Sons, 1977), p. 110.

(3) p. 3. He admonishes Watson...: Virginia Ellis, "Women Gain Clout in Capitol," *Los Angeles Times,* Nov. 6, 1991, p. A18.

(4) p. 3. Male managers at...: Bill Romano, "Nordstrom Clerk Sues, Says Store Invaded Her Privacy," *Seattle Post-Intelligencer,* July 8, 1990, p. A7.

(5) p. 3. A customer service...: Donna M. Stringer, Fran Pepitone-Arreola-Rockwell and Tamara Pearl, "Impacts on Employee of Abuse by Supervisors/Managers in the Workplace," 1990 (Unpublished).

(6) p. 3. The actor notes that...: Joy Horowitz, "Black Actresses Are Still Waiting for Starring Roles," *New York Times,* May 19, 1991, p. B1.

(7) p. 4. A university department head...: *9 to 5 Newsline,* 10, 5, 1991, p. 2.

(8) p. 4. One woman described...: Stringer et al., "Impacts on Employee...." (See n. 5.)

(9) p. 6. Dreyer heard via...: John M. Glionna, "Midshipman Recalls Her Rough Seas at Annapolis," *Los Angeles Times,* May 23, 1990.

(10) p. 7. Yet researchers also tell...: Helen C. Cox, "Verbal Abuse in Nursing: Report of a Study," *Nursing Management,* (November 1987), p. 47. This study of nurses subjected to verbal abuse, mostly from doctors, found that many nurses directly objected to the abuse. But when they discovered the tactic brought them few benefits, many tried to solve the problem by avoiding the perpetrators.

Donna Stringer, Fran Peptione-Arreola-Rockwell and Tamara Pearl interviewed twenty-five men and women about their experiences of emotional abuse at work. Seven worked with affirmative action officers or union representatives, and seven (some of whom may have been the same) responded in these ways: took control of meeting locations, confronted, performed well or walked out. Most other techniques were directed to reducing the impact of stress resulting from the abuse.

Michael Lombardo and Morgan McCall, *Coping with an Intolerable Boss* (Greensboro: North Carolina Center for Creative Leadership, 1984). A majority of the male managers in this study responded to impossible bosses by waiting for the boss to be transferred or retire.

(11) p. 9. [T]he abuse of power...: Jean A. Hamilton, Sheryle W. Alagna,

Linda S. King and Camille Lloyd, "The Emotional Consequences of Gender-Based Abuse in the Workplace: New Counseling Programs for Sex Discrimination," *Women, Power, and Therapy: Issues for Women,* ed. Marjorie Braude (New York: Haworth Press, 1987), p. 155.

(12) p. 9. A government study found...: Diana E.H. Russell, *Sexual Exploitation: Rape, Child Sexual Abuse, and Workplace Harassment,* Sage Library Social Research, Vol. 155 (Beverly Hills: Sage Publications, 1984), p. 270.

(13) p. 9. Mary Bularzik, a women's...: Ibid. p. 276.

(14) p. 10. Resigning because of...: Cox, "Verbal Abuse...," p. 49. (See note 10.)

(15) p. 11. I took a risk...: "Vickie Smith, Sprinkler fitter," Molly Martin, *Hard-Hatted Women* (Seattle: Seal Press, 1988), p. 147.

(16) p. 11. Women who consider...: Lynn Hecht Shafran, "Victimizing Victims," *New York Daily News,* reprinted in *On the Issues,* Spring 1992, p. 4.

(17) p. 11. Gigi, a tradeswoman...: Panel discussion at Women in Trades Conference, Seattle, Washington, May 4-5, 1990.

(18) p. 14. Werner Erhard has...: Walter Scott, "Personalities," *Parade Magazine,* Nov. 8, 1992, p. 1.

(19) p. 14. The investigation [of...: Susan Gilmore, "School Cuts Ties with a Founder," *Seattle Times/Post-Intelligencer,* Nov. 8, 1992, p. B10.

(20) p. 14. Defying ancient stereotypes...: Patricia Lee, "Sisters at the Border: Asian Immigrant Women and HERE, Local 2," in *Building Bridges: The Emerging Grassroots Coalition of Labor and Community,* ed. Jeremy Brecher and Tim Costello (New York: Monthly Review Press, 1990), pp. 38-46.

(21) p. 14. After years of enduring...: Cheryl Gomez-Preston, "Over the Edge," *Essence* (March, 1990), p. 125.

(22) p. 14. Now rehired, she...: Jane Gross, "Stanford Medical School Official Ousted," *New York Times,* Feb. 25, 1992, p. A7.

(23) p. 14. Office workers Ellen Cassedy...: Ellen Cassedy and Karen Nussbaum, *9 to 5: A Working Woman's Guide to Office Survival* (New York: Penguin Books, 1983).

Chapter 2: Naming Emotional Abuse on the Job

(1) p. 16. Not being able to name...: Shirley is a composite of several secretaries.

(2) p. 17. A Questionnaire to Name...: The questionnaire is adapted from the following sources: Ginny NiCarthy and Sue Davidson, *You Can Be Free* (Seattle: Seal Press, 1989), pp. 5–7, and Stringer et al., "Impacts on Employee," (See Ch. 1, n. 5.)

(3) p. 18. Rose Melendez worked in the...: Martin, *Hard-Hatted Women,* pp. 72–74 (See Ch. 1, n. 15.)

(4) p. 22. Lydia Vasquez, a single... Jean Schroedel, *Alone in a Crowd* (Philadelphia: Temple University Press, 1985), pp. 104–106.

(5) p. 30. If enough of them...: Diana Russell, *Rape in Marriage* (New York: Macmillan Pub. Co., 1982), p. 184. Categories reprinted from Amnesty International. Report on Torture (London: Gerald Duckworth, 1973), p. 49.

Chapter 3: The Special Case of Sexual Harassment

(1) p. 37. Out there, living and...: Cathleen Decker, "Sexual Harassment Laws Fall Short, Anita Hill Says," *The Los Angeles Times*, Nov. 16, 1991, p. A1.

(2) p. 38. It began to get weird...: Martin, *Hard-Hatted Women*, pp. 115-16. (See Ch. 1, n. 15.)

(3) p. 38. [They] would all come and...: Lin Farley, *Sexual Shakedown* (London: Melbourne House, 1978), pp. 117-18.

(4) p. 38. She says: "Right away...:" Constance Backhouse and Leah Cohen, *Sexual Harassment on the Job: How to Avoid the Working Woman's Nightmare* (Englewood Cliffs, N.J.: Prentice Hall, 1981), p. 27.

(5) p. 38. In 1980, the federal Equal Employment...: W.B. Nelson, "Sexual Harassment, Title VII and Labor Arbitration," *The Arbitration Journal*, 40, no. 4 (December 1985), pp. 55-65.

(6) p. 39. In 1986 the Supreme Court...: *Meritor Savings Bank vs. Vinson* (U.S. Supreme Court No. 85-1979).

(7) p. 40. Identifying Sexual Harassment....: Several items for this exercise were derived from: Louise Fitzgerald, et al., "The Incidence and Dimensions of Sexual Harassment in Academia and the Workplace," *Journal of Vocational Behavior*, 32, no. 2 (April 1988), pp. 152-175.

(8) p. 41. The women surveyed...: Donald Maypole and Rosemarie Skaine, "Sexual Harassment in the Workplace," *Social Work* 28 (Sept.-Oct. 1983), pp. 385-386; Sally Kaplan, "Consequences of Sexual Harassment in the Workplace," *Affilia: Journal of Women and Social Work*, 6, no. 3 (Fall 1991), pp. 50-65.

(9) p. 41. He got extremely abusive...: Farley, *Sexual Shakedown*, pp. 102-103. (See n. 3.)

(10) p. 42. They found that...: Sandra Tangri, Martha Burt and Leanor B. Johnson, "Sexual Harassment at Work: Three Explanatory Models," *Journal of Social Issues*, 38, no. 4 (1982), pp. 33-54.

(11) p. 42. Catharine MacKinnon, a legal...: Lois Price-Spratlen, ed., *Prevention of Sexual Harassment in Academe* (Seattle: University of Washington, 1986), p. 22.

(12) p. 43. Their response was to smile...: Backhouse, *Sexual Harassment on the Job*, p. 5. (See n. 4.)

(13) p. 44. If they work in jobs...: Alison Konrad and Barbara Gutek, "Impact of Work Experience on Attitudes Toward Sexual Harassment," *Administrative Science Quarterly*, 31, no. 3 (September 1986), p. 436.

(14) p. 44. This has been called...: Barbara A. Gutek and Bruce Morasch, "Sex Ratios, Sex-Role Spillover, and Sexual Harassment of Women at Work," *Journal of Social Issues*, 38, no. 4 (1982), pp. 55-74.

(15) p. 44. I like to think...: Arlie Hochschild, *The Managed Heart: Commercialization of Human Feeling* (Berkeley: University of California Press, 1983), p. 105. Emphasis in original.

(16) p. 45. I would say half...: Backhouse and Cohen, *Sexual Harassment on the Job*, p. 17. (See n. 4.)

(17) p. 46. [To his invitation] I...: Farley, *Sexual Shakedown*, p. 69. (See n. 3.)

(18) p. 46. If a woman has...: Konrad and Gutek, "Impact of Work Experience," p. 431. (See n. 13.)

(19) p. 47. Anita Hill's delay...: Marlene Cimons, "Both Thomas and Hill Fit Patterns of Harassment Cases, Experts Say," *Los Angeles Times*, Oct. 15, 1991, p. A8.

(20) p. 47. Closeted lesbians experience...: Beth E. Schneider, "Consciousness About Sexual Harassment Among Heterosexual and Lesbian Women Workers," *Journal of Social Issues*, 38, no. 4 (1982), p. 85.

(21) p. 47. One study found...: Farley, *Sexual Shakedown*, p. 22. (See n. 3.)

(22) p. 48. Indeed [you] must appear...: Catharine MacKinnon, *Sexual Harassment of Working Women* (New Haven, Conn.: Yale University Press, 1979), p. 44.

(23) p. 48. A secretary in a major...: Laurie Becklund and Chuck Philips, "Sexual Harassment Suit Targets Record Executives," *Los Angeles Times*, Nov. 15, 1991, p. A3.

(24) p. 48. We're an industry that...: Laurie Becklund and Chuck Philips, "Sexual Harassment Claims Confront Music Industry, *Los Angeles Times*, Nov. 3, 1991, p. A1.

(25) p. 48. She charged that a direct...: Stuart Elliott, "Suit Over Sex in Beer Ads Hits a Genre As It Changes," *New York Times*, Nov. 12, 1991, p. D22.

(26) p. 48. Sex is in the...: Elaine Dutka, "Scenes From the Home of the Casting Couch," *Los Angeles Times*, Oct. 15, 1991, p. F1.

(27) p. 49. The real problem is...: Backhouse, *Sexual Harassment on the Job*, p. 26. (See n. 3.)

(28) p. 49. Upset, she consulted...: Martin, *Hard-Hatted Women*, p. 179. (See Ch. 1, n. 15.)

(29) p. 49. Then he suggested...: Gomez-Preston, "Over the Edge," pp. 62, 120. (See Ch. 1, n. 21.)

(30) p. 50. Less than five percent...: U.S. Merit System Personnel, *Sexual Harassment in the Federal Government: An Update* (Washington, D.C.: U.S. Government Printing Office, 1988), pp. 24, 26-27.

(31) p. 51. In fact, even if you start...: Price-Spratlen, *Prevention of Sexual Harassment in Academe*, p. 61. (See n. 11.)

(32) p. 51. People in the sexual harassment...: Maypole and Skaine, "Sexual Harassment in the Workplace," p. 388. (See n. 8.)

(33) p. 51. Investigators of sexual harassment...: Helen Remick, Jan Salisbury, Donna Stringer and Angela Ginorio, "Investigating Complaints of Sexual Harassment," *Ivory Power: Sexual Harassment on Campus,* ed. Michele A. Paludi (Albany, N.Y.: State University of New York Press, 1987), p. 198.

(34) p. 52. But when you have children...: MacKinnon, *Sexual Harassment of Working Women,* p. 44. (See n. 22.)

(35) p. 52. They either quit...: T.S. Jones, M.S. Remland, and C.C. Brunner, "Effects of Employment Relationship, Response of Recipient and Sex of Rater in Perceptions of Sexual Harassment," *Perceptual and Motor Skills,* 65, no. 1 (August 1987), pp. 55-63; F.S. Coles, "Forced to Quit: Sexual Harassment Complaints and Agency Response," *Sex Roles* 14, nos. 1 and 2 (January 1986), pp. 81-95.

(36) p. 53. In fact Sally Kaplan, a social...: Sally J. Kaplan, "Consequences of Sexual Harassment in the Workplace," *Affilia: Journal of Women and Social Work,* 6, no. 3 (Fall 1991), pp. 50-65.

(37) p. 53. Coined only in 1976...: Joy Livingston, "Responses to Sexual Harassment on the Job: Legal, Organizational and Individual Actions," *Journal of Social Issues,* 38, no. 4 (1982), p. 5.

(38) p. 53. Following the Clarence Thomas...: Steven Goldsmith, "Thomas Hearing Prompts Calls on Harassment," *Seattle Post-Intelligencer,* Oct. 12, 1991, p. B1.

(39) p. 54. Organizations as diverse...: Mike Merritt, "City Council Gets Tough on Sexual Harassment," *Seattle Post-Intelligencer,* Jan. 14, 1992, p. B3; H.G. Reza, "Navy Toughens Sex-Harassment Rules," *Los Angeles Times,* Feb. 20, 1992, p. B1; Scott Sunde and Karen West, "Bosses and Workers Taking Cure for Sexism, Racism," *Seattle Post-Intelligencer,* Dec. 12, 1991, p. A1.

(40) p. 54. Four admirals and...: Eric Schmitt, "Senior Navy Officers Suppressed Sex Investigations, Pentagon Says," *The New York Times,* Sept. 25, 1992, p. 1.

(41) p. 54. A word like "Hon"...: Peter Kilborn, "Men Say Worry About Harassment Leads Them to Tone Down Conduct," *New York Times,* Nov. 7, 1991, p. A8.

(42) p. 54. Barney Rosenzweig, TV...: Elaine Dutka, "Scenes from the Home of the Casting Couch," *Los Angeles Times,* Oct. 15, 1991, p. F2.

Chapter 4: Are You Privileged, "Other" or Both?

(1) p. 57. Speaking Korean in...: Hyo-Jung Kim, "Do You Have Eyelashes?" in *Women, Girls & Psychotherapy: Reframing Resistance,* ed. Carol Gilligan, Anne G. Rogers and Deborah Tolman (New York: Haworth Press, Inc., 1991), p. 202.

(2) p. 64. I eventually began...: Debra A. Matsumoto, "One Young Woman in Publishing," in *Competition: A Feminist Taboo?* ed. Valerie Miner and Helen E. Longino (New York: The Feminist Press, 1989) p. 89.

Chapter 5: Myths of the "Working Woman"

(1) p. 82. But millions of women...: U.S. Bureau of the Census, *Statistical Abstract of the United States* (Washington, D.C.: U.S. Government Printing Office, 1991), Table 652, pp. 396-397.

(2) p. 83. Then one company decided...: Susan Cary Rice, Alice M. Price and Rachel Rubin, *Rights and Wrongs: Women's Struggle for Economic Equality* (New York: The Feminist Press, 1986), p. 47.

(3) p. 83. Half a million women...: Alice Kessler Harris, *A Woman's Wage* (Lexington, KY: University of Kentucky Press, 1990), p. 23.

(4) p. 84. For example, in Italy and Denmark...: Sylvia Ann Hewlett, *A Lesser Life: The Myth of Women's Liberation in America* (New York: William Morrow and Company, 1986), p. 73.

(5) p. 84. Women between the ages...: Sylvia Nasar, "Women are outgaining men in wage race, new data show," *The Seattle Post-Intelligencer*, Oct. 26, 1992, p. B1.

(6) p. 84. Economists noted in 1992...: Sylvia Nasar, "Women's Progress Stalled? Just Not So," *New York Times*, Oct. 18, 1992, p. 3-1, 3-10.

(7) p. 84. In law schools, the proportion...: U.S. Department of Education, *Digest of Educational Statistics* (Washington, D.C.: U.S. Government Printing Office, 1990), p. 273.

(8) p. 85. Girls in those playgrounds...: Eleanor E. Maccoby, "Gender Segregation in the Workplace," in *Women, Work and Health,* ed. Marianne Frankenhaeuser, Ulf Lundberg and Margaret Chesney, (New York: Plenum Press, 1991), pp. 5-6.

(9) p. 85. At times, children's behavior...: Carol Tavris, *The Mismeasure of Woman* (New York: Simon & Schuster, 1992), p. 290.

(10) p. 85. The differences continue...: Lenore J. Weitzman, "Sex-Role Socialization: A Focus on Women," in *Women: A Feminist Perspective,* ed. Jo Freeman (Palo Alto, Calif.: Mayfield Publishing Co., 1984), p. 160.

(11) p. 85. Mothers handle and talk...: Ibid., p. 161.

(12) p. 85. For girls, Mattel has made a doll...: Carol Lawson, "Who Believes in Make-believe? Not These New Toys," *New York Times*, Feb. 6, 1992, p. B1.

(13) p. 85. By the time people...: Tavris, *The Mismeasure of Woman*, p. 292. (See n. 9.)

(14) p. 85. Even when there is a...: Ibid., p. 42.

(15) p. 86. Husbands continue to...: Norma Williams, *The Mexican American Family* (Dix Hills, N.Y.: General Hall Inc., 1990), p. 1.

(16) p. 86. Studies disclose that...: Pamela Reid, "Socialization of Black Female Children," in *Women in Developmental Perspective,* eds. Phyllis Berman and Estelle Ramey (Washington, D.C.: Department of Health and Human Services, 1982), p. 144.

(17) p. 86. Schools also emphasize...: Denise Segura, "Labor Market Stratification: The Chicana Experience," *Berkeley Journal of Sociology*, (29) 1984, pp. 56-88.

(18) p. 87. In 1991 and 1992...: Barbara Laker, "Girls Still Feeling Gender Bias, AAUW Study Shows," *The Seattle Post-Intelligencer,* June 21, 1991, p. A1.; Susan Chira, "Bias Against Girls is Found Rife in Schools, With Lasting Damage, *New York Times,* Feb. 12, 1992, p. Al.

(19) p. 87. Teachers pay less...: Ibid.

(20) p. 87. By the end of high school...: Ibid.

(21) p. 87. Without math and science...: Lucy W. Sells, "Mathematics: The Invisible Filter," *Engineering Education* 70, no. 4 (1980), pp. 340-341.

(22) p. 87. Many Native American...: Ibid, p. 211; Lena Williams "Girl's Self-Image is Mother of the Woman," *New York Times,* Feb. 6, 1992, p. A1.

(23) p. 88. Paul Brandon, an education...: Paul Brandon, "Gender Differences in Young Asian Americans' Educational Achievement," *Sex Roles* 25, nos. 1/2 (1991), p. 46.

(24) p. 88. The Navajos have...: Hilary Lips, "Gender-Role Socialization: Lesson in Femininity," in *Women: A Feminist Perspective,* ed. Jo Freeman, (Mountain View, Calif.: Mayfield Publishing Co., 1989) p. 210.

(25) p. 88. I want to be...: Ruth Sidel, *On Her Own: Growing Up in the Shadow of the American Dream* (New York: Viking Penguin, 1990), p. 19.

(26) p. 89. Underneath I wanted...: Emily Hancock, *The Girl Within* (New York: E. P. Dutton, 1989), p. 130.

(27) p. 89. Carol Tavris, a social...: Tavris, *The Mismeasure of Woman,* p. 65. (See n. 9.)

(28) p. 89. Sara Snodgrass, a psychologist...: Sara Snodgrass, "Women's Intuition: The Effect of Subordinate Role on Interpersonal Sensitivity," *Journal of Personality and Social Psychology,* 49 (1985), pp. 146-155.

(29) p. 90. They looked over my...: *Seattle Times,* May 19, 1991, p. A 19.

(30) p. 91. Economists argue about...: Harris, *A Woman's Wage.* (See n. 4.)

(31) p. 91. You may have thought...: Lillian Rubin, *Worlds of Pain* (New York: Basic Books Inc., 1976), p. 40.

(32) p. 92. I'd never known...: Lips, "Gender-Role Socialization," p. 210. (See n. 28.)

(33) p. 92. Because I was raised...: Howe, *Pink Collar Workers,* pp. 41-42. (see Ch. 1, n. 2.)

(34) p. 93. Still, fifty-one percent...: "The road to equality," *Time,* Special Issue (Fall, 1990), p. 13.

(35) p. 93. In 1992, Carolyn Cowan...: Lawrence Kutner, "Parent & Child," *New York Times,* Nov. 12, 1992, p. B4.

(36) p. 94. The poll also revealed...: Laker, "Girls Still Feeling Gender Bias...." (See n. 22.)

(37) p. 94. "It is well known that...: "Girl Viewers Don't Rate," *New York Times,* May 8, 1991.

(38) p. 94. Half of accountants...: Nasar, "Women's Progress Stalled..." (See n. 7.)

(39) p. 94. After the November 1992...: Center for the American Woman and Politics, *Women Candidates and Winners in 1992* (New Brunswick, N.J.), Nov. 12, 1992.

Chapter 6: The Double Whammy of Stress and Abuse

(1) p. 95. Who is the worker?...: Wendy Kaminer, *A Fearful Freedom* (New York: Addison-Wesley Publishing Co., 1990), pp. 62-63.

(2) p. 96. As Faye Crosby, a social...: Faye Crosby, *Juggling* (New York: The Free Press, 1991), p. 63.

(3) p. 96. Lisa Silberstein, a social...: Lisa Silberstein, "The Dual-Career Marriage: A System in Transition" (Ph.D. Diss., Yale University, 1987), cited in Crosby, *Juggling,* p. 65.

(4) p. 96. If you answered yes...: Howard Karasek and Tores Theorell, *Healthy Work: Stress, Productivity and the Reproduction of Working Life* (New York: Basic Books, 1990), Chapter 4.

(5) p. 97. By 1991, that...: Susan Chira, "New Realities Fight Old Images of Mother," *New York Times,* Oct. 4, 1992, p. 1.

(6) p. 97. Public opinion polls show...: Mary Frank Fox and Sharlene Hesse-Biber, *Women at Work* (Palo Alto, Calif.: Mayfield Publishing Co., 1984), p. 13.

(7) p. 97. The few fathers...: Carol Lawson, "When Baby Beckons, Why is Daddy at Work? Just Ask His Employer," *New York Times,* June 16, 1991.

(8) p. 97. Yet, women who work outside...: Eleanor Grant, "The Housework Gap," *Psychology Today,* 22, no. 1 (January 1988), p. 10.

(9) p. 97. My work, it's hard...: Howe, *Pink Collar Workers,* p. 40. (See Ch. 1, n. 2.)

(10) p. 98. Right now, my...: Arlie Hochschild, *The Second Shift* (New York: Avon Books, 1989), pp. 95-96.

(11) p. 98. Since twenty-nine...: Chira, "New Realities Fight Old Images of Mother." (See n. 6.)

(12) p. 99. In fact, only five...: Nancy R. Hooyman and Osuman Kayak, *Social Gerontology* (Boston: Allyn and Bacon, 1988), p. 359.

(13) p. 100. Sometimes women say they...: Patricia Lunneborg, *Women Changing Work* (New York: Bergin & Garvey Publishers, 1990), p. 110.

(14) p. 100. I say to him...: Hochschild, *The Second Shift,* pp. 81-82. (See n. 11.)

(15) p. 100. I come home at...: Ibid., p. 105.

(16) p. 100. When Arlie Hochschild...: Ibid., p. 173.

(17) p. 100. Men aren't supposed...: Rubin, *Worlds of Pain,* p. 104. (See Ch. 5, n. 35.)

(18) p. 101. Marilyn French, a feminist...: Marilyn French, *The War Against Women* (New York: Summit Books, 1992), p. 39.

(19) p. 101. Louise Howe, an analyst...: Howe, *Pink Collar Workers*, p. 126. (see Ch. 1, n. 2.)

(20) p. 102. She sees it differently...: Hochschild, *The Second Shift*, p. 126. (See n. 11.)

(21) p. 102. It used to be that what...: Hugh Mulligan, "Corporate America Makes Workplace a Happier Place," *Seattle Post-Intelligencer*, May 28, 1991, p. B8.

(22) p. 103. Services ranged from...: Sheila B. Kamerman and Alfred J. Kahn, *The Responsive Workplace* (New York: Columbia University Press, 1987), p. 191.

(23) p. 103. But by 1985, thirteen...: Ibid., p. 236.

(24) p. 103. In 1990, a corporate...: Amy Saltzman, "A Question of Balance," *Seattle Post-Intelligencer*, Oct. 7, 1990, pp. El-E5.

(25) p. 104. Ten million children.... "Who Cares About Day Care," *Newsweek*, March 28, 1988, p. 73.

(26) p. 104. Child care in public...: Hewlett, *A Lesser Life*, pp. 127-128. (See Ch. 5, n. 4.)

(27) p. 104. Mothers received two years...: Ibid., pp. 171-172.

(28) p. 104. Someday this nation may join...: Tavris, *The Mismeasure of Woman*, p. 128. (See Ch 5, n. 9.)

(29) p. 105. On May 14, 1990...: Stuart Bass and Nathan S. Slavin, "Avoiding Sexual Discrimination Litigation in Accounting Firms and Other Professional Organizations: The Impact of the Supreme Court Decision in Price Waterhouse v. Ann Hopkins." *Women's Rights Law Reporter* 3, no. 1 (1991), pp. 21-34.

(30) p. 105. The men have to know...: Lunneborg, *Women Changing Work*, p. 50. (See n. 14.)

(31) p. 106. One of the bosses...: Ibid., p. 52.

Chapter 7: Discover Your Individual Voice

(1) p. 111. I wasn't a quitter....: Gomez-Preston, "Over the Edge," p. 120. (See Ch. 1, n. 21.)

(2) p. 111. As a woman living...: W.E.B. Du Bois, cited by Susan Stanford Friedman, "Women's Autobiographical Selves," in *The Private Self*, ed. Shari Benstock (Chapel Hill: University of North Carolina Press, 1988), p. 40.

(3) p. 112. It is a woman...: Mark Fineman, "Speaking Her Mind," *Los Angeles Times*, June 3, 1991, p. El.

(4) p. 113. I used to constantly...: Gomez-Preston, "Over the Edge," p. 62. (See Ch. 1, n. 21.)

(5) p. 114. [T]he threats started...: Ibid. p. 120.

Chapter 8: The Thought is Mother to the Feeling

(1) p. 132. The reality was... Janet Kragel and Mary Kachoyeanos, *Just a Nurse* (New York: Dell Publishing Co., 1989), p. 117.

(2) p. 140. Whenever you are ready..." The exercise, Focus On Your Feelings, is loosely adapted from Eugene T. Gendlin, *Focusing* (New York: Bantam Books, 1981).

Chapter 9: Passivity, Aggression or Assertiveness

(1) p. 151. Speak up, but...: Diane Fisher, a tradeswoman, panel; "Technical Upgrading," at Women in Trades Fair. (See Ch.1, n. 17.)

(2) p. 154. Forty-eight hours before...: Agnes De Mille, "The Dancer From The Dance," *Vanity Fair*, August 1991, pp. 138-139.

(3) p. 156. After a long...: Laura Pfandler, pipefitter, in Schroedel, *Alone in a Crowd*, p. 20. (See Ch. 2, n. 4.)

Chapter 10: Out on a Limb: Risks for You and Your Family

(1) p. 162. One time when I...: Louise Carter, "Coming of Age at 74," *View Magazine* (Nov./Dec. 1991), p. 30.

(2) p. 162. She found time to...: Ibid, p. 32.

(3) p. 164. Getting married (Single women...: Jesse Bernard, *The Future of Marriage* (New York: Bantam Books, 1973).

(4) p. 175. Groups for abused women...: Ginny NiCarthy, *Getting Free* (Seattle: Seal Press, 1986).

Chapter 11: Going It Alone: Other Individual Choices

(1) p. 181. That led to me...: Schroedel, *Alone in a Crowd*, p. 20. (See Ch. 2, n. 4.)

(2) p. 181. "I didn't have...: Ibid.

(3) p. 184. But when that tactic...: Cox, "Verbal Abuse in Nursing," p. 47. (See Ch.1, n.10.)

(4) p. 185. One of the guys...: *Tradeswomen Magazine*, 7, 1 (Spring 1988), p. 47.

(5) p. 185. No doubt taken aback...: *Dangerous Propositions* (Lifetime Television documentary hosted by Linda Ellerbee and Harry Hamlin), June 24, 1992.

(6) p. 185. That done, I proceeded...: Christine Craft, *Too Old, Too Ugly and Not Deferential to Men* (New York: Dell Publishing, 1988) p. 10.

(7) p. 186. Professor Regina Barreca states...: Regina Barreca, *They Used to Call Me Snow White...But I Drifted* (New York: Penguin Books, 1990) p. 125.

(8) p. 186. Ibid., p. 129-130.

Chapter 12: Your Boss and Power

(1) p. 194. Maria, a Latina packager in...: Maria is a composite picture derived from: Patricia Zavella, *Women, Work and Chicano Families: Cannery Workers in the Santa Clara Valley* (Ithaca: Cornell University Press, 1987).

(2) p. 194. A warehouse packer says:...: Howe, *Pink Collar Workers*, p. 39. (See Ch. 1, n. 2.)

(3) p. 195. As another example...: Asian Women United of California, ed., *Making Waves: An Anthology of Writings By and About Asian American Women* (Boston: Beacon Press, 1989), p. 174.

(4) p. 202. Organizational analysts have...: Rino Patti, "Organizational Resistance and Change," in *Change from Within*, ed. Herman Resnick and Rino Patti (Philadelphia: Temple University Press, 1980), pp. 114-131.

Chapter 13: Shadow Organizations

(1) p. 207. The problem may originate...: J. Robert Russo, *Serving and Survivng as a Human Service Worker* (Monterey, Calif.: Brooks/Cole Publishing Company, 1980), p. 80.

(2) p. 208. You can answer some....: Perry W. Buffington, "A Culture in the Workplace," *Sky Magazine*, April 1991.

(3) p. 209. You can also pick up...: Natasha Josefowitz, *Paths to Power* (New York: Addison-Wesley, 1980), p. 64.

(4) p. 213. One day when...: Farley, *Sexual Shakedown*, p. 85. (See Ch. 3, n. 3.)

(5) p. 214. A personnel manager told...: Ibid., p. 132.

(6) p. 215. They want respect at work...: M. R. Cooper et al., "Changing Employee Values: Deepening Discontent?" *Harvard Business Review*, 57, 1 (January/February 1979), pp. 117-125.

Chapter 14: Target Your Goal

(1) p. 238. One time, a doctor...: Kragel and Kachoyeanos, *Just A Nurse*, p. 117. (See Ch. 8, n. 1.)

(2) p. 239. Without asking...: "Terese M. Floren: Firefighter," in Martin, *Hard-Hatted Women*, p. 16. (See Ch. 1, n. 15.)

Chapter 15: The Nitty-Gritty of Assertive Confrontation

(1)   p. 240. I gradually became...: Stringer et al., "Impacts on Employees...," (See Ch. 1, n. 5.)

(2)   p. 255. We pass around jokes...: Molly Martin, editor, *Tradeswomen Magazine*, personal interview.

Chapter 16: Evaluation and Follow-Through

(1)   p. 262. I yelled at him...: Elaine Canfield, quoted in Schroedel, *Alone in a Crowd*, p. 39. (See Ch. 2, n. 4.)

(2)   p. 278. Her boss fired...: Philip J. Hilts, "Hero in Exposing Science Hoax Paid Dearly," *New York Times*, March 21, 1991.

(3)   p. 278. She says that...: Philip Weiss, "Whistlegate," *Mirabella*, June 1991, p. 100.

Chapter 17: You Don't Have to Go It Alone

(1)   p. 293. We developed a...: Martin, *Hard-Hatted Women*, p. 76. (See Ch. 1, n. 15.)

(2)   p. 294. An uncooperative administration...: Gomez-Preston, "Over the Edge," (See Ch. 1, n. 21.)

(3)   p. 299. But intervention by...: Personal conversation with Marlene Pedregosa, union organizer.

Chapter 18: Collective Action

(1)   p. 304. Regardless of what work...: Cassedy and Nussbaum, *9 to 5*, p. 133. (See Ch. 1, n. 23.)

(2)   p. 305. One of the women...: Ibid., p. 154. (See Ch. 1, n. 23).

(3)   p. 307. Later, many of the nurses...: Diane Sosne, Service Employees International Union (SEIU), 1199, interview with author, Seattle, Washington, June 7, 1991.

(4)   p. 308. Most of us came right...: Moe Seager, "Fighting for the Black Belt...and More," *Z Magazine* (June 1991), p. 52.

(5)   p. 309. Fifteen percent of women...: Bureau of Labor Statistics, *Employment and Earnings* 38, no.1 (Washington, D.C.: U.S. Government Printing Office, 1991), p. 229.

(6)   p. 309. For us, it began...: Cassedy and Nussbaum, *9 to 5*, p. 16. (See Ch. 1, n. 23.)

(7)   p. 310. Supervisors in an electronics...: Ann Bookman, "Unionization in an Electronics Factory: The Interplay of Gender, Ethnicity and Class," in *Women and the Politics of Empowerment*, ed. Ann Bookman and Sandra Morgan (Philadelphia: Temple University Press, 1988), p. 164.

(8) p. 310. In any way they could...: Cynthia B. Costello, "Women Workers and Collective Action: A Case Study from the Insurance Industry," Ibid., p. 121.

(9) p. 311. Although more women fill...: Barbara Wertheimer, "The United States of America," in *Women and Trade Unions in Eleven Industrialized Countries*, ed. Alice Cook, Val Lorwin and Arlene Kaplan Daniels (Philadelphia: Temple University Press, 1984), p. 297.

(10) p. 311. The only union...: Howe, *Pink Collar Workers*, p. 43. (See Ch. 1, n. 2.)

(11) p. 311. We don't try to justify...: Ibid., p. 44.

(12) p. 312. By 1989, that proportion...: Bureau of the Census, *Statistical Abstract of the U.S.* (Washington, D.C.: Government Printing Office, 1971), p. 233. Bureau of the Census, *Statistical Abstract of the U.S.* (Washington, D.C.: Government Printing Office, 1991), p. 425.

(13) p. 312. Currently, unions feel...: Wertheimer, "The United States of America," p. 301. (See n. 9.)

(14) p. 312. Working with others...: Ruth Milkman, *Women, Work and Protest* (Boston: Routledge & Kegan Paul, 1985).

(15) p. 313. Before the strike, I...: Costello, "Women Workers and Collective Action," p. 128. (See n. 8.)

(16) p. 313. It's very difficult...: Brecher and Costello, *Building Bridges*, p. 26. (See Ch. 1, n. 20.)

(17) p. 314. When asked whether...: Joseph Amato, David Nass and Thaddeus Radzialowski, "A Year on the Line," *The Progressive*, 43, no. 2 (February, 1979), p. 41.

(18) p. 314. Women whose work...: Joseph Amato, David Nass, David and Thaddeus Radzialowski, "The Women of Willmar," *The Progressive*, 42, no. 8 (August, 1978), p. 26.

(19) p. 315. Furthermore, women joined...: Bookman, "Unionization in an Electronics Factory," p. 171. (See n. 7.)

(20) p. 315. "As the strike progressed...: Costello, "Women Workers and Collective Action," p. 26. (See n. 8.)

(21) p. 316. The women felt they needed...: Ibid.

(22) p. 316. Have you learned nothing...: Teresa Amott and Julie Matthaei, *Race, Gender and Work: A Multicultural Economic History of Women in the United States* (Boston: The South End Press, 1991), p. 81.

(23) p. 317. Organizers found that the...: Naomi Almeleh, "Working Women Organizing for Comparable Worth: The Case of the CSA/District 925" (Vermont College, 1990), unpublished dissertation.

(24) p. 318. Since the successful fight...: Naomi Almeleh, Steve Soifer, Naomi Gottlieb and Lorraine Gutierrez, "Women Achieving Personal and Political Empowerment through Workplace Activism," *Affilia: Journal of Women and Social Work*, 18, no. 1 (Spring 1993), p. 34.

Chapter 19: Using the Law and Government

(1) p. 332. So the court awarded...: "Harassment of Women has $50,000 Price Tag," *Labor Law Reports—Employment Practices* (June 10, 1991), p. 4.

(2) p. 335. The woman has returned...: Jonathan Gaw, "$200,000 for Teacher in Harassment Suit," *Los Angeles Times*, Oct.19, 1991, p. B1.

(3) p. 336. The court denied her claim...: Wendy Pollack, "Sexual Harassment: Women's Experience vs. Legal Definitions," *Harvard Women's Law Journal* 13 (Spring 1990), p. 65.

(4) p. 336. In a court case in 1988...: Ibid., p. 77.

(5) p. 336. And in 1990, when...: Fair v. Guiding Eyes for the Blind, 42 Federal Supplement S.D. N.Y. (1990), p. 156.

(6) p. 336. In 1986, the Supreme Court...: Meritor Savings Bank v. Michele Vinson, 477 U.S. 57 (1986).

(7) p. 336. In 1991, two federal courts...: Arthur S. Hayes, "Courts Concede the Sexes Think in Unlike Ways," *Wall Street Journal*, May 28, 1991, p. B1.

(8) p. 336. The attorney for the women...: *New York Times*, Dec. 9, 1991.

(9) p. 336. As of 1991,...: Donna Walters and Stuart Silverstein, "Tackling a Very Tough Problem," *Los Angeles Times*, Oct. 10, 1991, p. D2.

Chapter 20: Where Do We Go From Here?

(1) p. 341. If the personal...: *New England Journal of Public Policy*, Special Issue, ed. Dawn-Marie Driscoll (Jan. 1991), reprinted in *Women's International Network News*, 17, no. 2 (Spring 1991), pp. 74-75.

(2) p. 343. With all this constant...: Anonymous, "Air-Conditioned Nightmare," pp. 12-14. (See Ch. 1, n. 1.) Emphasis is in the original.

(3) p. 343. The women need...: Lee Bowker, *Ending the Violence: A Guidebook Based on the Experiences of 1000 Battered Women* (Holmes Beach, Fla: Learning Publications, 1986).

(4) p. 353. It also states...: "Association Europenne Contre Les Violences Faites Aux Femmes Au Travail," *Women's International Network News* (Winter, 1990), p. 35.

(5) p. 353. Although the threat...: "Female Workers in Costa Rica Denounce Sexual Harassment," *International Network Against Violence Against Women Newsletter*, Winter 1989, p. 4.

(6) p. 353. It now concentrates...: Himanee Gupta, "Women Unite," *Seattle Times/Post-Intelligencer*, Nov. 1, 1992, p. C1.

(7) p. 354. A petition currently...: This petition is being distributed in several languages by the Center for Women's Global Leadership, Douglass College, 27 Clifton Avenue, New Brunswick, N.J. 08903.

INDEX

Abbott, Kimberley   320, 325-326, 335
Abuse at home   174-176
   See also Family violence
Abuse at work
   See Emotional abuse at work
Abused woman   344
Abuse of power   8, 32
Abuser
   See Abusive person
Abusive person   6, 67, 79
Accountants
   See Hopkins, Ann; Muriel
Accounting firms   105
Action plan   230
Actors   162
Addictions at work   210-213
Admiral style of boss   198
Advertising   43
   See also Nancy
Affirmations   117-118
African Americans, fluid gender roles
   among, 85-86
African-American women   3, 38,
   78-79, 91-92, 308
   See also Crystal; Dian; Gwen; Johnson,
   Margaret; Murphy, Rana
Age Discrimination Act   334
Aggression
   defined, described   155-156
   indirect or passive   182-183
   as tactic   181-182
Airlines *See* Flight attendants
Alana   78-79, 157, 215, 223, 243, 290,
   355
Alcohol abuse   207, 210-213
Alliances
   with co-workers, mentors   187
   with powerful people   242-243
Amato, Joseph   314
Anger   142-147
Anita (Hill) *See* Hill, Anita
Ann   98
Ann (Hopkins) *See* Hopkins, Ann
Anxiety   245-246
Architecture *See* Daphne

Asian Americans   14, 88 *See* Bloch,
   Julia Chang; Kim, Hyo-Jung
Assertive action   238-239
   See also Assertiveness, Assertive
   confrontation
Assertive confrontation
   See also Assertiveness
   evaluating success of   263-267
   follow-through on   271-277
   in public   252-254, 257
   need for records, witnesses   250-252
   planning time, arena, limits
      246-250
   request for change   235-236
   pressing for answer   267-269
   retreat   277-278
   with co-worker   254-257
Assertiveness
   See also Assertive confrontation
   defined and described   156-157
   evaluating   232-235
   setting goals   223-239
   guidelines   160-161
   hazards and benefits of   159-160
   practice   243-246
   reactions to   161
Associations   305
Attorneys *See* Lawyers
Automatic thoughts   122-128, 133
Backlash   347-348
Banks   284-285, 313-314
Barbara   201
Barreca, Regina   186
Bartender *See* Patty
Bassett, Susan   331-332
Battered woman   343
Beauticians   92, 97, 311-312
   See also Mary Ellen
Beauty salons *See* Beauticians
Beer industry   48
Belinda   173
Beryl   175
Blacks *See* African Americans
Black women *See* African-American
   women

Blame, of self   8, 32-33, 46-47
Bloch, Julia Chang   112
Bosses   198-203
    legitimate power of   196-198
    reaction to rejection   44
    styles: admiral 198; combination
        202-203; crazy, 201; crisis manager
        201-202; democratic, 200; dictator,
        198; manipulator, 199
Bosses, female *See* Women bosses
Bowker, Lee   343
Brainwashing   30-31, 33, 344
Brandon, Paul   88
Bularzik, Mary   9
Canfield, Elaine   262
Carolyn   64
Cassedy, Ellen   14, 309
Challenging abuse, effects on
    family   167-168, 170
    finances   168
    personal time   169
    relationships   170-71
Charlotte   16, 20
Child care *See* Jo, Daycare
Civil Rights Act of 1964   73, 334
Clothing store   3
Clients as sexual harassers   49
Coalition of Labor Union Women   312
Collective action *See* Unions, Unionizing
Comebacks   255-256
Community action   299
Community college *See* Alana
Comparable worth   316-318
Competence of women workers   10
Complaint process *See* Filing complaints
Computer work   175, 186-187
    See also Janice
Confrontation *See* Assertive confrontation
Conley, Frances   14
Connections with co-workers   79, 208
    See also Status
Construction industry   37-38, 181
Co-workers
    informal power of   207-209
    as harassers   49
    providing support   215-217
Craft, Christine   185-186
"Crazy-making"   5, 32
Crisis manager   201
Crosby, Faye   96
Crystal   128-130
Customers as sexual harassers   49
Customer service   3

Custodian *See* Abbott, Kimberley
Daphne   178-180, 184
Daycare   103-105
Deaf people   265
    See also Zoe
Debbie (Dritz) *See* Dritz, Debbie
Debra (Matsumoto) *See* Matsumoto,
    Debra
Delays in confronting abuse   188
Democratic boss   200
Department stores   98, 213
Depression   147-148
Dian (Murphy) *See* Murphy, Dian
Diane (Fisher) *See* Fisher, Diane
Dictator boss   198
De Mille, Agnes   153
Disabled men   7-8; women   91
Doctors   10, 238
Domestic workers   312
Doris   195
Dreyer, Gwen Marie   6
Drinkers' caucus   207-208
Dritz, Debbie   3, 343
Drug abuse *See* Addictions at work
Du Bois, W. E. B.   111-112
Ecologist   126
Edna   101
EEOC *See* Equal Employment
    Opportunity Commission
Elaine   52
Electronics industry   16, 314-315
Elliot   248-250
Emotional abuse at work
    defined, described   4-5
    effects of   4-5, 28-29
    excuses for   4
    media treatment of   14
    naming   4, 17-18
    public issue   81, 303-304
    reactions to   32
    related to alcohol or drug
        abuse   210-213
Employee Assistance Programs   212
Equal Employment Opportunity Com-
    mission   38-39, 323, 329-333
Equal Pay Act   334
Equal Rights Amendment   348
Erhard, Werner   14
Exercises on *See also* Questionnaires
    abusive person's status   67-69
    addictions at work   210
    anger   143-145
    automatic thoughts   125

behavior 226
brainwashing 33-34
complaint and plan 231-232
confrontation 241-242, 263-265
consequences of confronting
  abuse 171-172
emotional abuse 28
feelings 134, 137-140, 230
follow-through 271-272, 276-277
group action 289, 291-294
ideas 127, 130-131
informal organizations 208
learning from the past 165
privileged 62, 70 *See also*
  "Other" status
promises 273-274
risks 164-166
self-inventory 35
sexual harassment 40-41, 50-51
thoughts 30,120
Family 93, 113, 166-171, 218
Family and Medical Leave Act 103
Family violence 13-14, 175
Feelings 132-148, 224-230
"Feminine nature" 84-85
"Filer's remorse" 51
Filing complaints 322-334
Filipinos 299
Filmmaker 45
Firefighters 105, 238-239
Firings 172-173
Fisher, Diane 151
Flex-time 103
Flight attendants 44, 48, 313
Flirting 45
Floren, Terese 238-239
Follow-through 271-277
Food processing plant 194
Freedom from abuse 343-344
French, Marilyn 100-101
Friends 217-218
Future 351-356
Gay men 7, 351
Gender differences 85
Genvieve 41
Gifts 5
Gigi 11
Gigi (Martino) *See* Martino, Gigi
Girls, expectations of 93-94
Global thinking 122-123, 225-226
Gomez-Preston, Cheryl 14, 49, 111,
  113-114, 293-294
Government, women in 94

See also Charlotte; Muriel
Government agencies 320-324,
  326-335
Grace 298
Graham, Martha 153-154
Grievance procedures 324
Group action 281-302
  against boss 200
  risks of 282-283
  exploring 289
  large and long-term 285-288
  small and short-term 283-285
  timing 294
  trust factor 289-293
Gwen 177
Gwen Marie (Dreyer) *See* Dreyer, Gwen
  Marie
Hannah 172
Hattie 281, 285-288
Hazing 6
Health care industry 9-10, 195
  See also Conley, Frances; Helen; Janet;
    Jessica; Nurses; Polly; Rebecca
Helen 189-190
Hill, Anita 6, 37, 47, 53-54, 177
Hochschild, Arlie 100
Home and women 97 *See also*
  Housework
Homosexuals *See* Gay men; *See also*
  Lesbians
Hopkins, Ann 105
Hospitals 195, 248 *See also* Health care
  industry
Housework 92, 100
Howe, Louise 101
Human rights commissions *See* State
  agencies
Humiliation 5, 8
Humor as tactic 185-186
Hyo-Jung (Kim) *See* Kim, Hyo-Jung
Informal organization *See* Shadow
  organization
Injustice 194-196
Insults 181, 255, 258-259
  racial 259
  reaction 132
  of self 119-120
  of tradeswomen 156
Insurance companies 310, 313,
  315-316
  See also Rana
International coalitions 352-356
Investment firm *See* Kate

Janet 42-43
Janice 207-208, 211
Janine 248
Jessica 3, 76, 157-159, 161, 199, 248, 298
Jew *See* Valerie
Jo 180-181, 186, 215, 260
Job hunting 173-174
Jobs for Justice 313
Johnson, Margaret 331
Kaminer, Wendy 95
Kanter, Rosabeth Moss 341
Kaplan, Sally 52-53
Kate 31, 182, 184, 250
Kim, Hyo-Jung 57
Labor organizations *See* Unions
Latinas 194 *See also* Maria; Mexican Americans
Laws 334
Lawsuits 320-321, 334-338
Lawyers 64, 172, 213
Leah 181, 186, 215
Legal secretaries 304
Legal system, discrimination in 11
Lesbians 47, 91, 260
Lillian 98
Linda 97
Lockyer, Bill 3
Lydia (Vasquez) *See* Vasquez, Lydia
MacKinnon, Catharine 42
Management 310-311
Manipulation as tactic 183-184
Manipulator boss 199
Manufacturing 22, 308, 312
Marcia 27
Maria 194-195
Martha 126
Marital battering 8 *See also* Battered woman
Martin, Molly 255-256
Martino, Gigi 49
Marva 23, 183-184, 202-203, 285-288, 290-291, 296-297, 299-301
Maternity leave 104
Mary Ellen 75-76
Matsumoto, Debra 64
Media reports 345-346, 348
Melanie 98-99
Melendez, Rose 18, 293
Men
    attitudes toward abuse, 11; hazing, 11; sexual harassment and sexuality at work, 43

caring for children 97
coping with difficult situations 11
privilege of 349
as sexual aggressors 43-44
sharing domestic duties 12
status of 8
Men of color 7, 217
Mentors 187-188
Merchant marine 49
Mexican Americans 86 *See also* Latinas
Minority men *See* Men of color
Minority women *See* African Americans, African-American women, Asian Americans, Latinas, Mexican Americans, Native Americans, Women of color
Miranda 240
Mistreatment *See* Emotional abuse at work
Movie industry 45-46, 48
Muriel 24, 198
Murphy, Dian 313
Myths about women 81-86, 89-92
Name-calling 257, 267-269 *See also* Insults
Nan 132
Nancy 175-176
Native Americans 52, 88, 112 *See also* Elaine
Navy 6, 54
Negative thoughts 114-117, 121-123
Nettie 140-141
Networks 187-188
New Kids on the Block 94
Newspaper industry *See* Ruth
Nina 100
9 to 5 304, 308-310
Nonprofit organizations 311 *See also* Social agencies
Northern Exposure 162
Nurses 3, 9-10, 52, 306-307
Nussbaum, Karen 14, 309
Office workers' unions 304, 308-310, 317-318
"Old boy" networks 11, 187, 208
Older woman 259-260 *See also* Genvieve
Old-timers 209
Organizing 306, 318 *See also* Unions
"Other" status
    alliances and support 216-217
    causing anxiety 245-246
    defined and described 61-62
    and helplessness 71-72
    insults based on 258-260
O'Toole, Margaret 278

Overtime   230-231
Part-time work   102
Passivity   151-155
Pattern of emotional abuse   7, 27-28 *See also* Emotional abuse at work
Patty   134-136, 223
Paul   267-269
Pedregosa, Marlene   303
Pfandler, Laura   156, 181, 217
Phillips, Peg   162
Physicians *See* Doctors
Physicians' assistant   27
Planner *See* Charlotte
Police departments   18, 293-294
Police officers *See* Police departments
Politeness as tactic   180
Political movements   345
Polly   9-10, 152-153
Power
    abuse of *See* Emotional abuse at work
    defined   72
    demonstrations of   5
    at home related to work   45
    lack of   46
    legitimate, of boss   72
    and privilege   74
    and women   8
Powerful people   242-243
Pregnancy Discrimination Act   334
Priscilla   242-243
Privilege
    of co-workers   74-75
    defined and described   57-61
    effects on feelings   69-70
    linked to power and abuse   74
    loss differs from abuse   67
    of women   349-350
    of youth   66-67
Privileges   5
Profit making   194-195
Promises   269-271
Publishing industry   64
Questionnaires on *See also* Exercises
    degradation and humiliation   20
    demonstrating power   24
    exhaustion and lowered competency   26
    indulgences   23
    isolation   17-18
    naming emotional abuse at work   17
    threats   19
    unreasonable demands   22

Quitting jobs   52-53, 278
Racism   76
Rana   25, 214, 218, 251-252, 322-323, 328, 333-334, 337
Rape   8, 341-342
Real estate   106
Rebecca   169-170
Recording industry   48
Records of confrontations   250-252
Repair work *See* Dritz, Debbie
Resentment   145-146
Resigning jobs *See* Quitting jobs
Respect   215, 304, 309
Retreat   277-278
Risk-taking   162-166
    and evaluations   214-215
    consequences of   171-172
    and sexual harassment   176
Rodgers, Fran   97
Role playing   243-246
Rose (Melendez) *See* Melendez, Rose
Rosenzweig, Barney   54
Rubin, Lillian   91
Ruth   72-74, 81, 117-118, 136-137, 193, 202, 209, 225
Ruth-Anne (Miller) *See* Miller, Ruth-Anne
Sadie   213
Safeway   331-332
Sailor *See* Martino, Gigi
Sales *See* Nettie
Salt of the Earth (movie)   316
Schools   86-87, 248
Science *See* O'Toole, Margaret
Secretaries   4, 41, 201 *See also* Rebecca
Security investigator *See* Bassett, Susan
Self-change   178
"Self-help" for women   12
Self-inventory   35
Self-sabotage   116-117
Self-worth   46
Settlements   329-330, 337-338
Sex-based harassment   321
    See also Sexual harassment
Sex-role spillover   44, 105
Sex stereotyping in schools   86-87
Sexual attraction *See* Sexuality in workplace
Sexual attractiveness, as strategy   45
Sexual harassment   5-6, 37-54
    See also Sexualized jobs, Sexuality in workplace
    apprehension about   9
    by clients, customers, co-workers   49

complaint procedures   321
confronting harasser   50, 236-237
court decisions on   336
defined   38-39
differs from emotional abuse,   41;
    from dating,   42
identifying   40-41
history of   53-54
ignoring the problem   47
incidence among working
    women   41
quitting as a way out   52-53
reactions   42, 46
and risk-taking   176
and shadow organizations   213-214
Sexuality in workplace   42-43
    See also Sexual harassment
Sexualized jobs   48-49
Shadow organization   207-219
Sharpe, Joan   308
Shirley   16
"Shoulds"   123-124
Sidel, Ruth   88-89
Silberstein, Lisa   96
Silence   114
Single mothers   98
Small group action *See* Group action
Smith, Vickie   11
Snodgrass, Sara   89
Social agencies *See* Marva; Priscilla; Zoe
Socialization of women   92-93
Social workers *See* Zoe
Spokespersons   294-296
Sprinkler fitter   11
State agencies   333-334
Stress   96
Strikes   313-314 *See* Unions;
    Organizing
Stripper   49
Status
    complexity of   71
    differences in cultures,
        situations   65-66
    hidden aspects of   64-65, 77
    issues   65
    mix of privilege and Other   77
    need to check assumptions   78
Strategy against abuse *See* Tactics against
    abuse
Support of co-workers, friends   215-219
Supreme Court sexual harassment
    cases   39, 52
    See also Sex-based harassment

Symptoms as result of abuse   28
Systemic injustice   194-196
Systems, seeking change in   237
Tactics against abuse   177-190
    aggressive action   181
    alliances with co-workers   186-187
    bypassing confrontation   180
    calling the person's bluff   184
    encouraging others   189-190
    humor   185
    indirect or passive aggression
        182-183
    manipulation   183-184
    threats   235-236
"Tailhook" scandal   54
Tavris, Carol   89
Telecommunications industry   83
Telephone solicitors   38
Television industry   162
    See also Craft, Christine
Terese (Floren) *See* Floren, Terese
Therapist   218
Thomas, Clarence   6, 37, 53-54
Tina   23-26
Title IX of Education Act   84
Title VII of Civil Rights Act
    See Civil Rights Act
Toys   85
Trades   75, 185, 255-256
Troublemaker   214
Trudy   284
Trust   289-293, 298-299
Turnover   10
Unfairness *See* Injustice
Unionizing   314-315 *See also* Unions
Union organizer *See* Valerie
Unions   303-319
    history of women in   312-313
    not serving women   11, 311
    recent changes   351
United Nations   354-355
Universities   4, 190
Unpredictable boss   201
Valerie   146-147
Vasquez, Lydia   22
Vickie (Smith) *See* Smith, Vickie
Violence toward women, movement
    against   13, 341-342
Waitresses   3, 52, 101, 173
Watson, Diane   3
Whistle blower   214
White men   11, 60
Willmar bank tellers   313-314

Witnesses   51-52
Women bosses   8, 203-206, 350
Women for Sobriety   218
Women of color   194 *See also* African
    Americans, Asian Americans, Latinas,
    Mexican Americans, Native Americans
Women's networks   307-309
Women's unions   312-313 *See also*
    Unions
"Women's work," salary issues   89-90,
    316-318
Women workers
    earnings   84
    in high-paying or prestigious
        jobs   10, 82
    increasing share of some jobs   94
    job choices limited   90
    as managers   307

multiple roles   95-101
    in low-paid, low-status jobs   82
    need to work   9, 101-102
    in professions   84
    segregation of   10
    support in abuse cases   216
    "underemployed"   83
Women's movement
    benefits   53
    goals   346
    history   12
    mixed progress   93-94
    in other nations   353-356
Working-class women   350
World War II   83-84
Young women   31
Zoe   66, 168, 205, 237, 265, 290-291

AUTHOR BIOGRAPHIES

Ginny NiCarthy's name is familiar to tens of thousands of women as the author of *Getting Free: You Can End Abuse and Take Back Your Life,* the groundbreaking book on abuse of women by intimate partners that has now sold over 120,000 copies. Ms. NiCarthy is also the co-author of an easy-to-read version of this bestseller called *You Can Be Free* and co-author of two important books: *Talking It Out* and *The Ones Who Got Away* (all published by Seal Press). Ginny NiCarthy has been active in the movement to end violence against women for over 18 years as a writer and counselor. She has been instrumental in starting programs for rape victims and battered women, including groups for lesbians and women of color. She lives in Seattle.

Naomi Gottlieb is Professor at the School of Social Work at the University of Washington in Seattle. She has been on the faculty there since 1970 and was Associate Dean from 1974 to 1985. From 1975 to the present, she coordinated the development of a special curriculum sequence on women, the first in the country for graduate social work students. She was co-founder of the journal *Affilia: Journal of Women and Social Work.* Her books include *Alternative Social Services for Women, The Woman Client,* and *Feminist Social Work Services in Clinical Settings.*

Sandra J. Coffman is an Assistant Clinical Professor in the Clinical Psychology Department at the University of Washington. She co-authored *Talking It Out* with Ginny NiCarthy and Karen Merriam and has written many professional articles. A psychologist in independent practice in Seattle, she has provided training and supervision nationwide on the issues of physical and emotional abuse, trauma and depression.